WEST OF SUEZ
A PATRIOT FOR ME
TIME PRESENT
THE HOTEL IN AMSTERDAM

By John Osborne

Look Back in Anger
The Entertainer
Epitaph for George Dillon (*with Anthony Creighton*)
The World of Paul Slickey
A Subject of Scandal and Concern: *play for television*
Luther
Plays for England: The Blood of the
Bambergs and Under Plain Cover
Inadmissible Evidence
A Patriot for Me
A Bond Honoured
Time Present and The Hotel in Amsterdam
Tom Jones: *film script*
The Right Prospectus: *play for television*
Very Like a Whale: *play for television*
West of Suez

WEST OF SUEZ
A PATRIOT FOR ME
TIME PRESENT
THE HOTEL IN AMSTERDAM

FOUR PLAYS BY
JOHN OSBORNE

DODD, MEAD & COMPANY · NEW YORK

ISBN: 0-396-06659-3
Library of Congress Catalog Card Number: 72-3920
Printed in the United States of America
by The Cornwall Press, Inc., Cornwall, N. Y.

CONTENTS

CONTENTS

WEST OF SUEZ

TO J.R.B. AND G.T.

The first performance of *West of Suez* was given at the Royal Court Theatre, Sloane Square, London, on August 17, 1971, by The Royal Court Theatre and Tennent Productions, Ltd. The cast was as follows:

WYATT GILLMAN, a writer	*Ralph Richardson*
ROBIN, Wyatt's daughter	*Patricia Lawrence*
FREDERICA, Wyatt's daughter	*Jill Bennett*
EVANGIE, Wyatt's daughter	*Sheila Ballantine*
MARY, Wyatt's daughter	*Penelope Wilton*
EDWARD, Frederica's husband— a pathologist	*Geoffrey Palmer*
ROBERT, Mary's husband—a teacher	*Frank Wylie*
PATRICK, a retired brigadier	*Willoughby Gray*
CHRISTOPHER, Secretary to Wyatt	*Nigel Hawthorne*
ALASTAIR, a hairdresser, resident on the island	*Anthony Gardner*
OWEN LAMB, a writer, resident on the island	*Nicholas Selby*
HARRY, resident on the island	*Peter Carlisle*
MRS. JAMES, an interviewer from the local newspaper, resident on the island	*Sheila Burrell*
LEROI, Robin's and the Brigadier's servant	*Raul Neunie*
MR. DEKKER, American tourist	*John Bloomfield*
MRS. DEKKER, American tourist	*Bessie Love*
JED, American tourist	*Jeffrey Shankley*
ISLANDER	*Leon Berton*
ISLANDER	*Montgomery Matthew*

Directed by Anthony Page
Designed by John Gunter

ACT ONE

The loggia of a trim, attractive villa on a subtropical island, neither Africa nor Europe, but some of both, also less than both. Startling shrubs and trees. Bright, stippled patches, cold, dark places, a whisper of ocean and still heat. Chairs reclining in and out of the sun. FREDERICA *and* EDWARD, *her husband, are sitting beneath a trailing vine. She is just in the sun, her eyes closed, he in the shade, reading a newspaper. Presently, a brownish coloured servant in a white jacket,* LEROI, *comes over to the table beside them and laboriously puts down a glass of iced orange juice and a long exotic-looking drink in a taller glass.*

EDWARD: Thank you. That's fine. *[*LEROI *stares at the glass, hesitates]* Fine. Thanks. *[To* FREDERICA*]* Sure you won't have a proper drink?

FREDERICA: Sure. Alcohol and me before lunchtime in this climate just don't go. *[*LEROI *goes.]* It does something to women, anyway.

EDWARD: Well, there are misfortunes all sides. Nothing else, thanks, Leroi.

FREDERICA: He's gone. Not that he'd hear you.

EDWARD: They really do stand and stare.

FREDERICA: They're not waiters for nothing.

EDWARD: Yes. A sort of ethnic group. While they last.

FREDERICA: We *last*, you mean. It's an odd mixture.

EDWARD: What?

FREDERICA: Them. Lethargy and hysteria.

EDWARD: Oh, yes. I've noticed. Perhaps it's being a small island.

FREDERICA: Brutality and sentimentality.

EDWARD: Perched between one civilization and the next.

FREDERICA: Craven but pleased with themselves.

EDWARD: Listen to those birds.

FREDERICA: They're too pleased with themselves as well.

EDWARD: Jolly pretty.

FREDERICA: Not pretty enough. Like those same old native songs they sing every night. And those dreadful instruments. One of the worst things about England.

EDWARD: What?

FREDERICA: Bloody birds. Making a din, first thing you hear.

EDWARD: Only in the country.

FREDERICA: No, in London as well. Wake me up every day.

EDWARD: Don't know what we can do about your sleep.

FREDERICA: Neither do I.

EDWARD: Still, better than aeroplanes.

FREDERICA: Um?

EDWARD: Birds.

FREDERICA: Oh. Don't see why. I rather like the sound of aeroplanes. At least they're useful. I thought I'd be all right, marrying a doctor.

EDWARD: All right for what?

FREDERICA: Oh, everything. Getting to sleep, I suppose.

EDWARD: Well, I have *tried.*

FREDERICA: Oh, you all *try.*

EDWARD: Thanks a hump.

FREDERICA: I think doctors are an oddly narrow lot on the whole.

EDWARD: We try not to give rise to incident.

FREDERICA: Indeed. Don't forget to dispense negatives. Like civil servants. I didn't used to think so.

EDWARD: I suppose you're really a bit of a whore about medicine.

FREDERICA: Oh, I'll try anything once.

EDWARD: But not necessarily twice.

FREDERICA: Doctors are to be *used.*

EDWARD: Like bookmakers.

FREDERICA: Right. They never lose . . .

EDWARD: We all lose.

FREDERICA: Some sooner and quicker.

EDWARD: No. That's how we start out.

FREDERICA: Or faster and funnier.

EDWARD: No. Not very funny.

FREDERICA: Oh, I think so. Don't you really?

EDWARD: No.

FREDERICA: I do. What's dull is people who don't know they've lost already. Like Leroi.

EDWARD: That's a misnomer, I must say.

FREDERICA: They're all misnomers, if you ask me. Mr. and Miss Nomers . . .

EDWARD: I think you concern yourself a bit too much about sleeping.

FREDERICA: You mean I shouldn't?

EDWARD: No. But——

FREDERICA: But what?

EDWARD: You know what I was going to say, so what's the point?

FREDERICA: Perhaps you might surprise me for once.

EDWARD: I doubt it.

FREDERICA: Now *you* sound pleased.

EDWARD: You shouldn't incite me to repeat myself.

FREDERICA: Then why rise to it?

EDWARD: Why lay it?

FREDERICA: No quarry, no bait, I suppose is that answer.

EDWARD: It's a habit people have when they've lived at close quarters for long. People *can* live without too——

FREDERICA: Much sleep. Like you?

EDWARD: It can be acquired. Or not.

FREDERICA: What do you do instead?

EDWARD: Keep awake?

FREDERICA: And the options?

EDWARD: What you fancy.

FREDERICA: And if there's nothing you fancy?

EDWARD: Do nothing and don't panic.

FREDERICA: Keep the patient in a warm blanket, if possible, with hot sweet tea.

EDWARD: That sort of thing.

FREDERICA: Thanks, doctor. I don't know what we'd do without your medical skill.

EDWARD: Survive, in most cases. . . . Sure you won't have something stronger than that?

FREDERICA: Quite sure. What's that flowery thing you've got?

EDWARD: Rum with local flora and fauna.

FREDERICA: Looks disgusting.

EDWARD: It does. Bit cloying and pleased with itself, as you'd say. But quite pleasant. Try a bit.

FREDERICA: No thanks. I've had all the hangovers I want in this place.

EDWARD: Good for boredom.

FREDERICA: You mean I'm bored?

EDWARD: Didn't occur to me . . . Did you mean what you just said?

FREDERICA: What? About birds?

EDWARD: Well, that too . . .

FREDERICA: Why shouldn't I mean it? I didn't realize you were such a bird lover. If one can still use it in the feathered sense.

EDWARD: And about losing . . .

FREDERICA: You think I lie?

EDWARD: No. Only that——

FREDERICA: What? Only?

EDWARD: The ones who make an ethic out of truthfulness do incline to rhetoric.

FREDERICA: You mean I put on a show of feelings I don't have?

EDWARD: Not necessarily.

FREDERICA: Then what?

EDWARD: I don't know.

FREDERICA: Then why say it?

EDWARD: Say what?

FREDERICA: What you said.

EDWARD: I don't remember.

FREDERICA: Then you should. You've a trained, scientific mind.

EDWARD: Only in a very narrow discipline.

FREDERICA: I don't think you could call pathology narrow. Somewhat inhuman and requiring a detachment that's almost unscientific. *If* that's what I mean.

EDWARD: You see. It *is* difficult. So let's not pursue it, shall we?

FREDERICA: "Let's not pursue it, shall we?" If you really do think you've got the gift of scientific lucidity, you'd better brush up on your English a bit.

EDWARD: Blood and shit.

FREDERICA: A blood and shit man.

EDWARD: That's all I need to look at all day, just as——

FREDERICA: I always remind you.

EDWARD: As you do. Which isn't quite necessary as I'm only too conscious of it.

FREDERICA: Then why should I remind you of it?

EDWARD: Only you and God knows. You wouldn't, or what's even more likely, couldn't, and I don't see much chance of God revealing any of his prime moves or divine intention.

FREDERICA: Oh, that was quite good . . .

EDWARD: What was?

FREDERICA: That sentence. It had almost a syntactical swing about it.

EDWARD: But not quite.

FREDERICA: Not bad though.

EDWARD: "Syntactical" 's a pretty poor word to flash at anyone.

FREDERICA: Don't spar with me.

EDWARD: I wouldn't dream of it. I haven't the equipment.

FREDERICA: You haven't.

EDWARD: Or inclination.

FREDERICA: Or energy.

EDWARD: Or stamina.

FREDERICA: Or interest.

EDWARD: That either.

FREDERICA: Then why are you here then?

EDWARD: To have a refreshing, enhancing holiday with my wife.

FREDERICA: You don't really like holidays . . .

EDWARD: My sister-in-law's very pleasant villa with their family and friends.

FREDERICA: Or anything else for that matter.

EDWARD: That's right, actually. Sometimes, your open-ended tongue does tip over a real, palpable truth.

FREDERICA: What *are* you interested in?

EDWARD: I told you: blood and shit.

FREDERICA: Something passive.

EDWARD: The specimens I see are very active indeed.

FREDERICA: You should have married someone like Robin.

EDWARD: Like looking down a volcano sometimes. I think I *have* said I think your sister's quite a nice girl but a trifle more dull with it than I'd have thought necessary.

FREDERICA: Or Evangeline.

EDWARD: I thought we——

FREDERICA: Oh, yes, you don't like intellectual women.

EDWARD: It's the truth.

FREDERICA: So you keep saying.

EDWARD: No. So you keep asking. Like most men——

FREDERICA: Of your background, yes——

EDWARD: I'm dim and dismal enough to find them intimidating.

FREDERICA: Intimidating? She's pathetic.

EDWARD: Not specifically attractive I'd have thought, but pathetic no, no more than the rest of us. She's got a thumping success of a career, which is what she says all the time is the only really important thing.

FREDERICA: You mean it isn't?

EDWARD: To her it is, so she always tells me whenever I talk to her. I can't believe it's just a common . . . or a gambit or whatever. Being a man, as you say, I've never had to define myself about a career. Just a plain old blood and shit man who does it because it's the one skill he's managed to more or less master and the one he can pay the bills with in any sort of comfort . . .

FREDERICA: I think you're taken in by her.

EDWARD: I've always been prone to being taken in, as easily as a pussy cat's laundry.

FREDERICA: Now you're straining.

EDWARD: She's certainly no more pathetic than Robin.

FREDERICA: What do you mean?

EDWARD: You know quite well what I mean. You've said it often enough yourself.

FREDERICA: She's *my* sister.

EDWARD: Running off with the old Brigadier.

FREDERICA: I thought you said you liked him?

EDWARD: I do. I certainly don't hold him in the contempt you do.

FREDERICA: He's too old and doddery by half.

EDWARD: He'll outlast *her*.

FREDERICA: While the money holds out.

EDWARD: But then contempt comes easily to you.

FREDERICA: I keep most of it for myself.

EDWARD: Then try spreading the load or turning down the pressure or something.

FREDERICA: I happen to like high standards, starting with number one.

EDWARD: Perhaps you should have a go at observing them, whatever they are. Like try charity for a bit. Give *that* a whirl.

FREDERICA: Don't start giving me St. Paul. That's the prig's first.

EDWARD: You think you *don't* sound priggish?

FREDERICA: The woman was made for the man, not the man for the woman or whatever it is.

EDWARD: If only he'd pop in on one of his journeys now——

FREDERICA: He'd be made welcome. I'm sure. Visiting fireman.

EDWARD: Well, he *did* say better to marry than to burn. Perhaps he meant it the other way round. Bad translation. Sort of Hebraic inversion. . . . Anyway, I think the Brigadier's quite happy.

FREDERICA: So he should be.

EDWARD: Why should he be? Because he's a nice simple old stick and he's happy pottering around all day building his little walls and grottoes and making his dreadful old wine for a bob a gallon?

FREDERICA: And drinking it. . . . He'll not divorce that wife.

EDWARD: It doesn't seem as if he's able to.

FREDERICA: Doesn't want to.

EDWARD: And he's got his children . . .

FREDERICA: Oh, don't. He's so sentimental about them. They're both six feet five and about thirty and doing better than the old man. I can't understand how he ever held down while he was in the army.

EDWARD: The army's never been short on either sentiment or incompetence. And quite rightly. Anyway, Robin's not exactly a chicken, and even if she is, she's not my idea of the prize of the battery.

FREDERICA: You accept her hospitality.

EDWARD: I do. And the fact that I'm not enjoying it too well is no fault of hers.

FREDERICA: You mean it's mine?

EDWARD: No, it isn't, Frederica. It's mine. We can't be——

FREDERICA: Responsible for others.

EDWARD: Well, I believe it.

FREDERICA: So you always say.

EDWARD: Yes. As I always say. It's my responsibility if I am tired, unspontaneous, or pretty insubstantial . . .

FREDERICA: You're sounding pleased again.

EDWARD: Or *seeming* pleased with myself, which I only wish were sometimes true even.

FREDERICA: Come.

EDWARD: If I am unhappy, it is my own responsibility.

FREDERICA: *Are* you?

EDWARD: Responsible?

FREDERICA: Unhappy?

EDWARD: Fair to Middling to occasional Full Speed Ahead.

FREDERICA: Thanks.

EDWARD: I thank myself.

FREDERICA: You should. Be generous.

EDWARD: I try to be.

FREDERICA: To yourself?

EDWARD: I try not to give myself *too* hard a time . . .

FREDERICA: It's the others.

EDWARD: Others what?

FREDERICA: Give you a hard time?

EDWARD: No. That would be a delusion.

FREDERICA: You're not being very clear.

EDWARD: That's because I'm not what I appear to be.

FREDERICA: And what are you?

EDWARD: A middle-aged blood and shit man trying to mop up a bit of sunshine and eat, drink, and swim too much, at least not in that order . . .

FREDERICA: I wouldn't like you to test *my* blood.

EDWARD: Well, I've sampled enough of the other.

FREDERICA: Shit, you mean. Ah!

EDWARD: I'm sure your blood is just as lively . . . Well, here's to the Brigadier *and* his wife.

FREDERICA: You wouldn't say that if they were out there.

EDWARD: I see no reason to be ungrateful or unkind.

FREDERICA: What *is* your reason then?

EDWARD: And to his children, all six foot five of 'em. Perhaps they'll jolly him along when he's tired of it all.

FREDERICA: Of Robin?

EDWARD: No. Just tired. She's past that, anyway.

FREDERICA: You mean *he* is.

EDWARD: I'd say he was quite a good old rattler. Gets his oats twice a day like an old horse on his holidays.

FREDERICA: If he can get it up, more likely. Anyway, why should she want to have a child by him even if he could?

EDWARD: Or *she* could.

FREDERICA: And what makes you think she couldn't?

EDWARD: Well, she hasn't and she *was* married before for twenty years or whatever.

FREDERICA: So?

EDWARD: So.

FREDERICA: People are capable of making a clear decision about these things.

EDWARD: Like us.

FREDERICA: Like me is what you meant.

EDWARD: Whatever I meant, it turned out you were quite right. And if I ever thought different, I can see how wrong I was . . .

FREDERICA: How much do you really hate me?

EDWARD: I don't know the answer to that one.

FREDERICA: Why not? You're an intelligent man.

EDWARD: You're an intelligent woman.

FREDERICA: You don't think so.

EDWARD: So you say. And as your father would say, I think that is really an opinion posing as a question.

FREDERICA: You disapprove of his going on the telly all the time, don't you?

EDWARD: And *you* certainly can't reply to a question that expresses its own hatred——

FREDERICA: Don't *you?*

EDWARD: I don't disapprove any more than I do of the Brigadier and his wine making, as long as I don't have to drink it too much.

FREDERICA: You don't though. And how can you compare the Brigadier with my father?

EDWARD: I wasn't and you know it . . .

FREDERICA: What is it that's so fascinating in the newspaper?

EDWARD: The Brigadier is retired and not particularly distinguished even though he's my host and I like him and your father is a busy working writer and very distinguished indeed. All of which is quite different and a waste of my breath and your ears, except they don't function too well.

FREDERICA: They function all right.

EDWARD: It's because I respect what he's done.

FREDERICA: Ah, past tense.

EDWARD: And will quite inevitably do.

FREDERICA: I thought you didn't go much on literature.

EDWARD: I don't. There's enough trouble . . .

FREDERICA: As it is.

EDWARD: Exactly. But looking up occasionally from my smears and slides, I do think someone who is as distinguished and been such a figure, yes, been, is, will still be, continue to be, in nearly all our lives or Western Europe's or at least a few schools and universities and weekly periodicals and newspapers, shouldn't have to clown about doing interviews and literary quiz games and being a fireside character or sage or whatever he is to people, which I've no idea what that is and don't care and neither will they for different reasons and in five minutes either before a new series or after the next programme even. Even . . .

FREDERICA: I don't understand that sentence.

EDWARD: Nor me. But there was some bacteria jumping about in there if you can be bothered and we neither of us can . . .

FREDERICA: You were saying?

EDWARD: I just hope he gets paid all he can get and gets some innocent pleasure out of it, which he's entitled to without censorious philistines like me overreacting to . . . As for this paper, I quite agree with you that it's pretty deadly——

FREDERICA: Do you think you're getting your sense of humour back again?

EDWARD: As usual . . . I never lost it. It was taken from me by force.

FREDERICA: By me?

EDWARD: No. By the mysterious, satanic little creatures that even sober English ladies, colonels' ladies, residents' and missionaries' ladies used to occasionally spot after daylong tennis parties in the dusk of forgotten . . . colonial days.

FREDERICA: No. Not forgotten.

EDWARD: No, remembered in white and pink Georgian buildings . . . and the reef piloted through by Nelson himself, and the harbour where the American tourists throw their litter and cartons and beer cans and coke, on the way to the gift shops with their tour guides, and "hello folks," the package smiles and surliness and black feeling all round, all, all of a dimness . . .

FREDERICA: This place really has got you down.

EDWARD: No it hasn't. And the reason I read the paper is because the Brigadier goes into town and gets it specially for me every morning.

FREDERICA: That's his excuse.

EDWARD: He can't afford it.

FREDERICA: You mean Robin can't.

EDWARD: And I know that he'll want to talk about it page by page

from the home news to the leader and letters, to the racing
at Catterick and the obituaries and court circular.

FREDERICA: Fascinating.

EDWARD: Not at all fascinating. But probably as much or as more
as he gets from Robin . . .

FREDERICA: Why do you have to knock my sisters?

EDWARD: I don't. As you know. You know better than I do.

FREDERICA: Come on.

EDWARD: What?

FREDERICA: Please.

EDWARD: Please come on? Come on what?

FREDERICA: Be friends.

EDWARD: We *are* friends.

FREDERICA: Married—friends.

EDWARD: Yes. Married—friends . . .

FREDERICA: You are having a good time, aren't you?

EDWARD: Yes. Are you?

FREDERICA: Sure. Can I have some of your drink?

EDWARD: I'll call Leroi.

FREDERICA: No. I'll have a sip of yours.

EDWARD: I'll get another. Leroi!

FREDERICA: What have I done now?

EDWARD: Leroi! Come on, you sullen, charmless, unbeautiful,
black bastard.

FREDERICA: Don't get one for *me*.

[LEROI *ambles in*]

EDWARD: Are you sure? Well, I will, anyway. Another one please,
Leroi. [LEROI *leaves into the cool of the house*] Sorry to be
a bother!

FREDERICA: I wonder what it was like then, when Nelson or Hood
or poor old Admiral Byng used to drop in.

EDWARD: Rather pleasant after being aboard those ships, I should
think.

FREDERICA: Would you like to go back?

EDWARD: Where?

FREDERICA: Home.

EDWARD: What for?

FREDERICA: You're restless.

EDWARD: One thing I'm not ever is restless, at home or abroad
. . . He said, trying to sound as pleased with himself as possible.

FREDERICA: We're all right, aren't we?

EDWARD: Fine. All right . . .

FREDERICA: You don't sound sure.

EDWARD: Neither do you. But I take your word for it . . .

FREDERICA: Do you?

EDWARD: I did just say so . . .

FREDERICA: Do you think Robin and the Brigadier *will* have any
children?

EDWARD: If they can and want to. Why don't you ask her?

FREDERICA: I don't like to.

EDWARD: Would you like *me* to?

FREDERICA: No. It's too personal.

EDWARD: Indeed.

FREDERICA: Private. [LEROI *comes in and they watch him go
through the slow business of putting the drink on the table.
He goes]* Why do you get cross when I ask questions?

EDWARD: I don't. Only when you expect answers.

FREDERICA: Friends? [*She puts out her hand to him*]

EDWARD: Friends.

FREDERICA: I *did* put out my hand.

EDWARD: Yes. I know. *First.*

FREDERICA: Don't say anything . . . I try to be detached.

EDWARD: Why not? If it makes you feel more real?

FREDERICA: Real. What's *that,* for God's sake?

EDWARD: You can produce effects in *real* people. Including me,
even. As if you *were* them. Or me.

FREDERICA: I'm afraid I don't understand that. And I shouldn't
think you can.

EDWARD: No. Sometimes I don't feel I can understand a word of
anything anyone says to me. As if they were as unclear as
I am . . .

FREDERICA: Too abstract for me.

EDWARD: If you're wayward.

FREDERICA: *Way*ward?

EDWARD: Oh, or impossible or just dotty enough, you escape every, any coherence or intent that might be in the way . . .

FREDERICA: What'll we do today? Swim before lunch?

EDWARD: Don't think *I* will.

FREDERICA: Do you good.

EDWARD: I know. I've put on weight.

FREDERICA: You have.

EDWARD: Robin's cooking.

FREDERICA: Well I think *I'll* go.

EDWARD: I'll come down with you . . .

FREDERICA: Are you sure you wouldn't rather go home?

EDWARD: Sure.

FREDERICA: You wouldn't like to get back to your work?

EDWARD: No. I don't find work so irresistible.

FREDERICA: That's because you're lucky. You know it's there, waiting for you.

EDWARD: There are equally attractive alternatives to work.

FREDERICA: Like?

EDWARD: Idleness, for one. You can always make a choice.

FREDERICA: Not all of us. It's *behind* us.

EDWARD: Can we leave that one alone for a bit.

FREDERICA: Of course . . . I'll get changed. I can't bear abstractions. Sort of labour-saving devices.

EDWARD: *That* sounds like an abstraction.

FREDERICA: Does it? Well, I'll go for the concrete any time.

EDWARD: That can be just as evasive. Don't ask me what I mean.

FREDERICA: I wasn't going to. I've given all that up . . .

EDWARD: Just as well.

FREDERICA: Um?

EDWARD: I think I'll have a quick dip after all.

[Enter MARY, FREDERICA'*s youngest sister. Her husband,* ROBERT, *with her. Both about mid-thirty]*

FREDERICA: Where have you been?

MARY: Just for a walk, keeping away from the tourists from the cruise ship.

FREDERICA: Not another lot!

MARY: I think these are only here for the day. We went along the beach.

EDWARD: Oh, you hardly ever see them there. They don't like the idea of walking.

FREDERICA: Don't think they *can*, you mean.

ROBERT: Few little Nips popping away with cameras and an odd Kraut or two, bellowing at their *Fraus*.

EDWARD: Didn't you notice the little fleet of old cartons and coke bottles coming round this way? You can see it from here even. Regular armada out there.

ROBERT: Also, we thought we'd nip off early so that we didn't have to say good-bye to the Brigadier's mama.

FREDERICA: She has gone, I hope?

MARY: Unless the plane's crashed.

FREDERICA: As long as she's *on* it, that's fine.

MARY: Robin went with them, to see her off. And the Brigadier's getting the papers and a few other things.

FREDERICA: We stayed in bed till we thought she'd gone . . .

EDWARD: Well, the Brigadier seems quite fond of her.

FREDERICA: He doesn't have to put up with her like the rest of us. He's too busy with his vines or in his workshop making some object. Anyway, I don't think you should call him "Brigadier."

EDWARD: Well, he is, isn't he?

FREDERICA: I suppose he is, though I've got my doubts about it. But people don't call you "Doctor." Besides, you're the only one who calls him it to his face.

EDWARD: Why not?

FREDERICA: Because it sounds as if you're sending him up.

EDWARD: I don't mean to.

FREDERICA: Maybe.

MARY: I think you're all a bit mean about his mother. She's not that bad. And she *is* quite old.

FREDERICA: That is no mitigation any more than youth. She's a crabbed old rat bag. If I'd have known she'd be here I don't suppose I'd have come. Damn it, one of the reasons we came out here was to get away from having to have Edward's mother another Christmas.

MARY: *And* see Robin and everyone.

FREDERICA: Sure. But I tell you, I'd have got on the nearest dog-sled to the South Pole to get away from one more Christmas with that old gangster. Complaining, and wailing, and scheming, impossible to please. Like having an incontinent, superannuated Mafia in your sitting room all day. Even Edward can't stand her, though he never tells her to her face and he really—and he really—hates her more than I do.

ROBERT: Men's mums *are* usually worse.

FREDERICA: The Christmas before, I nearly went into the London Clinic afterwards for the rest of the year. Actually, I'll say this, which isn't much, for the Brigadier's mama—she's got a bit more class than Edward's, even if she does pretend she's not deaf. At least, she doesn't look as if she's had the curse every day for the past sixty-five years.

ROBERT: She's got chronic menstruation,
     Never laughs, never smiles,
     Mine's a dismal occupation,
     Cracking ice for Grandma's piles.

EDWARD: Oh, *I* remember that.

FREDERICA: Men——

EDWARD: What's the verse after that?

ROBERT: Even now the baby's started,
     Having epileptic fits;
     Every time it coughs it farts,
     Every time it farts it shits.

FREDERICA: If it's grubby-minded, *they'll* remember it.

EDWARD: That's it:
     Yet we are not broken hearted,
     Neither are we up the spout.

FREDERICA: Or schoolboy enough.

ROBERT: Auntie Rachel has just farted,
     Blown her arsehole inside out.

EDWARD: Or—innocent enough.

MARY: Who needs men?

FREDERICA: I think—mostly—other men.

MARY: Perhaps we should do without 'em altogether.

EDWARD: I hope you all shall.

MARY: Be careful.

FREDERICA: Yes. You're all likely to be taken up on it any moment.

EDWARD: We have looked upwards at the heavens and seen the signs brooding over us, and taken . . . due note.

FREDERICA: Good. [To MARY] Coming for a swim?

MARY: Oh. I don't know really. I've got an odd sore on my thigh. It doesn't seem to heal.

FREDERICA: Nothing does here. Come on.

ROBERT: I think she's a bit self-conscious about it.

FREDERICA: In front of her sister and her husband—come on. Even the salt water in this sea must have *some* salty old natural antiseptic in it somewhere.

ROBERT: Do you mind if I have a drink first?

FREDERICA: If you don't mind waiting for Flash Leroi, the genie of the island.

ROBERT: Oh, yes. [Calls] Leroi!

FREDERICA: You'll have to do better than that. He'll just pretend he's not heard.

ROBERT: LEROI!

EDWARD: LEROI!

FREDERICA: Either he'll have heard it or we'll be trampled under a turtle stampede.

EDWARD: [To MARY] Would you like me to look at that sore place for you?

MARY: No, thanks. I've bought some stuff at the chemist and old Harry's given me something.

FREDERICA: Harry's got more medicines than Edward ever has.

EDWARD: Mosty local herbs and stuff but they're probably more effective than anything you'll buy. He's full of local folklore and benevolent witchcraft.

FREDERICA: Harry must be the only American to stay here longer than a week.

EDWARD: Maybe *they're* right.

FREDERICA: Maybe.

MARY: He must be the oldest—I was going to say European—well, resident.

FREDERICA: I think that palm goes to Lamb. He was clattering his golden typewriter out there just after the war.

ROBERT: *Our* war, you mean?

FREDERICA: Yes. Ours.

MARY: That makes Robin and the Brigadier practically newcomers.

EDWARD: Until the next wave. It's what I think they call "ripe for development."

FREDERICA: Nothing heals, everything goes rotten or mildewed. Slimy. It's like a great green bombed garden . . .

ROBERT: Look at those birds.

FREDERICA: Don't *you* start.

ROBERT: What are they, tern?

FREDERICA: We've named them "the duffers."

MARY: Why?

FREDERICA: Mr. and Mrs. Duffer. Because they're so helpless. Helpless and hopeless. They managed to bang out some eggs, half of which I think they broke themselves. They half built a nest, then it blew down. And when they finished one finally they can hardly remember where they put it.

EDWARD: I find that quite likable.

FREDERICA: I don't know which of them is worse, him or her. Both hopeless.

EDWARD: Tending your own garden's not a bad resort, even if it *is* the last one *and* bombed at that.

FREDERICA: Well, if no one's coming, I think I'll have my dip before Robin and the Brigadier come back to tell me I mustn't spoil the lunch.

MARY: I'd come but Alastair's coming and he'll get cross if my hair's all full of salt and greasy.

FREDERICA: Is he coming to crimp your hair?

MARY: Yes. He's doing it this afternoon.

FREDERICA: Would you ask him to do mine? I've nothing to do.

MARY: Right.
EDWARD: I'll come and watch you.
FREDERICA: Just as you like . . .

[EDWARD *follows her off*]

MARY: Did I say anything?
ROBERT: She's *your* sister.
MARY: I don't know what any of them are thinking. I never have done. Robin or Evangie neither.
ROBERT: Nor does Edward.
MARY: You *are* enjoying yourself?
ROBERT: The fare was expensive. But otherwise it's cheap. And the company's good.
MARY: Who?
ROBERT: *You*, dozey . . . The one thing about Frederica. She's adroit. She can even make Edward feel he's created a situation when it's all hers. We're all relatively innocent.
MARY: Do you think anyone's enjoying it?
ROBERT: Me.
MARY: And Robin and the Brigadier?
ROBERT: They have to. They've chosen to live here.
MARY: Yes. Odd to think of them actually *living* here.
ROBERT: Improvising. Getting things done. Plumbing, a new bathroom and shower, or extra guest room . . .
MARY: Yes, but swimming and sunshine.
ROBERT: Every day.
MARY: No taxes.
ROBERT: Hardly
MARY: It seemed as if we were all on holiday again at first . . . Leroi never came.
ROBERT: I think one day we'll call and he'll not be there. And someone, Robin and the Brigadier anyhow, will be on their own.
MARY: I think I know what you mean . . .
ROBERT: Still, as you say, for the meantime, there's still tennis and riding and water skiing. The Club, long drinks. Golf course.
MARY: And Americans. Do you think they'll stay?

ROBERT: The Americans? Oh, build more hotels I dare say.

MARY: No, Frederica and Edward?

ROBERT: Don't know. They're rich enough to cut holidays short. Remember, with her, it's all or nothing, and as you can't get all, not really anywhere . . .

[Enter ROBIN *and the* BRIGADIER*]*

ROBIN: Hullo. Where's everyone gone to?

ROBERT: Your dad's gone for a walk and to buy a new hat against the sun. And Fred and Ted have gone for a dip. At least, *she* has.

ROBIN: What about the others?

MARY: Well, Alastair should be here soon. And I expect Daddy won't be long.

BRIGADIER: Isn't Lamb coming?

MARY: I expect he'll pick up Alastair in his car.

ROBIN: Only the Brigadier's making one of his soufflés and he's already had too much at the airport *and* the Club while I was shopping.

BRIGADIER: I didn't.

ROBERT: Did the old lady get off all right then?

ROBIN: Usual delays.

BRIGADIER: Only thing left over from the *ancien régime* and that's red tape and it grows like flowers in this climate.

ROBIN: Examined her passport, money, search for firearms. Everything. She'd even managed to convince herself she'd had a good time before she got there. And then . . .

BRIGADIER: Better see what Leroi's up to. I can get the salad going, at least, and the wine.

ROBIN: I told *him* to do all that.

BRIGADIER: I know. Drinks all charged? Good. *[He goes out]*

ROBIN: And there's always Harry. He'll drop in any old time.

MARY: Can I help?

ROBIN: No. You're here to relax. After all, we *live* here. . . . Do you think they're having a good time?

MARY: Frederica?

ROBIN: Yes.

ROBERT: Enormous. . . . You know what people are like.

ROBIN: That's the trouble. I don't. I just gave up, years ago. Even my sisters, no, mostly my sisters, except perhaps Mary here. And they've given *me* up too.

MARY: Well, you do live what's called "out of the way."

ROBIN: I know. But that's why we came here in the first place. Evangie's working on her book I suppose?

MARY: Somewhere.

ROBIN: She never seems to let up. I said to her: come for a "holiday."

MARY: You know Evangie. Work is everything.

ROBIN: Not if it's never play as well. Worrying about the reviews——

ROBERT: Which hardly anyone reads anyway.

ROBIN: Worrying about the next thing she's going to do.

ROBERT: And the one after that. And after *that*. No one owes *that* to posterity. What does it do for you?

ROBIN: I think Christopher may be right about the past after all.

MARY: What do you mean?

ROBIN: Looking over his shoulder all the time, living off the things daddy's done, rather than what he's doing himself now.

ROBERT: Well, the future owes no one a living. After all, it's done nothing for you . . .

ROBIN: Still, it's a strange thing, giving yourself up to the reputation of an old man. And an old man so demanding . . . and self-protective. It isn't that the old thing is some *giant*.

MARY: We may not be the judges of that. He's not half bad . . .

ROBERT: Even if he's only half good, one shouldn't be on trial by one's daughters. It would make parlour King Lears out of a lot of us.

ROBIN: Perhaps having children of your own puts one in a different position to your own father, and that's why Frederica and I are more critical of him.

MARY: I may be just less critical. . . . But Evangie worships him.

ROBERT: That might be because she feels in blood competition.

ROBIN: As a writer too.

MARY: *His* achievement.

ROBIN: An example.

ROBERT: Of excellence. Or, as you say, *nudging* it.

ROBIN: Christopher feels that obviously. Robert, as someone said, if you've no world of your own, it's rather pleasant to regret the passing of someone else's.

MARY: I think Evangie's a bit keen on him.

ROBIN: Is she really? I'd have thought he wasn't successful enough, too much of a disused hulk. Anyway, I can't see Christopher turning his head forward to an affair with someone like Evangie.

MARY: Or marriage?

ROBIN: Least of all. He's left that behind him. Just so much discarded wreckage and messy debris. Like bits of old cars dumped in the woods.

MARY: I can't think he can feel as bleak as all that, otherwise he couldn't be so cheerful at devoting all his time to daddy and nannying him like he does.

ROBERT: I don't know. It might be a case of fatigue. Shaky structure. Apologetic for what one is, afraid of what we may become.

MARY: You make him sound such a mediocrity.

ROBERT: I don't think he is. He may want too much, and unlike Evangie, he's given up. People do sometimes choose mediocrity.

MARY: But can you really *choose* it?

ROBERT: I don't see why not. It's a way out of feeling isolated. Like a horse's twitch, you apply pain to the nose—to divert it from the knife cutting into it from behind. Or wherever it may be . . .

ROBIN: I think if he's got eyes for anyone, it's Frederica.

ROBERT: Not much joy there, I'd have thought.

ROBIN: No. She and Edward are at least matched.

ROBERT: That would be swapping one twitch for another. She'd eat him before breakfast.

ROBIN: I don't know about that. But it would certainly be hurtful all round. Still, I've watched him with her. He's certainly fascinated by all those straight, masculine gestures of hers and what he thinks is openness.

ROBERT: Instead of a disguise?

ROBIN: Yes.

MARY: Do you imagine Edward's noticed?

ROBIN: Probably. But she knows there's not much pain she can cause there. Besides, I don't think she has much regard for Chris. Though, that might not matter, of course.

ROBERT: Could be the opposite.

ROBIN: And, he may be, even he, well, getting a bit tired of coping with the old man . . . I say, we do observe one another and speculate and chatter on about the others.

ROBERT: Perhaps it's being sisters. All four of you. Even to an outsider, there's something fascinating to watch in it. An inner circle of lives. One's almost tempted to try each one in turn.

MARY: Not any more, I hope.

ROBERT: I'm too near the circle.

ROBIN: Yes. And sharing the same parents. But all different.

MARY: And living different lives, having husbands and lovers or not, or children or not.

ROBERT: In-laws.

ROBIN: Don't. At least I know mine's safely on the plane for another twelve months anyway. Sometimes I don't give the Brigadier her letters to him. It often kills the morning. He sits out in his old shed, brooding and smoking and then drinks too much of his own wine for lunch and has to lie down for the rest of the day. What's going on today, anyway?

MARY: Well, Robert, I expect, will do nothing again. Alastair's coming to do my hair.

ROBIN: Ah, yes. I hope he doesn't bring anyone. Oh, well, doesn't matter. You all seem to like him.

MARY: He's thoughtful and attentive. And kind. He amuses daddy. And the Brigadier likes him. And *he's* keen on Frederica. She's beautiful and she makes *him* laugh.

ROBIN: And she's got hair he calls "good stuff." Not like my mop.

ROBERT: Everyone *does* like him. He gives you a feeling he's just about to do or say something brave. Instead of just camp.

MARY: You're right about daddy.

ROBERT: Oh, yes, he's always saying to me "When's that nice little queer boy coming round?"

ROBIN: Yes, he's always asking me the same things about people he's going to meet. "Will I like him?" Then "Is he a bugger or a Jew?"

[Enter CHRISTOPHER *and* EVANGIE*]*

CHRISTOPHER: You're talking about Wyatt. Behind my back.

ROBIN: Why not? We *have* known him quite a long time.

CHRISTOPHER: Sure. Longer than I have. Before I'd *heard* of him.

EVANGIE: He's said that as long as I remember. "Will I like him?" And then "Do you think he'll like *me?*"

CHRISTOPHER: I've been asleep. Apart from a phone call. Then Evangie's typewriter woke me——

EVANGIE: Sorry.

CHRISTOPHER: I should have been up. I made her come out for some sea air. Where's the old boy?

ROBIN: Up first thing. Gone for his walk. And a new hat. I said I'd throw the old one away.

EVANGIE: I think he inherited it from George Moore or somebody.

CHRISTOPHER: Yeats, I think.

EVANGIE: Oh. Sorry.

CHRISTOPHER: Don't. It's not very important.

EVANGIE: It is—to him.

CHRISTOPHER: Not necessarily.

ROBIN: Alastair's coming for lunch. Do you want your hair done?

EVANGIE: Oh, yes.

ROBIN: What's Wyatt up to after lunch?

CHRISTOPHER: I've arranged an interview for him. With the island newspaper, whatever it is . . .

MARY: He'll hate that.

ROBIN: No he won't. He'll make us and Christopher *think* he does. Or try to.

EVANGIE: And why not?

ROBERT: Why not?

CHRISTOPHER: Indeed.

ROBERT: You can't make people like Wyatt do things he doesn't really want to do. Even Christopher. It's a mistake one's inclined to make.

[Enter WYATT. *He is about seventy, flushed and hot from his walk*]

WYATT: What's that? What are you saying? You can't be talking about me. Gosh, I'm in a soak from all this sun! What a *day* it is! Think of all those people freezing in the Home Counties, hoping the rails and points won't ice up again! Ice and floods to *come*, I dare say. And everybody'll be *so* astonished. As usual. I *have* had a time. Spoke to such a nice lot of people. Charming lot in the shops, and I went to that smashing little market. Got a splendid new hat. Do you like it?

ROBIN: Quite an improvement.

WYATT: Couldn't bear to part with the old one. Poor old thing. They put it in this parcel for me, all done up. Can't remember who gave it me.

EVANGIE: George Moore.

WYATT: No, it wasn't him.

CHRISTOPHER: Yeats.

WYATT: No. Someone . . . I say, you *do* look in the pink, all of you. How nice. You're such a good sight to come back to. I'm quite tired. Been walking since breakfast. Old Leroi can be quite good, you know. I know you don't go on him much but lovely poached eggs he got. Asked him what he thought about the English, and do you know what he said: "I'm glad they've gone, sir, but an English millionaire is still worth more than an American millionaire."

ROBERT: Depends on how many millions.

ROBIN: He means we're better tippers.

WYATT: Went all round the bay. Quite empty. Not an American in sight. Not even old Harry.

ROBIN: He's not exactly a tourist.

WYATT: No. Sweet old thing. Had a good squiz at all the coral. Remarkable. Real Captain Cook, Darwin sort of thing. Saw

Nelson's little place. If ever it was, anyway, all jolly nice. What's for lunch?

ROBIN: Salad and soufflé. And some fish. The Brigadier's laid it all on today.

WYATT: Good old Brigadier. Officer material all right. I often think of him in the war and all that. All I ever did was fill in forms for supplies in Delhi most of the time. What have you all been doing?

ROBIN: Chatting, seeing off mothers . . .

WYATT: She go off all right?

ROBIN: Yes, but it seemed like touch and go for a while. When it took off I had a large brandy.

WYATT: Oh, dear, she's not all that much older than me. I hope you don't have to have large brandies after seeing me off.

ROBIN: Don't be silly, papa. You know you're welcome as long as you like.

MARY: The thing is you're too restless to stay anywhere too long.

EVANGIE: Besides, you do, at least, seem to enjoy everything— while it lasts, anyway.

ROBERT: Instead of looking like a professional spare prick at a wedding.

WYATT: Oh, that *is* good!

MARY: Robert! Really . . .

WYATT: Oh, dear, do I seem easily bored? I don't think I am. No, I just like to waddle off in all directions. While I'm still able to. She seemed quite a sprightly old trout. Of course, I suppose we had odd common points of interest, people we both knew. That's one of the things about age, you find less and less people who remember the things you do. Of course, the Brigadier's father was in the Colonial Service, like your grandfather, so there was all that. Then there was the war. She remembered that.

ROBERT: Yours or ours?

WYATT: Mine, I suppose, though I don't remember much of it. I remember yours, as you call it, all the ration books and being snubbed and kept waiting at the Food Office.

ROBIN: Don't!

EVANGIE: Most of the people I meet don't even remember *that*. Or they've forgotten.

MARY: Or they think you mean Korea or even Vietnam.

WYATT: Only things I remember well are the list of names of old boys killed or wounded being read out by the housemaster in chapel. That and being chased by a horde of women, very middle-class sort of women, half way across Southsea because I wasn't in uniform. Jolly thankful I was too. Too feeble to be a conchie and too much of a funk to face all that mud and bullying and limbs blown off. Oh, no. Of course, I was only about fourteen but "tall for my age," as they said then. "Outgrowing my strength." School was bad enough, at least I suppose it wasn't *quite* as bad. Do you know, I was asking the Brigadier the other day why this house was called "Mesopotamia"? Apparently, his father was there in 1917 or whenever it was. Always thought if I'd had to go, or be dragged off, I'd rather have gone there. Expect I'd have been stung by a wasp and died like poor little R. Brooke. Funny end for a poet, I mean *genuinely* funny. I think I'd prefer to be stung to death rather than to wake up in some agonising ward with half of me shot away and the rest in torment. Don't you?

ROBERT: Right. What school *did* you go to?

WYATT: Marlborough. That was *my* Western Front. Perhaps it wasn't so bad, though all the ones I've spoken to who were there then who say they were happy are the most awful types. Overweaning little swots or thumping great Prussian sons of Great Albion. All become florid M.P.s or sarky-tongued bullies at the Bar; clammy old bishops and arch-bishops or those huge surgeons who tower over you in green and rubber wellies and call their patients "the meat." Of course I was the only one who didn't go to Eton. My father went, so did all my elder brothers.

CHRISTOPHER: Why was that?

WYATT: For one thing I was a skinny, runtish thing, although I was tall and none of my brothers' clothes ever fitted me. Because, of course, being the last, I wore their cast-off jackets and even trousers. Always had a patch on sleeves just below the elbows, so I always felt cold and had chilblains. Anyway, Father decided I needed "toughening up" at a really tough school. *Actually* it was because he'd already sent five sons to Eton and the year I left my prep school, the roof of the house had to be completely renewed and the old boy said he couldn't afford the fees at Eton, even with reductions. So: that's how I got to Marlborough. Though I believe it's quite a jolly place nowadays, pop music and even girls, girls! What it *could* have been like! Do you know what the cure for chilblains was then? Soaking your feet and hands in your own pee. *Most* unpleasant—you ponged all over the classroom and weren't even warm when you dunked yourself.

ROBIN: Well, *I'd* better rescue the Brigadier from Leroi. I hope Frederica isn't too late for lunch. The old chap gets awfully upset if his cooking is spoiled.

MARY: Start without them.

ROBIN: No. He likes everyone to sit down.

WYATT: Quite right. We'll wait for her. I say, the old boy's jolly clever with his cooking, isn't he? Must be nice for you, old thing. I could never cook an *egg*, not even at Oxford, where everybody seemed to.

ROBIN: Well, it's better than relying on *my* cooking and anything's better than Leroi. You'll get lunch about tea time.

CHRISTOPHER: Shall I go and look for Frederica?

ROBIN: No, she'll come in her own time. Edward's with her, anyway. He'll hurry her somehow.

CHRISTOPHER: Pretty exhausting—hurrying people up. Like picking up a child's clothes for him.

MARY: *You* should know . . .

EVANGIE: I think when you love someone you should do so, knowing that one day you will hate them.

WYATT: I say, *what* an interesting remark!

EVANGIE: I've seen it happen too often——

MARY: To others?

EVANGIE: Most of us.

WYATT: Do you know, I haven't thought of it? I suppose I must be a thundering old nuisance. Am I, Christopher?

CHRISTOPHER: You're scrupulous about the things that matter.

WYATT: No, Evangie's right as usual.

EVANGIE: I wish I *were* "right as usual."

CHRISTOPHER: Do you? I don't. But I don't expect it. Certainly not of myself.

WYATT: No. I *am* disorganized. I forget things, leave things about, crash in everywhere, like some maddening old toddler. I *must* watch it. Otherwise, you'll *all* need large brandies when you see the back of me. . . . Your mother was a bit like that and I never realized it till she was dead. I must have enjoyed a few brandies since that funeral. Awful thing to say, but I think that was almost the most enjoyable day of my life. When those ropes slid down into that grave, I had to lower my head right down so that no one could see my face . . . I must be very unfeeling indeed, I mean not to feel anything but, no, not relief, merriment, that's the word for it, merriment at my own wife's funeral! Even good old Cranmer's words didn't affect me. Well, of course, none of you really remember her. Except Robin, I suppose?

ROBIN: Not much. Try and hurry them up. *[She goes out]*

WYATT: Is that nice little queer boy coming?

MARY: Yes. He's crimping the entire family.

WYATT: Oh, good. I do like him. I didn't know what'sit, crimping, was such an interesting business. Like being in the mess or common room. Wish he'd do *mine*. He's got a splendid head of hair.

MARY: It's a wig.

WYATT: Good heavens—a wig! Is it really?

MARY: Yes, *really*, daddy.

WYATT: Perhaps he'd get *me* one. How do you *know* it is?

MARY: Some of us do notice these things.

WYATT: Did *you* know?

EVANGIE: Yes.

WYATT: Robert?

ROBERT: Yes, but he told me too. First time we met he said "You know I'm just an uptight little bald Scots queen under this red rug. They all send me up and call me either the Virgin Queen or Mary, Queen of Scots! It used to upset me but now I'm not bothered."

WYATT: Did he say that? Poor little devil! I suppose he must really be bothered, in fact.

EVANGIE: It's not only hairdressing that's cutthroat in his line.

WYATT: Yes, I see what you mean. Gosh, I'm so glad I didn't mention it to him. It would have seemed most unkind. I wish I noticed things like *you* all do.

MARY: I think you do, really, daddy. You don't miss the tricks.

WYATT: Devious, you mean? Yes. I see you do. That's not a nice trait either. Pretending not to notice when all the time you do.

EVANGIE: We forgive you.

MARY: Like your calling Robin "old thing."

WYATT: But I call everyone "old thing." Why, oh, even Leroi.

MARY: Exactly, it makes her feel old.

WYATT: It's just that she *is* the oldest of you all.

MARY: And inferior and played out.

WYATT: I honestly didn't mean to . . .

MARY: Whether you did or didn't, it still sounds disparaging and unkind. To her, anyway.

WYATT: Oh dear, I am sorry. You make me feel quite awful.

MARY: Like you never call Frederica "old thing" or me even. Or call her Fred, Fred and Ted, like some do, because you know she hates it. She gets "lovely long legs and hair like your mother . . ."

WYATT: Do I do that? Oh, dear. Poor old Robin. There I go again! It's just that I think of you all differently, different parts of my life. Robin, well, the eldest, first born then, you the young, pretty one with your own babies, and Evangie the intellectual one.

EVANGIE: Thanks. I know what a pejorative "intellectual" is to you.

WYATT: Not at all. I'm just frightened of people who are cleverer than me. They are even worse than the physical bullies at school. You could always *despise* them, even when they were making you cry.

EVANGIE: Men don't want "intellectual" daughters any more than they do wives.

WYATT: Oh, my dear, I seem to have hurt you all. I never meant to . . .

EVANGIE: Not Frederica. She was the only one who couldn't care.

WYATT: It's just that a lot of things I don't understand, and I suppose I've stepped over them or discarded them like my boots on the floor. I never even knew what "growing out of your strength" meant when it was said to me as a boy. Though I said it to Evangie, I know. Oh, dear . . . This hat's not as good as the old one. I feel quite hot. I'd better go into the shade, I think . . .

MARY: Alastair's probably coming with Lamb.

WYATT: Lamb? What's that?

MARY: The writer.

EVANGIE: Is he? Gosh, how good.

WYATT: Not a *writer?* Oh, Lord, I hate meeting writers.

EVANGIE: But why?

WYATT: They *know* about you usually. They can trip you up if they've a mind to. If they're better than me, I get all yellowy and envious, and if they're worse it just depresses me. For them. And then again, if they're bad, they perform themselves so *well* and amuse everyone. And if they're really good, they don't bother to perform at all, quite rightly, all lordly. Oh, dear, Lamb is it? But he's frightfully successful, isn't he, invented tax havens and things and writes best sellers?

CHRISTOPHER: I shouldn't worry about all that. Anyway, he's quite shy.

WYATT: Is he a bugger?

CHRISTOPHER: Almost certainly.

EVANGIE: But not necessarily literally.

MARY: And not Jewish.

WYATT: Is that why he's coming with little Alastair?

EVANGIE: Possibly. Alastair would tell you if you ask him.

WYATT: Oh, no. How awful. I wonder if he takes his wig off in bed. Lamb . . . Lamb. I remember him. We got frightfully drunk together in some club somewhere years ago. Savile or somewhere like that. But he's frightfully impressive. Rather good too, they tell me. I remember he asked me why I pretended to be an ageing schoolboy all the time and I was so embarrassed I didn't go out for a month afterwards. Then he said to me "How queer are you?" And I was so nonplussed because we didn't talk about that much at that time. So, like an awful coward, because I was pretty sure he *was*, I said a bit too airily, "Oh, about forty-five per cent." And he said "Are you? How interesting, I'm ninety-five. You see, I don't trust women." And I said something foolish and gauche. Like "Oh, but all your best friends must have been women."

ROBERT: What did *he* say?

WYATT: "Oh, *exactly,*" or something of the sort. I was so confused by him. Do you think he'll remember?

EVANGIE: Might do.

WYATT: Oh, dear. He must have thought me the most unbearable little prig. I do hope he doesn't. I mean he's really *famous,* isn't he?

CHRISTOPHER: Not in the way *you* are, and he'll know it.

WYATT: You know, I thought of him then as being lots older than me, but, if anything, I suppose he's even a bit younger. He wasn't at Marlborough, I do remember. Eton or Winchester, much grander altogether.

CHRISTOPHER: Don't worry. He'll be more worried than you are. Anyway, you've got this interview this afternoon.

WYATT: What interview?

CHRISTOPHER: With the island newspaper.

WYATT: Oh, no, I say, can't we cancel it?

CHRISTOPHER: He sounds quite a nice young man.

WYATT: Can't put him off? Oh, he'll expect me to be clever and say witty things instead of just being an old duffer who happens to be a writer.

EVANGIE: I think you'll manage.

MARY: Just say all the things you usually say. They won't have heard them out here.

WYATT: What a good wheeze! After all, they all ask the same questions, like have you moved further to the Right; should writers be seen on television; are they any longer relevant to the global village, wherever that is; or just plain do you use a pen or a typewriter? Is he a native? An islander?

CHRISTOPHER: Well, he—she's not English.

WYATT: Then she should be all right I'd think.

CHRISTOPHER: As Mary says, it doesn't matter, anyway.

ROBERT: If it doesn't matter, why does he need to do it?

WYATT: Look a bit childish I suppose. And you know how sensitive they can be in these little places. Especially ex-colonies or whatever they're called.

EVANGIE: Independent states.

WYATT: That's right.

[*Enter* ALASTAIR *with* JED. *Both in their early twenties, but* JED *with shoulder-length black hair. Behind them is* LAMB, *expensively dressed and with a club tie*]

ALASTAIR: Don't talk to me about independent states. This place is just Tel Aviv, U.S.A. in Atlantic. Have you seen that lot come in this morning on that boat? My dear, they've been in all morning in their Mickey Mouse glasses and Florida Blue dilly-dilly hairdo's. As if I'd touch the one of them. Complaining and carrying on, they didn't like Fiji, they liked Australia better. *Australia!* All those beaches, none of which they'd dare go near, but India was worse, and, as for *Europe,* that was worse, even the culture they didn't see much of. Or *think* much of, anyway. Talk about your Young Geriatrics Tours, Inc. "Can you tell me the way to the Gift Shop, young man? Oh, because we've lost our tour guide." I wish we'd lose *them!*

WYATT: Oh, Alastair! How nice it is to see you! You *are* a jolly old thing. *Do* tell us about the Americans.

ALASTAIR: Don't ask—oh, well, I'm bound to bore you about it, anyway. They just make me *mad. You* know. Oh, I don't think you know Mr. Lamb, any of you?

WYATT: My dear Lamb, how nice, what a pleasure to see you here. Do you remember? I was just saying—we met once and got awfully drunk and sorry for ourselves at the Savile—or was it the Travellers?

LAMB: Somewhere like that.

WYATT: This is my daughter Evangie and my youngest, Mary. That's her old man, Robert. Seems a bit surly when you first talk to him but he's North Country, East Riding I think, *and* a schoolteacher so it's not all his fault and he's a cracking good sort underneath it all, aren't you, old thing?

ROBERT: A little cracker.

WYATT: Then there's Frederica, my other daughter and her husband, Eddie. But they're down at the beach. She's rather beautiful, but I'm not supposed to say it and *you* certainly mustn't. She's a frightful flirt, even with me and I know she doesn't care for me over much. Evangie, she's awfully brainy and *writes*. She'll probably trap you in a corner, so I should watch it. Mary's the youngest and prettiest and quite the least trouble of any of them, enjoys everything, doesn't carp, well, not much, does as she's told and smiles and has lots of lovely little kiddies, which the others don't and who can blame them if they're as selfish as me? I never bothered with *my* children. Some people would say I was selfish and maybe it's so but I've always been fascinated by myself long after everyone else was bored to death with me.

ALASTAIR: Stop it! How can you *do* it in this weather?

WYATT: Who else is there? Oh, old Harry. He's not here yet but we think he'll turn up sometime. He's an American but not like the others at all.

LAMB: I know.

WYATT: Well, of course, you must know him better than any of us.

ALASTAIR: This is Jed. He's a student. He's just on his way.

WYATT: How do you do, Jed. Where are you on your way to?

JED: Wherever . . .

WYATT: Yes. I know what you mean. When Alastair says you are a student, are you an eternal student like say, Trefimov?

ALASTAIR: He's an eternal student, you can take it from me. Shall we get ourselves a drink inside? I'll have a word with Robin

to let her know we're here. Is she with Leroi and the Brigadier? Oh, she'll be wanting help then.

[The three of them, ALASTAIR, JED, *and* LAMB, *go in]*

MARY: *[After them]* I expect lunch is ready.
WYATT: Was I all right?
CHRISTOPHER: Fine. He was nervous. I think I'll go and see if I
can find Frederica and Edward.
MARY: I shouldn't worry. They'll come if they want.
CHRISTOPHER: I'll just have a look. All right, Wyatt?
WYATT: Fine, dear boy, fine. Oh, I say, I forgot to introduce you.
CHRISTOPHER: It doesn't matter. *[He goes off]*
WYATT: Do you think I hurt his feelings?
EVANGIE: No.
WYATT: I do hope not. He's such a dear boy.
MARY: Let's go in. I'm hungry.
ROBERT: Me too.
EVANGIE: Right.

[They rise]

WYATT: I feel a bit tired. Anyway, I think I'll wait for Christo-
pher and Frederica.
EVANGIE: Just as you like.
WYATT: Won't be a jiffy ...

*[They go off. He closes his eyes for a few moments. Then
opens them as* HARRY, *an enormous figure in late middle age,
comes in]*

Harry, my dear boy. We were talking of you.
HARRY: Yes? Americans, I suppose? *[He lowers his great frame
into a chair]* Ah! That's better.
WYATT: Not like *you,* Harry. Not like you. You're *special.*
HARRY: That's what we're here for, Wyatt. That's what we're here
for.
WYATT: Are you all right? You look awfully tired.
HARRY: I'm O.K. You know. You get, just tired, and in this
climate ...

WYATT: Yes. I know what you mean, old thing. I wonder where
    Frederica's got to . . . I miss the cold and the damp and the
    colours that change all the winter and then . . . I miss it . . .
    I wish I didn't . . .

HARRY: Well, guess I'd better make myself known to Robin and
    the Brigadier and warn 'em I'm here. *[He rises]* You coming?

WYATT: Later, dear boy. I think I'll wait a little longer.

HARRY: O.K. You'll miss the Brigadier's *plat de maison.*

[He goes into the house. WYATT *closes his eyes against the
sun]*

CURTAIN

ACT TWO

scene 1

After lunch. The same scene. Resting in the shade are WYATT, ROBERT, CHRISTOPHER, LAMB, *and* EVANGIE. *Only* FREDERICA *is standing, looking across the bay.*

WYATT: *[Presently]* I *thought* this new hat was a mistake.

FREDERICA: Sit in the shade, you old silly.

WYATT: Oh, *aren't I? [He moves his chair]* Gosh, it's a scorcher!

FREDERICA: There's a great breeze if you stand up here.

WYATT: Couldn't stand anywhere after all that lunch the Brigadier got for us. I say, he *is* hot stuff in that department, isn't he? But he *was* quite a soldier.

FREDERICA: I suppose it usually is.

WYATT: What?

FREDERICA: Quite a scorcher. Here.

WYATT: Oh.

LAMB: There's a cool season. It rains and there's mist and the mildew sprouts for a few weeks. But it never lasts long.

WYATT: *[Resettled]* Oh, yes, that's more like it.

ROBERT: It'll be cold at home.

WYATT: Perishing. Nice though.

FREDERICA: What are you thinking about?

WYATT: Me?

FREDERICA: Anyone. Don't go to sleep. Robert, keep awake.

ROBERT: Sorry. I was trying *not* to think about the new term start-

43

ing next week. Breath on the grey playground, frozen lava-
tories and Irish stew and sweating middens of cabbage.

WYATT: My dear boy! Don't! How awful for you.

FREDERICA: They're only children.

ROBERT: We're all children once.

FREDERICA: What a pious remark. We may be, but some are more
so than others. And leave it behind more quickly.

ROBERT: I'm sorry I sounded pious.

FREDERICA: Now you're piqued.

WYATT: I didn't think so at all.

LAMB: No. It's like saying: what's 1950 got to do with 1980?

FREDERICA: Well, *what?*

LAMB: We'll be the same people.

FREDERICA: Will we? What were *you* thinking?

LAMB: What I usually think of after lunch here. Walking down
Bond Street in midafternoon with a nice evening to look forward to at Covent Garden or somewhere and time for tea at
the Ritz and money to buy myself a present or, even better,
someone else as well.

FREDERICA: Daddy?

WYATT: Blackfriars Station and George Moore.

FREDERICA: You're making it up.

WYATT: No, I'm not. I was thinking of the beastly cold like
Robert. Of waiting for trains and then looking up at the front
of Blackfriars Station and seeing it inscribed in the stone:
Broadstairs; Dresden; Cheltenham; and *St. Petersburg.* So I
asked the booking clerk for a cheap return to St. Petersburg.

ROBERT: What did he say?

WYATT: "I'm afraid you'll have to go to Victoria."

LAMB: When was this?

WYATT: Nineteen sixty-one. What was the other thing?

ROBERT: George Moore.

WYATT: Nothing. I did meet him a couple of times when I was
a young man. Ebury Street, I think, he lived. Anyway, he
always looked dreadfully ill at ease in company, especially
mixed company, keeping his hands in his pockets all the
time. And one day someone asked him why and he said:

"Well, you see, whenever I stand up I'm afraid my under-
pants will fall down and it's a very uncomfortable feeling
in company. Especially mixed company." And so, whoever it
was, said: "But George, do you not have those little tabs inside to put your braces through?" And Moore replied: "Oh—
those. Do you know I've always been wondering what those
were for!"

FREDERICA: I know why you like that story.

ROBERT: Why? I'd not heard it.

FREDERICA: Because he likes writers being made out to be divine
simpletons or holy innocents, and himself most of all.

WYATT: Unholy. I think we're a dismal bunch, on the whole, to
meet, anyway. Don't you think so?

LAMB: The *performers* are the worst.

WYATT: That's true enough! Indeed. When I think . . . I was
dreading meeting *you*. What a relief it's turned out. He's a
modest old thing, don't you think?

LAMB: I'm not proud of living out in the sunshine if you mean
that?

WYATT: Certainly not. Where people choose to live is their own
business.

ROBERT: Listen . . .

FREDERICA: Not those bloody birds?

ROBERT: The surf.

FREDERICA: What about it?

ROBERT: I can't get used to the sound of it.

FREDERICA: I can. That's the trouble.

WYATT: Not like Cornwall.

ROBERT: Or Pembroke.

FREDERICA: Or Northumberland. Or Brighton. Do *shut up*, both
of you! You're being like those people who are never bored
again and we know what a deadly lot those are.

LAMB: It makes quite a fair old row——

FREDERICA: In the wet season.

ROBERT: Robin's never bored.

FREDERICA: No. She never was.

ROBERT: Neither's the Brigadier.

WYATT: No. Not him.

ROBERT: Cooking.

FREDERICA: Washing up.

ROBERT: Digging, watching his vines and waterfalls and rock gardens.

FREDERICA: Smoking his pipe. I wish men wouldn't smoke pipes.

WYATT: Oh, don't you like it? You used to say you liked the smell of mine.

FREDERICA: I did. I do. It's just *some* men. The way they *do* it. Putting you in your place . . .

ROBERT: Watching, observing, feeding the lizards——

WYATT: Oh, birds. Birds of boredom. What does that make me think of?

FREDERICA: Trafalgar Square . . . How strange you all seem sometimes.

LAMB: We are. And not. And you?

FREDERICA: I don't feel that. No. Not at all.

WYATT: Tedious flight of tern,
　　　How I wonder what you'd earn.

ROBERT: Did you make that up?

FREDERICA: What else?

WYATT: If you fumbled in the sky for words
　　　Would you still just bore like birds? . . .

ROBERT: Good.

WYATT: No . . . Chatter. Frederica is right as usual. Birds chatter and *that* is their mortal flaw. Chatter sins against language and when we sin against the word, we sin against God. Gosh, I *am* pompous.

FREDERICA: I wasn't going to say it.

WYATT: Must be the Brigadier's cuddly, loving little grape. Where's your old man got to?

FREDERICA: He's out there on the beach talking to Jed.

LAMB: Oh, *does* he talk?

ROBERT: I think *there is* someone who could sin against language if he could bring himself to it.

WYATT: Do you, really? Seemed a quiet little chap to me. I tried talking to him but he never said a word.

FREDERICA: Why should he? He despises us.

WYATT: Oh, do you think he does? Yes. Of course. You're right. Oh, dear. . . . Perhaps I said the wrong thing . . . I only asked him about himself.

FREDERICA: He doesn't want your interest. Or anyone's.

WYATT: I thought dear little Alastair was his chum.

FREDERICA: He despises him too.

WYATT: What a shame. Perhaps I should try again?

FREDERICA: Don't. Anyway, you know you've no intention. You dislike him as much as the rest of us. No. More. He frightens you more.

WYATT: I wonder if I should have a sleep and then a walk. Or a walk and *then* a sleep. What do you think?

FREDERICA: Either. On the other hand: both.

ROBERT: The first. Except chatter a bit.

WYATT: Oh. Shall I? I'll annoy old Fred there.

FREDERICA: Would that stop you? I wonder if you can get lung cancer from smoking pot?

ROBERT: Ask Jed.

FREDERICA: I will. There's something about that boy . . .

ROBERT: What?

FREDERICA: I don't know. But he shouldn't *be* here.

LAMB: Well, he is. And plenty more.

FREDERICA: I shan't be sorry to leave this place.

WYATT: Well, don't let old Robin and the Brigadier know.

FREDERICA: Oh, I know. They've taken such pains to give us a good time.

ROBERT: And they live here.

FREDERICA: I'm sorry. I know. [To LAMB] And so do you.

LAMB: That's all right, my dear. I see everyone think it. The ones who come to visit, I mean. Friends. They sit in the sun, and are waited on and bathe and chat, barefoot on the white evening sand, watching the sea and—thinking . . .

ROBERT: That they're glad not to be you.

LAMB: Not to be rich enough to be an exile, browned and at-tended on by sun and by the regular wind and service. But

back to cold, uncertain tides and striving pavements. And the
marriage of anxieties . . . domestic . . . oh . . . extremes . . .

FREDERICA: Where were you born?

LAMB: Me? Kuala Lumpur. Natch.

FREDERICA: Yes. But it doesn't—warm you—as it should do. No. It
leaves you open to all the chills when you come back . . .
over the other side.

LAMB: You?

FREDERICA: Kandy. Ceylon . . . Robin too.

LAMB: You?

EVANGIE: Singapore.

ROBERT: As they used to say, "their father had a bike."

WYATT: What's that?

EVANGIE: Grandpa was in "the Service."

WYATT: Papa? Oh, I'll say he was.

ROBERT: Where were *you* born?

WYATT: Srinagar. Kashmir. Shalimar. Bit like the Thames near
Henley. Lots of lush and vegetables and Weybridge-type
curry and pink blancmange in little elephant moulds. Oh,
the old boy wanted *me* to go in it, of course. All I did was
sire four daughters at his various postings. Trying to be A
Writer. But you *can* write and give Some Service as well.
Give some service. Well, I never did. Just his non-paying
guest. With a wife and four thumping daughters. Well—*he*
gave service. Old thing . . .

LAMB: And your husband?

FREDERICA: Rangoon.

WYATT: What about you, old thing?

ROBERT: Hastings Royal Infirmary.

WYATT: Hastings Royal Infirmary! What about the Brigadier?
Where do you suppose *he* was born?

FREDERICA: Mesopotamia.

WYATT: Mesopotamia. Of *course*.

ROBERT: That's why the house is named.

WYATT: To: Mesopotamia. You can see him . . . setting out. Or
someone . . .

FREDERICA: I wish Edward would stop talking to that boy. Man . . .

WYATT: Who? Little Alastair?

FREDERICA: No. Not little Alastair. Jed.

ROBERT: Perhaps it's his scientific curiosity: "the young mind."

FREDERICA: No. The young, whatever they are, bore him even more than I do.

WYATT: My darling Fred, he adores you.

FREDERICA: Maybe. But he's not a pathologist for nothing.

ROBERT: Examining blood.

FREDERICA: All day.

EVANGIE: Frederica's right.

WYATT: Of course. She always is.

EVANGIE: About being born. Away from home.

FREDERICA: Home?

EVANGIE: Whatever . . .

WYATT: Out of all . . . hearts . . .

EVANGIE: Do you remember grandfather's study?

WYATT: What? The old boy's?

FREDERICA: I'll say.

WYATT: All my life . . .

EVANGIE: The joss sticks and Burmese guns. Saddle oil . . .

FREDERICA: Even the books smelt of curry powder. The Casino Palace, Port Said.

EVANGIE: Back numbers of the *Times of Natal*. A Zulu grammar.

FREDERICA: Manuals in Urdu.

EVANGIE: Rawhide shields and dried python skins and brass iguanas. And the photographs.

FREDERICA: Brown. Brown to yellow.

WYATT: The Casino Palace!

EVANGIE: The Groups.

WYATT: What did the old boy say? I know—"The Royal Navy always travels first class."

EVANGIE: Probyn's Horse, the Peshawar Vale Hunt, tennis parties.

WYATT: Signed photograph of Lord Minto.

EVANGIE: Tent pegging. "Robin: aged one year." A cricket match on the parade ground; amateur theatricals.

FREDERICA: Mummy as Lydia Languish in *The Rivals.*

WYATT: Daddy on the prompt book.

EVANGIE: Field batteries, elephant batteries! I never understood them going into torches . . . The Newcastle Mounted Rifles.

FREDERICA: Inspected by grandfather. Men *do* inspect.

ROBERT: England Inspects . . .

EVANGIE: Frederica on grandmother's pony.

FREDERICA: In a white party frock.

EVANGIE: A timetable of the South India Railway, the oars of Jesus College; *In China with the British*—two vols. *Setting sail aboard the* Rawalpindi.

WYATT: Old *Pindi*—torpedoed first month of the war.

EVANGIE: Taking arsenic instead of baking powder. Talk in the mess. The club.

FREDERICA: In the club. Mummy four times. Lizards on the ceiling above the mosquito net, sweat, the mail. Knick-knacks. Junk and boa constrictors . . .

WYATT: I'm surprised you remember so much. *I* don't. You were all such *children* . . .

FREDERICA: Ah—home to England.

WYATT: *I* don't. At least I don't think so. Do I? Yes. I suppose so. I took it for granted then. Busy being a "writer." God, Lamb, why do we do it?

LAMB: For the money. And being treated well, or better than you *should* be by any rights . . .

FREDERICA: The sky is *so* clear . . . the trees seem even darker than they are. . . . What was it like before?

LAMB: Before? Oh, not so very different, I suppose. The governor general's house is still there though he's called something else now; royalty of some sort came out. New flag went up. The police band played the dreadful national anthem, all deliciously out of tune; you couldn't believe it, the comedy and pain of it. I think someone actually recorded it as a collector's item. Some relief, I suppose. A bit of apprehension but not over much. The climate was the same, the people were the same, we were the same. Except . . . You see. . . . There was despair in a lot of hearts. Even in those who . . . who . . . oh, who . . .

WYATT: Yes. I can see all that. Can't you? The lady-in-waiting; the umbrellas; the marquee.

LAMB: It was comic then. And it's comic *now*. If anyone could ever think of it or remember it. But it was full of pain. *And* some quite good people. Thing about pain. It changes as *you* change. But it doesn't go, does it? *Does* it? Or am I mad as I often think I am when I'm alone, or begging Robin and the Brigadier's pardon? . . .

WYATT: You're not mad, old thing . . .

LAMB: Wish you weren't all going.

WYATT: Still a bit of time.

LAMB: There's me and Robin. The Brigadier. Alastair chatting up the tourists in his crimping parlour. Going on his crying jags, threatening us all with his too many sleeping pills, falling in love with young Americans he despises and who despise him. Looking to an old Etonian queen like me, who's respectable only because he's rich and famous. Turning to Jed, who hates him slightly less than the rest of us . . .

WYATT: Oh, dear . . .

LAMB: Mortified by the sunlight on his wig join.

FREDERICA: That could have been a song once. When you think of it. "Sunlight on My Wig Join."

LAMB: I'm sorry.

FREDERICA: No.

LAMB: It's just that we shall miss you. But I shouldn't have really said so.

FREDERICA: Why not? You *thought* it.

LAMB: Do *you* say everything you think?

FREDERICA: No. People think I do. Sometimes *I* think I do.

LAMB: Robin will miss you.

ROBERT: Sisters are strange things.

FREDERICA: We all travesty ourselves. It seems unavoidable. Totally . . .

WYATT: *[Reading paper]* Good God!

LAMB: What?

WYATT: Do you know what we're missing on B.B.C.! At this almost very moment? Robert, *you* read it. You've got good, young eyes.

ROBERT: *[Reads]* "Europe Since 1945. The fifth of twelve programmes on economic and social change in Western and Eastern Europe since the end of the Second World War. Next: New Structures in Society . . ."

LAMB: Oh, no . . .

ROBERT: "To what extent have such factors as economic growth increased educational opportunity, and welfare of post-European societies both east and west, towards a single type of industrial society? . . ."

FREDERICA: Help!

ROBERT: "By the Professor of Social and Industrial Studies at the Sorbonne. *Worker Participation Control:* A discussion of different forms of worker power in industrial management, from participation French style, through West German cooperation to Yugoslavia's worker-control. Thursday: Managing the economy Number Seven. Prospects for an Incomes Policy. How to contain rising prices is something that has baffled one government after another . . ."

WYATT: Baffled!

FREDERICA: Stop!

LAMB: Oh, yes. Please.

ROBERT: "Does the present exercise in regulating prices and incomes offer any real chance of a breakthrough?"

FREDERICA: Can't wait! Let's go home *now*.

ROBERT: "*People in Towns.* Urban Sociology. A course. The existence of social problems in our towns has produced its equal and opposite reaction—the social work movement."

FREDERICA: Even the birds look good after that.

ROBERT: "The Lecturer for Social Work Training . . ."

WYATT: Social Work Training?

ROBERT: "Talks about——"

WYATT: What does the Old Thing talk about?

ROBERT: "About social workers and about the work of the Seebohm Committee, of which he was a member . . ."

FREDERICA: Poor soul.

ROBERT: "Further publications relating to this series include: *Second Year Russian.* Eight shillings. *Starting German.*

Books One and Two, price four shillings each. *Europe Since 1945. Study Notes I,* five shillings. *Study Notes II,* seven shillings. *People in Towns* will cost you eighteen shillings. *Manet* (colour slides) two pounds; *Renaissance Exploration,* eleven shillings; *Helping Your Neighbour,* three shillings and *Problems of Learning, Study Notes,* three shillings."

WYATT: My goodness! What you're missing, old thing!

ROBERT: Mustn't be patronizing now.

FREDERICA: Why not? I'm always being patronizing.

ROBERT: That's because you're more clever and assured than most people.

FREDERICA: Oh, no, I'm not. Evangie's the clever one.

EVANGIE: I'm not. Still a lot of people do . . . No, I won't say it.

LAMB: Why not?

EVANGIE: Because it sounds priggish and what people think I am.

LAMB: Which is?

EVANGIE: A rather voracious intellectual.

WYATT: Oh, come!

EVANGIE: It's true. Isn't it?

FREDERICA: Yes.

EVANGIE: True—or what people think?

FREDERICA: Both I should think. Don't ask me. They're all cleverer than I am . . .

WYATT: I rather like *"Helping Your Neighbour" Study Notes . . .*

EVANGIE: No. I'm sure you're right.

FREDERICA: You said it.

EVANGIE: And you agreed.

FREDERICA: Shouldn't I?

EVANGIE: Yes. I think you should. It's hard on me but probably harder for you.

FREDERICA: It's not hard at all.

EVANGIE: Then it should be. Even if it is your sister . . . I'm off to the beach, I think. Daddy?

WYATT: Think I'll stay in the shade a bit, old thing. I'm so *feeble.* We'll have a walk before dinner, right?

EVANGIE: Right. *[She goes. Pause]*

FREDERICA: You all think I'm a shit, don't you?

LAMB: *I* don't think so. Not me, anyway. But then I *am*. You're a
  clown. With all the privileges and penalties. You say what
  is obvious but not necessarily true, or the whole truth, at
  least. But that's something else and in the meantime there's
  the performing dog act of partiality.

FREDERICA: Thanks.

LAMB: Don't thank me. Everyone is grateful to you.

FREDERICA: Meaning?

LAMB: Please don't pick a fight with me, my dear. I like and admire you though, of course, don't know you or ever will. I
  may not, and I don't wish to, be able to hurt you. But this I
  do know: that nothing you could say or do would ever hurt
  me. Which is *my* misfortune.

FREDERICA: That was a bit glib, even for you, wasn't it?

LAMB: Not really. I tried a little more with you but it didn't come
  off. Quite clearly . . . I was thinking the other day about
  moon landings . . .

WYATT: God, the sun does BURN, doesn't it?

FREDERICA: The birds *sing*.

ROBERT: The surf—what? Pounds, I suppose.

WYATT: Why are we all so cruel to one another?

FREDERICA: *You're* not.

WYATT: Yes. I am.

FREDERICA: Yes. You are.

ROBERT: Frankly.

FREDERICA: Frankly. But no one thinks you're a shit. They think
  your lovable.

LAMB: Don't be intemperate. You lose your style.

FREDERICA: I don't know what intemperate means, or what you
  mean by it and I'm too proud to find out, do you mind? And,
  as for style, I haven't.

LAMB: I don't know you any more than I know your father but
  he has some concern for himself, as we all have. You mustn't
  grudge that.

FREDERICA: Why not?

LAMB: Because I feel it.

FREDERICA: There! That's all.

LAMB: Of course, you're right.

WYATT: She always is.

LAMB: No more than that.

WYATT: Always was. Evangie *seemed* the clever one. But she's not, poor old thing. Oh, dear, I must stop saying that.

ROBERT: What?

WYATT: Old thing.

FREDERICA: Quite. You should.

WYATT: I know.

FREDERICA: It isn't half as cute as everyone thinks or thinks they think.

WYATT: Yes. Pretty nauseating really. Well: I am.

FREDERICA: Don't sound pleased about it.

WYATT: I'm not. Actually. I don't quite know how to make it ring true. Or. Indeed . . . anything. I think moon landings must be pretty morose, don't you, I mean as we're being morose and we are, at least I am . . . [To CHRISTOPHER] You're very quiet, old thing.

CHRISTOPHER: Am I?

FREDERICA: Yes. Exhausted.

CHRISTOPHER: No. Tired. It's a tiring island.

FREDERICA: It is. So are we.

WYATT: Should we get him a doctor?

FREDERICA: Is that a real question?

CHRISTOPHER: I'm all right. I was just wondering if I should go for a swim or walk or something with Evangie.

WYATT: Too hot . . . Phew!

FREDERICA: She's all right.

CHRISTOPHER: Is she though?

FREDERICA: She's thinking about writing a piece about this place. Or some book. Or some insight she's fishing around for.

CHRISTOPHER: If it's well enough done and for the right reasons.

LAMB: I never know what the right reasons are.

FREDERICA: Oh, for *its* sake. And your's. Or neither—Who knows?

LAMB: Clearly, *you* don't.

ROBERT: Who would you send to the moon?

FREDERICA: Oh, the usual. Me, I expect.

WYATT: Yes, who *would* we?

FREDERICA: I wonder why people have children. Do they *want* you? What do you think, Robert?

[*At this stage* ROBIN, *the* BRIGADIER, ALASTAIR, JED, *and* HARRY *came out onto the porch and join the company*]

[*To* ROBERT] That man's dying.

ROBERT: Who?

FREDERICA: Harry. The hulking American.

WYATT: There you are, old things. I say, we did have a good lunch. Brigadier, you're a genius. We were just talking about moon landings and who we'd send up there.

ROBIN: Customs officers.

WYATT: Naturally.

LAMB: Women journalists.

WYATT: Good.

ALASTAIR: American tourists.

FREDERICA: But not Harry.

ALASTAIR: Harry's not exactly a tourist. He dropped in with Nelson. Anyone who goes on cruises. Do you know who we've got in today? The American Folk Dance Society. Eight hundred of them?

BRIGADIER: All local officials.

ROBIN: The high commissioner.

ALASTAIR: The high commissioner's wife.

FREDERICA: People who give poetry readings.

WYATT: Oh, I say, yes. [*They all settle into their chairs and relax in the shade*] I was just thinking about what the girls were saying.

BRIGADIER: What were they saying?

WYATT: Don't think you were here, old thing. About the old boy, papa. The way he'd talk about the Black Noons and sage and the gazelle and the bustard and all those camel-mounted soldiers, shuffling along in a freezing night with the animals gurgling and moaning and the men in their Section messes . . . and singing . . .

FREDERICA: We'll all be home soon.

ROBERT: Except for Robin and the Brigadier.

WYATT: Well, it's their home. And old Lamb's of course.

ALASTAIR: And mine, God help me. Why I should be crimping in a place like this I'll never know.

ROBERT: *[To* JED*]* What about you?

JED: Any place is home for me. So who cares?

*[*LEROI *enters with* MRS. JAMES*]*

LEROI: Mrs. James is here to see Mr. Gillman.

WYATT: *[Shouting off]* Christopher! *[To* MRS. JAMES*]* How nice of you to come and see me.

MRS. JAMES: Not at all. It's quite an honour. I was told you wouldn't give interviews.

*[*CHRISTOPHER *appears]*

WYATT: This is Mrs. James, Christopher. She's come to have a chat.

FREDERICA: Do you want us to all go?

WYATT: Not at all. I shan't feel half as self-conscious if I've got my chums around me.

CHRISTOPHER: Do sit down, Mrs. James. Thank you, Leroi.

WYATT: How very nice to meet you.

MRS. JAMES: I hope it will be.

CHRISTOPHER: Shall we start off right away? Or can I get you a drink or something?

MRS. JAMES: No, thank you.

CHRISTOPHER: Only he gets a little fatigued in this heat.

MRS. JAMES: So do we all. I shan't take much of your time. If you've no objection, I'll just turn on this little tape-recorder. I hope it works all right.

CHRISTOPHER: They all say that.

MRS. JAMES: Do they? Well, I'll try and get it working. Could you just say a few words for level?

WYATT: Who, me?

MRS. JAMES: It is you I've come to interview.

WYATT: Right. What about politics? Well, I'm just an old radical who detests progress. But then nobody hates it more. Don't you think, Mrs. James?

MRS. JAMES: You're the one being interviewed. I'll just play that back. [She does so]

MRS. JAMES: That's fine.

WYATT: Well, where shall we begin?

MRS. JAMES: Wherever you like.

CHRISTOPHER: You're the one conducting the interview.

WYATT: I don't really know why you should want to talk to me at all. I've got no interesting views or opinions about anything. Never have done. I don't believe in much, never have done, never been inspired by anything. I'm simply overtalkative, vain, corpulent, and a bit of a played-out hulk, as I think most of the world knows and I'm surprised the news hasn't even reached this delightful little island of yours.

MRS. JAMES: Isn't it a bit early to start being patronizing?

WYATT: I am never patronizing. I am in no position to be so. And never have been.

MRS. JAMES: How do you feel at the moment? How do you feel at the moment?

WYATT: Just about the same as usual. Except hotter. Always weary, ineffably bored, always in some sort of vague pain and always with a bit of unsatisfying hatred burning away in the old inside like a heartburn or indigestion.

MRS. JAMES: I can see we may not get very far.

WYATT: Does it matter?

MRS. JAMES: Not to you. I've simply been sent to do a job. Well, let's take an easy one first: what do you think of your fellow writers?

WYATT: Fellow writers! What a dreadful expression!

MRS. JAMES: I'm sorry, I couldn't think of anything else to describe the people who practise the same profession.

WYATT: I try not to think of my fellow writers. If they're better than I am, I am disturbed. If they're worse, which is unusual, I simply feel sorry.

MRS. JAMES: What do you think about the state of English literature at the moment?

WYATT: Nothing at all.

MRS. JAMES: Would you say that you strike postures with people whom you regard as provincials?

WYATT: Very likely, I'm afraid. But not in your case. You're quite clearly very sophisticated. I mean, you wouldn't have much trouble getting the edge on me. You can never win an interview if you are being interviewed.

MRS. JAMES: I'm not trying to win anything. I'm simply trying to arrive at some sort of approximation of the truth.

WYATT: Do you think there is such a thing?

MRS. JAMES: I don't think you should ask me facile questions, even if you are a famous man and paying us a visit.

WYATT: I'm not paying you a visit. I am visiting my daughter and her husband. And staying with my other daughters and friends.

MRS. JAMES: Do you think we should give up this interview?

WYATT: I think that onus is entirely upon you.

MRS. JAMES: Quite right. What do you think of as being Utopia?

WYATT: A place without pain, passion, or nobility. Where there is no hatred, boredom, or imperfection.

MRS. JAMES: What do you think of man?

WYATT: As a defect, striving for excellence.

MRS. JAMES: Do you really think that?

WYATT: No, but presumably you want me to say something, however dull. However, I do think that there is a disastrously false, and very modern, idea that you can be absolutely honest.

MRS. JAMES: How do you feel about your present work?

WYATT: At the moment I don't really have any present work to speak of.

MRS. JAMES: But has any of it been an advance?

WYATT: The idea of advance is only something that is nurtured by uncreative people and critics.

MRS. JAMES: You are well known for being oversensitive to criticism.

WYATT: Am I? I simply dislike it like a dog dislikes fleas.

MRS. JAMES: Didn't Doctor Johnson say that?

WYATT: Probably, but I should have thought the old boy would have put it a bit better, don't you?

MRS. JAMES: Do you deliberately adopt a public pose?

WYATT: Yes.

MRS. JAMES: Why?

WYATT: Because it makes life slightly more tolerable. The same applies to private life.

MRS. JAMES: Then why do you consent to be interviewed?

WYATT: I need the money.

MRS. JAMES: But we can't afford to pay you.

WYATT: I'm afraid Christopher didn't tell me that.

MRS. JAMES: What do you think about religion today?

WYATT: I think about religion if I think about it at all as it was in any time in human history. I think about it as the exercise of law as applied by each man to himself, even if that law be anarchy, negation, or despair. If you're really interested, and it's pretty clear that you can't be interested in a pontificating old English buffer like me, I also believe in what St. Augustine called "the harsh necessity of sin." It's a ponderous phrase but probably no worse than "make love not war" and, of course, I've always been very keen on the King James Bible and the English genius to boot, which it is being booted very swiftly, oh, and good old Cranmer's Book of Common Prayer. It's like the Bible, it combines profundity without complexity.

MRS. JAMES: What do you think about protest movements?

WYATT: Protest is easy. But grief must be lived. As dear old Yeats said, dear old thing, be *secret* and *exult*. Secret . . .

MRS. JAMES: Would you say that you are a neurotic?

WYATT: On the whole, yes, all neurotics are bullies. But then so are most interviewers.

MRS. JAMES: Going back again to one of your favourite topics, critics . . .

WYATT: One of yours too, so it seems.

MRS. JAMES: What would you say was the function of critics, if any?

WYATT: Critics are sacrosanct. You must make it clear to your readers that they are simply and obviously more important than poets or writers. That's why you should always get in with them. You see, what we chaps do may be all right in its little way but what really counts is the fact that if it weren't for the existence of critics, we shouldn't be around at all or would just be on the dole or running chicken farms. Never make cheap jokes about critics. You've got to remember this: the critic is above criticism because he has the good sense never to do anything. He's up there helping us poor little guys to understand what the hell we're doing, which is a jolly helpful thing, you must agree. And if he stops you from writing at all then he's done the best job possible. After all, who wants to read or listen to what some poor old writer has pumped out of his diseased heart when he can read a balanced and reasoned judgement about life, love, and literature from an aloof and informed commentator.

MRS. JAMES: Now that you have reached a certain stage in life, what, in fact, do you think about things like being in love?

WYATT: I think: thank God I don't have to be in love any more.

MRS. JAMES: What do you think you are?

WYATT: I think I'm probably what my daughter Frederica says she is, just a lot of hot shit, if you'll pardon the expression, blood, vanity, and a certain prowess.

MRS. JAMES: There is a rumour that you have given up writing altogether.

WYATT: Heard that, did you? Hear that, Christopher? God, that was the rumour I tried to spread about myself.

MRS. JAMES: In these changing times, do you still believe that words in themselves have any meaning, value, or validity?

WYATT: I still cling pathetically to the old bardic belief that "words alone are certain good."

MRS. JAMES: Do you still live in London for any reason?

WYATT: Same reason as dear old Yeats again. Lived in Dublin. Great hatred. Little room.

MRS. JAMES: Do you see art as going in any particular direction now?

WYATT: I can hardly see the table in front of me. All art is simply criticism now. Posturing as art, self-evaluating, categorizing, constitutional, branded, hectoring, and elbowing everyone out of the way.

MRS. JAMES: What do you think about friendship?

WYATT: A lost art. You should be able to discuss your friend's colds or toothaches as if they were railway disasters. As long as you both know they're not.

MRS. JAMES: Now, to a difficult question, as I know you have not been here long. What are your feelings about the island and the people you've met?

WYATT: All the good things I've see of the island seem to be legacies of the British, the Spanish, and the Dutch, particularly in the buildings and what's left of any proper dispensation of the law. As for the people, they seem to me to be a very unappealing mixture of hysteria and lethargy, brutality and sentimentality.

MRS. JAMES: Would you like me to turn this thing off?

WYATT: Not for my sake. I'm past protection. Aren't I, Christopher?

MRS. JAMES: Women have figured a great deal in your life.

WYATT: That sounds like a criticism veiled as a question.

MRS. JAMES: What would you say your feelings are about women nowadays?

WYATT: I have very little to do with women nowadays. As you can see, I've never been particularly attractive and if you want to ask that sort of question, and you clearly do, I'm pretty well past it anyway. The trouble with women is that I've always made a cardinal mistake: of treating them as friends and equals which they patently are not. Women only really love bullies.

MRS. JAMES: Don't you think that's a sweeping statement?

WYATT: Yes.

MRS. JAMES: What do you think about the class situation in England?

WYATT: I'm very fond of it. It provides a great deal of entertainment, fun, and speculation for people who have nothing better to do. Like many of the upper class, I've liked the sound of broken glass.

MRS. JAMES: What about God?

WYATT: I say, we are getting down to it, aren't we? Are you sure you won't have a drink? I've always had a bit of a leaning towards him. I think perhaps people nowadays, people probably make the mistake of thinking of God as some sort of competitive family concern. You know, who might be pushed out of the market by a bit of smart operation.

MRS. JAMES: You seem to keep referring to boredom. Is it an obsession with you?

WYATT: No, I'm a bit too keen on myself. But I think everyone should have a daily ration of it.

MRS. JAMES: Going back to literature——

WYATT: Oh, is it still there?

MRS. JAMES: Do you believe in the New Testament idea of the Gift of Tongues?

WYATT: Yes, I do. Mine was just a rather flabby, flailing thing. Everyone said I was rhetorical rather than recondite. And I think they were right.

MRS. JAMES: How would you describe yourself politically?

WYATT: I wouldn't attempt to. For one thing it isn't interesting enough. I believe in work but not in work to keep out all this desolation we live in. I believe in charity and I don't mean in the American sense, which is having buddies so that you can get on. I don't think I really believe in going on strike, even when some poor devil's in the right. My father believed that. Do you know one thing I'm really ashamed of? I drove a bus in the general strike. I thought I was such a dashing fellow.

MRS. JAMES: Everyone always thinks of you as a very English writer——

WYATT: Oh, do they really?

MRS. JAMES: You know perfectly well. Do you think that there is still something special about being English rather than some other nationality?

WYATT: I don't know. I always think that there's something like a certain form of, say, cloud formation, called the English imagination. And if ever there was a critic's phrase, I think that's probably one.

MRS. JAMES: Do you think of yourself as an artist?

WYATT: Everyone nowadays is apparently an artist.

MRS. JAMES: But do you believe it?

WYATT: No. I believe in special gifts. Just as I believe some people are better than others.

MRS. JAMES: Do you believe in the family?

WYATT: I don't believe in its continuance, if that's what you mean. I do think it had its pleasures while it lasted and I was fortunate enough to have enjoyed and suffered them. I had a father whom I loved and now I have daughters whom I love, no doubt largely selfishly. But I wouldn't call it a write-off either for them or for me. Or indeed their mother. Like the passing of empires and pride of tongue.

MRS. JAMES: Do you think that the relation between the sexes is healthier now than when you were a young man?

WYATT: Yes. But less pleasurable and less enduring. But that is not a question to ask an old man.

MRS. JAMES: What do you think of young people?

WYATT: I try not to. But then I've always preferred the instinct of friendship to that of the herd.

MRS. JAMES: What do you think of as real sin?

WYATT: The incapacity for proper despair. About talking about loss of faith as if it were some briefcase you've left behind you on the tube.

MRS. JAMES: What do you look on as virtue then?

WYATT: True innocence.

MRS. JAMES: Lastly, Mr. Gillman, what do you dread most at this stage of your life?

WYATT: Not death. But ludicrous death. And I also feel it in the air.

[*Long pause. Enter* TWO AMERICAN TOURISTS. *They are* MR. *and* MRS. DEKKER]

FREDERICA: Yes?

MRS. DEKKER: Oh, we were just looking for the gift shop.

FREDERICA: Well, I'm afraid this isn't the gift shop.

MRS. DEKKER: Oh, dear, I'm so sorry. It's just that my husband

and I, Mr. Dekker here, wanted to buy a few things to take back home. We've bought something from every place we've been.

FREDERICA: I think the place you're looking for is just down the road.

MRS. DEKKER: Oh, dear, I'm so sorry. This must be a private home.

FREDERICA: That was what my sister hoped.

MRS. DEKKER: Only you see, Mr. Dekker and I are on this cruise and they told us the gift shop was just down the road.

FREDERICA: Well, it is. But I'm afraid we've nothing to sell.

MRS. DEKKER: We're with the Folk Song and Dance Society of America.

ALASTAIR: How nice for you. You all have such lovely hair.

MRS. DEKKER: Do you live here? You actually live here?

FREDERICA: My sister and her husband live here and so do two of these gentlemen. The rest of us are what is known as "passing through."

MR. DEKKER: Having intruded upon you in this way, may I ask you a small favour?

BRIGADIER: Certainly.

MR. DEKKER: May we take a photograph of your beautiful home?

BRIGADIER: By all means. Garden as well if you like.

MRS. DEKKER: And could we take a picture of you all as well?

FREDERICA: Why not go the whole hog?

MRS. DEKKER: My husband, Mr. Dekker, just loves to take momentos.

FREDERICA: Yes, they are nice, aren't they?

[They all pose quickly while MR. DEKKER *takes his photographs]*

MRS. DEKKER: Well, thank you all so much. It was a real pleasure meeting you all.

FREDERICA: Likewise, Mrs. Dekker.

*[*MR. *and* MRS. DEKER *wave farewell and go out. Pause]*

HARRY: *[To* FREDERICA*]* You didn't have to be like that, you know. They're harmless.

FREDERICA: You think so?

HARRY: I know so.

FREDERICA: Why do you really live here? Is it really just because you want to bring water down from the mountains to a lot of people who aren't that bothered anyway?

WYATT: I thought they were a nice couple of old dears.

FREDERICA: No, you didn't. You pretend that you did. Like you've pretended to so much else always.

ROBIN: Frederica—leave Father alone.

FREDERICA: Why should I? *[To* WYATT*]* The trouble with you is that you've always been allowed to get away with it. Yes, I mean, get away with it. Like some of us can't. You get away with it all. Bad manners. Laziness. Cowardice. Lateness. Hurtful indiscretion. And we're all supposed to be stunned by the humour and eccentricity of it.

[Pause]

WYATT: I *am* a clown . . . People laugh at me in the street when they see me. But, as you say, it's my own fault. *[*WYATT *gets to his feet]* Think I need a bit of a walk after that lunch with the Brigadier.

[They all watch him go off in the direction of the beach]

CURTAIN

SCENE 2

The same evening, as before. The air seems still and there is a strange noise of resentful-sounding music in the distance. Dogs howl. FREDERICA *picks up a cushion dropped by* LEROI. *She goes for a cigarette and, having got it, turns and almost bumps into* CHRISTOPHER.

FREDERICA: Edward's talked to that boy down on that beach nearly all day long. Why can't *he* shut him up! Or Robin! She's supposed to be such a hostess. Any of you. You. You're Wyatt's

Great Protector . . . Aren't you? But, no, you all let the boy just go on and on—and daddy pretending to be deaf . . . all the while. Don't bother to answer . . .

CHRISTOPHER: I won't. Even if I could. *[She offers him a cigarette]* Strange sound . . .

FREDERICA: What?

CHRISTOPHER: The music.

FREDERICA: Not very attractive. I suppose they think it has a simple, brooding, native charm and vitality. Which is about the last thing any of them have got. Anyway, they never stop playing it.

CHRISTOPHER: Tourists like it, I suppose.

FREDERICA: They would. . . . Why did you leave your wife and give up everything for the old man? It can't be much fun. Or is it?

CHRISTOPHER: You do ask direct questions, don't you?

FREDERICA: Only when I think I might get a direct answer. Rather charmless really.

CHRISTOPHER: Well . . .

FREDERICA: No. You needn't tell me if you don't want. Or fictionalize just to please me.

CHRISTOPHER: I want to please you.

FREDERICA: Please *me?* Why?

CHRISTOPHER: Because, well, I've simply got a thing, this thing about you. For you.

FREDERICA: Why?

CHRISTOPHER: Oh, lots of reasons. You're in pain at lot of the time.

FREDERICA: I don't need a nurse, thanks. Anyway, you've got the old man and he needs ten blooming nursemaids and God knows what.

CHRISTOPHER: No. I didn't fancy my chances.

FREDERICA: Right. There's no future in me. Not for anyone. One day it'll be just . . . *out.* . . . Tell me about your wife.

CHRISTOPHER: She just, didn't fancy me, that's all.

FREDERICA: Perhaps you weren't very fanciable.

CHRISTOPHER: Indeed. So I left her the house, most of the money . . . and the child . . . I minded that . . .

FREDERICA: The child?

CHRISTOPHER: Yes.

FREDERICA: I wonder if you really did. Or was it the house and the money? Is the old boy a fair exchange?

CHRISTOPHER: I think so . . . I admire him.

FREDERICA: Do you?

CHRISTOPHER: Do you think I'm bent?

FREDERICA: No. Just a bit potty. Like most of us . . .

CHRISTOPHER: There was another woman who didn't fancy me either. So I just gave up.

FREDERICA: Faint of heart.

CHRISTOPHER: Quite.

FREDERICA: You're quite attractive.

CHRISTOPHER: Not very. . . . You know that boy Jed. He reminds me of a young S.S. man I killed in the war. Unarmed prisoner. A G.I. tried to stop me so I shot him too.

FREDERICA: Now, that's *not* attractive.

CHRISTOPHER: No. . . . Not at bit . . .

FREDERICA: Did you get away with it?

CHRISTOPHER: Oh, yes. It's amazing what you can.

FREDERICA: Don't we all know? . . . Why does he pretend to be deaf and in front of Jed?

[Pause. The rest of the company come in from the dining-room. They all look uneasy, particularly ALASTAIR, *who is hysterical]*

ALASTAIR: *[To everyone]* I told him to go! I told him to go! But he won't! He just won't! Oh God! *[*ALASTAIR *sits down and weeps silently]* Just another of my crying jags . . .

*[*JED *looks down at* ALASTAIR *contemptuously and then turns to address everyone else]*

JED: You all, you all bastards . . . I sit here listening to you. Having your fancy dinner and your wine from France and England. You know what I think of you? What *we* think of you? What we think of you? Fuck all your *shit*—that's what we think. One person, not like any one of you here, even if he's the God-damnest cretin, I'd make him God, yes, man, rather than you. You hear? Hear me. Listen to me if you can hear anything but the sound of your own selves and present. I'm not interested in your arguments, not that they are, of your so-called memories and all that pathetic shit. The only thing that matters, man, is blood, man. Blood. . . . You know what that means? No, no, you surely as to hell don't. No, no, when you pigs, you pigs go, it ain't going to be no fucking Fourth of July. All I see, and I laugh when I see it, man, I laugh, is you pigs barbecued, barbecued in your own shit. *We're,* yes, we're going to take over and don't you begin to forget it. Man, I feel real sorry for you lot. No, I don't . . . You got it coming. And you *have soon.* Think of the theatre of the mind, baby, old moulding babies, except you won't. We count and we *do,* not like you, we *really,* really do. . . . Why, we fall about laughing at you people, not people, you're not people, you pigs. We are people. *We* are. But not you. You don't understand and why should you because, believe me, babies, old failing babies, words, yes I mean words, even what I'm saying to you now, is going to be the first to go. Go, baby. Go. You can't even make love. Do you understand one word, those old words you love so much, what I mean? No. And you won't. If it ain't written down, you don't believe it. . . . There's only one word left and you know what that is. It's fuck, man. Fuck. . . . That's the last of the English for you babies. Or maybe shit. Because that's what we're going to do on you. Shit. That's what you'll all go down in. One blissful, God-like shit. *You* think we're mother-fucking, stink-ing, yelling, shouting shits. Well that's what we are, babies. And there's nothing, not nothing you or anybody else can do about it. Jesus is sort of shit. But you're not even *shit.* We thing, we fuck and we shit and that's what we do and you're on the great gasping end of it. Because you're pigs. Just take one little look at yourselves. You're pigs, babies. Pigs. And we're gonna shit you out of this world, babies. Right out of this mother-fucking world. You know what? I just had an idea. Like that old prick writer there. Colonialism is the

fornication of the twentieth century. You can't be young. . . .
So all you'd better do, all you *will* do, is die, die, baby. And
pretty soon. Just real soon. Like tomorrow. Or even tonight.

[*There is a short pause*]

CHRISTOPHER: I remember killing someone like you. Only he was
blond.
JED: Yes? Well, just remember it. Because you may not remember it much longer.

[*Pause*]

WYATT: I was never a *young* man. I think I always felt old. I was
always wrinkled somehow. More than I am now. Well, nearly.
Now I am sort of old. No, old. But something always kept
telling me I was young. Very young. But, of course, I never
was. Something started without me. Too slow. Never got off
the old ground. Never got off the ground. Wasn't sure about
the ground at all. Never capable of inspecting it. Or, anyway,
closely. Not closely. . . . Not closely. . . . I think I ought to
go to bed.

[*As* WYATT *rises to go, several armed islanders appear out of
the darkness. He looks at them with their firearms pointing
at the group and turns to run away. They shoot him down*]

[*Pause*]

EDWARD: There's an old English saying. Don't suppose you'd know
it . . .
JED: So? What is it?
EDWARD: My God—they've shot the fox . . .

CURTAIN

A PATRIOT FOR ME

The first performance of *A Patriot for Me* was given at the Royal Court Theatre, Sloane Square, London, on June 30, 1965, by the English Stage Society, by arrangement with the English Stage Company. It was directed by Anthony Page and the décor was by Jocelyn Herbert.

The musical adviser was John Addison. The cast was as follows:

ALFRED REDL	*Maximilian Schell*
AUGUST SICZYNSKI	*John Castle*
STEINBAUER	*Rio Fanning*
LUDWIG MAX VON KUPFER	*Frederick Jaeger*
KUPFER'S SECONDS	*Lew Luton, Richard Morgan*
PRIVATES	*Tim Pearce, David Schurmann, Thick Wilson*
LT.-COL. LUDWIG VON MÖHL	*Clive Morton*
ADJUTANT	*Timothy Carlton*
MAXIMILIAN VON TAUSSIG	*Edward Fox*
ALBRECHT	*Sandor Eles*
WAITERS AT ANNA'S	*Peter John, Domy Reiter*
OFFICERS	*Timothy Carlton, Lew Luton, Hal Hamilton, Richard Morgan*
WHORES	*Dona Martyn, Virginia Wetherell, Jackie Daryl, Sandra Hampton*
ANNA	*Laurel Mather*
HILDE	*Jennifer Jayne*
STANITSIN	*Desmond Perry*
COL. MISCHA OBLENSKY	*George Murcell*
GEN. CONRAD VON HÖTZENDORF	*Sebastian Shaw*
COUNTESS SOPHIA DELYANOFF	*Jill Bennett*
JUDGE ADVOCATE JAROSLAV KUNZ	*Ferdy Mayne*
FLUNKEYS	*John Forbes, Richard Morgan, Peter John, Timothy Carlton*

HOFBURG GUESTS	*Cyril Wheeler, Douglas Sheldon, Bryn Bartlett, Dona Martyn, Virginia Wetherell, Jackie Daryl, Sandra Hampton, Laurel Mather*
CAFÉ WAITERS	*Anthony Roye, Domy Reiter, Bryn Bartlett, Cyril Wheeler*
GROUP AT TABLE	*Dona Martyn, Laurel Mather, Bryn Bartlett, Cyril Wheeler*
YOUNG MAN IN CAFÉ	*Paul Robert*
PAUL	*Douglas Sheldon*
PRIVATES	*Richard Morgan, David Schurmann, Tim Pearce, Thick Wilson*
BARON VON EPP	*George Devine*
FERDY	*John Forbes*
FIGARO	*Thick Wilson*
LT. STEFAN KOVACS	*Hal Hamilton*
MARIE-ANTOINETTE	*Lew Luton*
TSARINA	*Domy Reiter*
LADY GODIVA	*Peter John*
BALL GUESTS	*Cyril Wheeler, Richard Morgan, Timothy Carlton, John Castle, Edward Fox, Paul Robert, Douglas Sheldon, Tim Pearce*
FLUNKEY	*David Schurmann*
SHEPHERDESSES	*Franco Derosa, Robert Kidd*
DR. SCHOEPFER	*Vernon Dobtcheff*
BOY	*Franco Derosa*
2ND. LT. VIKTOR JERZABEK	*Tim Pearce*
HOTEL WAITERS	*Bryn Bartlett, Lew Luton*
ORDERLY	*Richard Morgan*
MISCHA LIPSCHUTZ	*David Schurmann*
MITZI HEIGEL	*Virginia Wetherell*

MINISTER	*Anthony Roye*
VOICES OF DEPUTIES	*Clive Morton, Sebastian Shaw, George Devine, Vernon Dobtcheff, Cyril Wheeler*
MUSICAL DIRECTOR	*Tibor Kunstler*
MUSICIANS	*Reg Richman (Bass), Michael Zborowski (Piano), Ray Webb (Guitar)*

AUSTRIA-HUNGARY

Lemberg, Warsaw, Prague, Dresden, Vienna

1890–1913

ACT ONE

A gymnasium. Of the Seventh Galician Infantry Regiment at Lemberg, Galicia, 1890. It appears to be empty. From the high windows on one side, the earliest morning light shows up the climbing bars that run from floor to ceiling. From this, a long, thick rope hangs. Silhouetted is a vaulting horse. The lonely, slow tread of one man's boots is heard presently on the harsh floor. A figure appears. At this stage, his features can barely be made out. It is ALFRED REDL, *at this time lieutenant. He has close cropped hair, a taut, compact body, a moustache. In most scenes he smokes long black cheroots, like Toscanas. On this occasion, he takes out a shabby cigarette case, an elegant amber holder, inserts a cigarette, and lights it thoughtfully. He looks up at the window, takes out his watch, and waits. It is obvious he imagines himself alone. He settles down in the half light. A shadow crosses his vision.*

REDL: Who's there? *[Pause]* Who is it? Come on! Hey!
VOICE: Redl?
REDL: Who is it?
VOICE: Yes. I see you now.
REDL: Siczynski? Is it? Siczynski?
VOICE: Thought it was you. Yes.

[A figure appears, AUGUST SICZYNSKI. *He is a strong, very handsome young man about the same age as* REDL, *but much*

79

more boyish looking. REDL *already has the stamp of an older man]*

SICZYNSKI: Sorry.

REDL: Not at all.

SICZYNSKI: I startled you.

REDL: Well: we're both early.

SICZYNSKI: Yes.

REDL: Still. Not all that much. Cigarette? *[*SICZYNSKI *takes one.* REDL *lights it for him]* Almost light. I couldn't sleep anyway. Could you?

SICZYNSKI: *[Smiles]* I haven't the style for that. Von Kupfer has, though. Expect he's snoozing away now. *[Looks at his watch]* Being wakened by his servant. Um?

REDL: He gave a champagne supper at Anna's.

SICZYNSKI: Who was invited?

REDL: Half the garrison, I imagine.

SICZYNSKI: Did you go?

REDL: I'm your second . . .

SICZYNSKI: Is that what prevented you being asked?

REDL: It would have stopped me going.

SICZYNSKI: Well then, he'll have stayed there till the last moment, I should think. Perhaps he'll have been worn down to nothing by one of those strapping Turkish whores.

REDL: I doubt it.

SICZYNSKI: His spine cracked in between those thighs. Snapped. . . . All the way up. No, you're most likely right. *You're* right.

REDL: He's popular, I suppose.

SICZYNSKI: Yes. Unlikable too.

REDL: Yes. He's a good, what's he, he's a good officer.

SICZYNSKI: He's a gentleman. And adjutant, adjutant mark you, of a field battery at the ripe old age of twenty-one. He's not half the soldier you are.

REDL: Well . . .

SICZYNSKI: And now he's on his way to the War College.

REDL: *[Quick interest]* Oh?

SICZYNSKI: Of course. If you'd been in his boots, you'd have been in there and out again by this time, you'd be a major at least, by now. *[Pause]* Sorry—didn't mean to rub it in.

REDL: Kupfer. Ludwig Max von Kupfer . . . it's cold.

SICZYNSKI: Cigarette smoke's warm.

[Pause]

REDL: How are you?

SICZYNSKI: Cold.

REDL: Here.

SICZYNSKI: Cognac? Your health. Here's to the War College. And you.

REDL: Thank you.

SICZYNSKI: Oh, you will. Get in, I mean. *You* just have to pack in all the effort, while the Kupfers make none at all. He'll be sobering up by now. Putting his aristocratic head under the cold tap and shouting in that authentic Viennese drawl at whoever's picking up after him. You'd better, make it, I mean. Or you'll spend the rest of it in some defeated frontier town with debts. And more debts to look forward to as you go on. Probably the gout. *[Pause]* I just hope there isn't ever a war.

[They smoke in silence. Slightly shy, tense. SICZYNSKI leans against the vaulting horse]

REDL: You may underestimate Kupfer.

SICZYNSKI: Maybe. But then he overestimates himself. *You've* tremendous resources, reserves, energy. You won't let any old waters close over your head without a struggle first.

REDL: What about you?

SICZYNSKI: *[Smiles]* I'm easily disheartened.

REDL: He's destructive, *very* destructive.

SICZYNSKI: Who?

REDL: Kupfer.

SICZYNSKI: Yes, yes. And wilful. Coldly, not too cold, not disinterested.

REDL: That's why I think you underestimate him.

SICZYNSKI: But more vicious than most. You're right there. He's a killer all right.

REDL: Someone'll chalk him up . . . sometime.

SICZYNSKI: What about me?

REDL: That would be very good. Very good.

SICZYNSKI: Just not very likely . . .

REDL: Have you done this before?

SICZYNSKI: *[Smiles]* No, never. Have you?

REDL: Only as a bystander.

SICZYNSKI: Well, this time you're a participant. . . . I'd always expected to *be* challenged a hundred times. I never thought *I'd* do it. Well, picked the right man. Only the wrong swordsman. May I? *[He indicates Cognac. REDL nods]* Have you seen him?

REDL: Seen? Oh, with a sabre. No. Have you?

SICZYNSKI: No. Have you seen *me?*

REDL: Often.

SICZYNSKI: Well, there it is.

REDL: *[Softly]* More times than I can think of.

SICZYNSKI: They say only truly illiterate minds are obdurate. Well, that's me and Kupfer.

REDL: Why do you feel like this about him? He's not exactly untypical.

SICZYNSKI: Not by any means. For me, well, perhaps he just plays the part better. He makes me want to be sick. Over *him* preferably.

REDL: I don't understand you. You're more than a match for his sort.

SICZYNSKI: I just chose the wrong ground to prove it, here.

[Pause]

REDL: Look, Siczynski, why don't I, I'm quite plausible and not half a bad actor, for one . . . reason and another, why don't you let me, sort of . . .

SICZYNSKI: Thank you, Redl. You can't do anything now.

REDL: Very well.

SICZYNSKI: Don't be offended.

REDL: Why should I?

SICZYNSKI: [Wry] Someone who looks as good as me ought to be able to handle himself a bit better, don't you agree?

REDL: Yes.

SICZYNSKI: At least—physically. . . . A *little* better don't you think? Why did you agree to be my second?

REDL: Why did you ask me?

SICZYNSKI: I thought you'd agree to. Did you get anyone else?

REDL: Steinbauer.

SICZYNSKI: As a favour to you? No, I didn't think you'd have to be persuaded.

REDL: No.

SICZYNSKI: Mine's gone out. [REDL *offers him a cigarette, from which he takes a light*] I thought you always smoked those long Italian cigars. [REDL *nods*] Expensive taste. What is it?

REDL: I was only going to ask you: *are* you a Jew?

SICZYNSKI: [Smiles] Grandmother. Maternal grandmother. Quite enough though, don't you think? Oh, she became Catholic when she married my grandfather. Not that she ever took it seriously, any more than him. She'd a good sense of fun, not like the rest of my family. You think it doesn't matter about Kupfer's insult, don't you? Well of course you're right. I don't think it would have mattered *what* he said. Oh, I quite enjoyed his jokes about calling me Rothschild. What *I* objected to, from him—in the circumstances—was being called Fräulein Rothschild. . . .

REDL: You shouldn't gamble.

SICZYNSKI: I don't.

REDL: On people's goodwill.

SICZYNSKI: I don't. *You* do.

REDL: I do? No, I don't . . . I try not to.

[*He is confused for a moment.* SICZYNSKI *watches him thoughtfully, through his cigarette smoke. It is getting lighter, colder*]

SICZYNSKI: You smell of peppermints.

REDL: Nearly time. [*He stands*]

SICZYNSKI: Kupfer's breath stinks.

REDL: I hadn't noticed.

SICZYNSKI: You mean you haven't got near enough? You don't need to. *He* should chew peppermints. *[Pause]* Have some of your brandy.

REDL: Thanks.

SICZYNSKI: It's a cold time to be up, to be up at all.

REDL: I've hardly ever had warm feet. Not since I went to Cadet School.

SICZYNSKI: You work too hard.

REDL: What else can I do?

SICZYNSKI: Sorry. Of course, you're right. I'm just waiting. Can't think much any more. *[*REDL *would like to help if there were some means. But he can't]* Go on. If you can, I mean. Don't if you can't . . . Won't be long, now . . .

REDL: We've never talked together much, have we? We must have both been here? What? Two years?

SICZYNSKI: Why couldn't you sleep?

REDL: Don't know. Oh, yes, I had a dream . . .

SICZYNSKI: But then you're not what they call sociable, are you?

REDL: Aren't I?

SICZYNSKI: Well! Asking for extra duties, poring over all those manuals.

REDL: You don't make it sound very likeable.

SICZYNSKI: It isn't—much.

*[*REDL *takes out his watch]*

REDL: I told Steinbauer two minutes before. He's pretty reliable.

SICZYNSKI: Anyway, you're taking a risk doing *this.* But I suppose Kupfer will draw the fire.

REDL: And you. You specially.

SICZYNSKI: The Galician Jew, you mean? Yes. But that's only if I win.

REDL: It needn't come to that.

SICZYNSKI: It will.

REDL: I'll see it doesn't.

SICZYNSKI: No, you won't. You can't. . . . What, what does one, do you suppose, well, look for in anyone, anyone else, I mean.

REDL: For?

SICZYNSKI: Elsewhere.

REDL: I haven't tried. Or thought about it. At least . . .

SICZYNSKI: I mean: That isn't clearly, really, clearly, already in oneself?

REDL: Nothing, I expect.

[Pause]

SICZYNSKI: Tell me about your dream.

REDL: Do you believe in dreams?

SICZYNSKI: Not specially. They're true while they last, I suppose.

REDL: Well, it wasn't—— *[There is the sound of boots. Walking swiftly, confidently, this time. The two men look at each other]* Steinbauer. On the dot. *[STEINBAUER enters]* Morning, Steinbauer. *[STEINBAUER nods, slightly embarrassed. Clicks his heels at SICZYNSKI]* Cold.

STEINBAUER: Yes.

SICZYNSKI: Got the cutlery? Oh, yes, I see.

STEINBAUER: All here.

SICZYNSKI: Redl was telling me his dream. Go on.

REDL: It's nothing.

SICZYNSKI: That hardly matters does it?

REDL: Not really time.

SICZYNSKI: Please.

[STEINBAUER takes out his watch]

REDL: Just, oh, I was, well later, I was, I won't tell you the first——

SICZYNSKI: Why not?

REDL: It's too dull. So is *this* too. Anyway: I was attending a court martial. Not mine. Someone else's. I don't quite know whose. But a friend of some sort, someone I liked. Someone upright, frank, respected, but upright. It was quite clear from the start what the outcome would be, and I was immediately worrying about having to go and visit him in gaol. And it wasn't just because I knew I would be arrested myself as soon as I got in there. It wasn't for that. Anyhow, there I was, and I went and started to talk to him. He didn't say anything. There was just the wire netting between us . . . and then of course, they arrested *me*. I couldn't tell whether he was pleased or not. Pleased that I'd come to see him or that they'd got me too. They touched me on the shoulder and told me to stand up, which I did. And by that time he'd gone. Somehow.

[Sound of several pairs of boots clattering on the unyielding floor into the gymnasium. REDL *frowns anxiously at* SICZYN- SKI, *who smiles at him. As soon as* KUPFER *and his seconds arrive, they get to their feet. Both sides salute each other and prepare for the duel in silence. Sabres are selected. Tunics discarded, etc. All brisk. The duel begins. The four men watch almost indifferently at first. But the spectacle soon strips away this. Blood is drawn, sweat runs, breathing tightens. At one point* REDL *steps forward.* KUPFER *orders him back curtly. All settle down for the end. It comes fairly soon.* SICZYNSKI *cries out and falls to the ground.* KUPFER *begins dressing almost immediately. He goes out with his companions, who are trying to be composed]*

STEINBAUER: Shall I? Yes, I'd better get the doctor.
REDL: Yes, I suppose so.

*[*STEINBAUER *follows the others out.* REDL *wipes the blood from* SICZYNSKI'S *mouth, cradling him in his arms. He is clearly dead]*

FADE

SCENE 2

Office of the Commandant, Seventh Galician Infantry Regiment. The Commandant, LIEUTENANT-COLONEL VON MÖHL, *is seated at his desk. A sharp rap at the door.* VON MÖHL *grunts. The door is opened smartly by the* ADJUTANT.

ADJUTANT: Lieutenant Redl, sir.

[REDL *enters, salutes, etc.*]

MÖHL: Is Taussig there?

ADJUTANT: Yes, sir.

MÖHL: Good. All right. [ADJUTANT *goes out*] Redl, Redl, Redl: yes. [*He looks up*] Sit down, please. [REDL *sits.* MÖHL *scrutinizes him*] Well, Redl. You've quite a good deal of news to come it seems to me. Yes.

REDL: Yes, sir?

MÖHL: You may think that a young officer gets lost among all the others, that he isn't observed, constantly, critically, and sympathetically. You might think that an officer with an unremarkable background, or without rather dazzling connections of one sort or another would go unnoticed. Do you think that, Redl?

REDL: Sir, my own experience is that genuine merit rarely goes unnoticed or unrewarded. Even, particularly in the army.

MÖHL: Good. And quite correct, Redl, and for a very obvious reason. The future of the Empire depends on the army, probably the future of Europe, on an alert, swift machine that can meet instant crisis from whatever quarter it may come. It's taken us a long time to learn our lesson, lessons like Solferino. Expensive, humiliating, and inglorious, but worth it now. Only the very best kind of men can be entrusted in the modern army. [*He waves at the map of pre-1914 Europe, with Austria-Hungary in the middle, behind him*] No one's going to be passed over, every man'll have his chance to prove himself, show what he could do, given half the chance. I don't say there still aren't short cuts for people who don't appparently deserve it, but that's not for you or me to argue. What we *can* do is make sure the way's made to virgin merit, someone with nothing else. What do you say?

REDL: I'm sure you're right, sir.

MÖHL: Oh?

REDL: It always seems quite clear to me, sir, the officers who complain about privilege are invariably inferior or mediocre.

*[*REDL *speaks coolly and carefully. He is anxious to be courteous and respectful without seeming unctuous, or sound a false, fawning note. He succeeds]*

MÖHL: Exactly. The real good 'uns don't ever really get left out, that's why so much nonsense is talked, especially about the army. You can't *afford* to ignore a good man. He's too valuable. A good soldier always knows another one. That's what comradeship is. It's not an empty thing, not an empty thing at all. It's knowing the *value* of other men. And cherishing it. Now: Redl. Two reasons I sent for you. I'll, yes, we'll, I think we'll deal with the best first. *[He pauses.* REDL *waits]* As you know, as commander, it's my duty to recommend officers for War College examination. This year I only felt able to recommend von Taussig, von Kupfer, and yourself. The result I can now tell you, after the final examination and interview, is that you have all three been granted admission, a very fine achievement for us all. Four hundred and eighteen candidates for thirty-nine places. Well, von Taussig has been admitted number twenty-eight, yourself twenty-six, and von Kupfer seventeen. Congratulations.

REDL: Thank you, sir.

MÖHL: Well, I'm very pleased indeed myself, with the result. All three accepted. It's quite something for me too, you know, especially over you. I was pretty sure about the other two, well, of course. . . . But you, well, I knew you had the education, enough . . . There it is. Now you've done it.

REDL: I'm very grateful, sir.

MÖHL: By yourself. You. Number twenty-six! Please. Smoke, if you wish. Here—one of these. *[Offers him a cigar. Takes one himself.* REDL *lights both of them]* So: How do you feel?

REDL: Very proud—and grateful, sir.

MÖHL: I don't think you realize, you've made quite an impression. Here, listen to this. Arithmetic, algebra, geometry, trigonometry—all excellent. Elementary engineering, construction, fortification, geography, and international law, all eighty-five percent, all first class. Riding—required standard. That's the only begrudging remark on any of your reports, required standard. Anyway, get that horse out in the school a bit. Yes?

REDL: Yes, sir.

MÖHL: Let's see now, what does it say, do you speak Russian?

REDL: No, sir.

MÖHL: No matter. You will. Native language?

REDL: Ruthenian.

MÖHL: German—excellent. Polish, French—fair. Punctilious knowledge military and international matters. Seems to know Franco-Prussian campaign better than anyone who actually took part. Learned. All the qualities of first-class field officer and an unmistakable flair for intelligence. No. Wait a minute, there's more yet. Upright, discreet, frank and open, painstaking, marked ability to anticipate, as well as initiate instructions, without being reckless, keen judgement, cool under pressure—*that's* Erdmannsdorfer, so that's good, very good indeed—Yes, cool, fine interpreter of the finest modern military thinking. Personality: friendly but unassertive, dignified and strikes everyone as the type of a gentleman and distinguished officer of the Royal and Imperial Army. Well, what do you say?

REDL: I'm overwhelmed, sir.

MÖHL: Well, I like to see this sort of thing happen. Kupfer and Taussig are one thing, and I'm proud of them. But you're another. . . . Yours is effort, effort, concerted, sustained, intelligent effort. Which: Brings me to the Siczynski affair. Of course, you realize that if your part in that incident had been made properly known, it would almost certainly have prejudiced your application?

REDL: Yes, sir.

MÖHL: However, we chose to be discreet.

REDL: I'm more grateful than I can tell you, sir.

MÖHL: Well, of course, with Kupfer, it was more difficult. However, he has been in trouble of this kind before, and, let's be honest about it, he does have advantages. He is able to get away with incidents like Siczynski occasionally, though even he can't do it too often. Of course, he was a principal in this case and you weren't, but I must tell you it was a grave error on your part ever to have consented to become involved in an affair which ends in a brother officer's death. I'm saying this to you as a warning for the future. *Don't* get involved.

REDL: Yes, sir. May I ask where is Lieutenant von Kupfer, sir?

MÖHL: Temporarily transferred to Wiener Neustadt. . . . Was Siczynski a friend of yours?

REDL: No, sir.

MÖHL: What was your opinion of him?

REDL: I hardly knew him, sir. *[Realizes quickly he needs to provide more than this]* He struck me as being hypercritical, overskeptical about things.

MÖHL: What things?

REDL: Army life and traditions, esprit——

MÖHL: Religion?

REDL: We never discussed it. But—yes, I suspect so, I should think . . .

MÖHL: Jewish . . .?

REDL: Yes, sir. I believe.

MÖHL: Galician, like yourself.

REDL: Yes.

MÖHL: You're yes, Catholic, of course.

REDL: Yes, sir.

MÖHL: What about women?

REDL: Siczynski? *[Nod from* MÖHL*]* As I say, I didn't know him well.

MÖHL: But?

REDL: I never thought of him, no one seemed to, as a ladies' man.

MÖHL: Precisely. Yet he was very attractive, physically, wouldn't you say?

REDL: That's a hard question for another man to answer——

MÖHL: Oh, come, Redl, you know what women are attracted——

REDL: Yes. Of course, I should say he was, quite certainly.

MÖHL: But you never heard of any particular girl or girls?

REDL: No. But then, we weren't exactly, and I don't——

MÖHL: You are a popular officer—Redl—Siczynski wasn't. He had debts, too. And quite hefty ones. Oh, one expects all young

officers to have debts. It's always been so, and always will,
till they pay soldiers properly. Every other week, a fund has
to be raised for this one or that. Fine. But this officer had,
or so it seems, and frankly it doesn't surprise me, no friends,
was in the hands of moneylenders, of his own race, naturally,
and why? Women? Of course, one asks. But who? No one
knows. No family. Who was worth nine thousand kroner in
debts.

REDL: Nine . . .

MÖHL: Do you think I can find out? It *is* odd, after all. Young
officer, apparently attractive in many ways, work excellent,
intelligence exceptional, diligent, manly disposition and all
the rest of it. Then: where are you?

REDL: Perhaps?—I don't think he was ever in his right element.

MÖHL: Well. There it is. Incident closed now, including your part
in it.

REDL: Thank you, sir.

MÖHL: Only remember. Involvement. Debts—well, you'll be all
right. Also, you have friends, and *will* have. As for women,
I think you know what you're doing.

REDL: I hope so, sir.

MÖHL: What about marriage?

REDL: I'm not contemplating it, not for quite some time, that is.

MÖHL: Good. You've got ideals and courage and fortitude, and
I'm proud and delighted you'll be going from this regiment
to War College. You're on your way, Redl. Taussig! [ADJU-
TANT *enters*] Send in Taussig. [ADJUTANT *clicks heels. Enter*
TAUSSIG *presently*] Ah, Taussig. Come in. You know Redl.
You two should have something to celebrate together to-
night.

FADE

SCENE 3

ANNA's. *A private cubicle. In the background a gipsy orches-*
tra, and flash young officers eating, drinking, swearing, sing-
ing, entertaining ANNA's *young ladies.* REDL *is alone in the*

*cubicle. He leans forward, scoops a champagne bottle from
its bucket to pour himself another glass. It is empty. He
draws the curtain aside and bawls into the smoke and noise.*

REDL: Anna! Anna! Hey! You! What's your name?! Max! Leo!
Anna! Damn! *[He gives up. Looks in his tunic for his cigar
case. Takes one out, a long, black, Italian cheroot.* A YOUNG
WAITER *enters]* Ah, there you are. Thank God. Another—
please. Oh—you've got it. That's clever.

WAITER: I guessed you'd be wanting another, sir.

REDL: Good fellow. Open it, would you?

WAITER: At once, sir.

REDL: Which one are you then?

WAITER: Which one, sir?

REDL: You're not Leo or that other stumpy creature, what's his
name . . .

WAITER: I am Albrecht, sir.

REDL: You're new then.

WAITER: Seven months, sir.

REDL: Oh. I didn't notice you.

WAITER: You don't often do us the honour, sir.

REDL: Light this for me. *[WAITER does so]* I can't afford time for
this sort of caper very often.

WAITER: What a magnificent cigar case, sir.

REDL: What? Oh. Yes. Present. From my uncle.

WAITER: Very fine indeed. Shall I pour it now?

REDL: Yes.

WAITER: Pol Roger eighty-one, sir.

REDL: *[Shortly]* Fine.

WAITER: Would that be crocodile, sir?

REDL: Eh? Oh. Yes. Have you seen my guest anywhere among
that mob?

WAITER: Lieutenant Taussig, sir?

REDL: Well, who else?

WAITER: He is talking with Madame Anna.

*[REDL sips his champagne. The WAITER has increased his rest-
less, uneasy mood. He can't bring himself to dismiss him yet]*

REDL: Rowdy, roaring mob you've got in there.

WAITER: Yes, sir.

REDL: Why do they have to make such a damned show? Howling and vomiting or whoring. *[They listen]* Drunk. . . . Why do they need to get so drunk?

WAITER: End of the summer manoeuvres they tell me, sir. Always the same then.

REDL: This place'll get put out of bounds one day. Someone should warn Anna.

WAITER: I think she just does her best to please the young officers, sir. Giving them what they ask for.

REDL: They'll get it too, and no mistake. What's that young officer's name?

WAITER: Which one, sir? Oh, with the red-haired girl, Hilde—yes, Lieutenant Steinbauer, sir.

REDL: So it is.

WAITER: Very beautiful girl, sir.

REDL: Yes.

WAITER: Very popular, that one.

REDL: Garbage often is.

WAITER: That's true too, of course, sir.

   [Pause]

REDL: Taussig! Where the hell is he?

WAITER: Shall I tell him you want him, sir?

REDL: No. Better not. I'm getting bored sitting here on my own.

WAITER: Can I do anything else, sir?

REDL: No. *[Detaining him]* Do you remember Kupfer?

WAITER: Lieutenant Kupfer? Oh yes, he used to be in here nearly every night, sometimes when he shouldn't have been. We were sorry when he was re-posted.

REDL: And Lieutenant Siczynski? Do you remember him?

WAITER: No, sir, I don't.

REDL: You don't come from Lemberg?

WAITER: No, sir. From Vienna. Oh, you mean the one who was killed in the duel? He used to come in sometimes, usually on his own. But no one seemed to take much notice of him. He

didn't exactly avail himself of the place. Like Lieutenant
Kupfer. *He* used to have this cubicle regularly.

REDL: You must miss Vienna.

WAITER: I do, sir. There are always so many different things to
do *there*. In Lemberg everybody knows who you are and
everything about you. . . . Well, no doubt you'll be in Vienna
yourself before long. May I congratulate you, sir?

REDL: Thank you.

WAITER: On the General Staff, I've no doubt, sir.

REDL: We'll see. *[A roar and banging of tables]* What the devil's
going on?

WAITER: Lieutenant Steinbauer has passed out, sir. They're passing him over their heads . . . One by one . . . Now he's being
sick. I'd better go.

REDL: Well, he's better off: see someone takes him home, if you
can.

WAITER: I'll do my best, sir. So, as I say, you'll soon be seeing for
yourself.

REDL: What?

WAITER: Why, Vienna.

REDL: Oh. All I'll see is work. Maps, tactical field work, riding drill,
Russian language, maps.

WAITER: Oh, of course.

REDL: That'll be enough for me.

WAITER: Yes, sir.

[Pause. Enter TAUSSIG*]*

TAUSSIG: Well, I've fixed us up.

REDL: What?

TAUSSIG: Girls. One each. I've been arguing ten minutes with
Anna, and she insisted she'd only got one spare, that lovely
great black gipsy with the mole on her cheek. There.

WAITER: Zoe.

TAUSSIG: That's the one. So I said to her, I know she's a big girl,
but I know my friend Lieutenant Redl won't go much on
sharing, especially on an occasion like this evening.

REDL: Please forget it. I'm bored with the place.

TAUSSIG: So am I. We'll take another, oh, you've got another, we'll take some more champagne upstairs with us and be entertained properly, me by big black Zoe, and you, you my friend by Hilde. And very lucky you are, doubly lucky, because she was tied up by young Steinbauer until a few moments ago, but he's now safely on his face in the cellar, he won't be capable of fulfilling his little engagement tonight, he'll be lucky to stand up on parade in the morning, and Hilde, red, pale, vacant, and booked this moment by me is all yours.

REDL: It doesn't matter.

TAUSSIG: Of course, it doesn't. It's all fixed. Fixed by me and paid for.

REDL: Taussig, I can't allow it.

TAUSSIG: Nonsense. It's done. [WAITER *pours champagne.* TAUSSIG *drinks*] You insisted on buying the dinner and champagne. And now, *more* champagne. Now, *I* insist on treating you. Your health. [*He glances quickly at the* WAITER] To black Zoe and her gipsy mole. And Hilde and her red whatever special she's got in there. Drink up. [REDL *drinks*] [*To* WAITER] What are *you* standing about for?

REDL: He was opening the champagne.

TAUSSIG: Well, take another one up. On *my* bill.

REDL: Are you sure?

TAUSSIG: Of course I'm sure. We're going to need it. Come on, I'm glad to see you smoking a cigar again. Can't stand the smell of those peppermints. I've always wanted to tell you. I say, that's a pretty classy case.

REDL: My uncle.

TAUSSIG: I didn't know you had rich relatives.

REDL: Only him.

TAUSSIG: Perhaps I should have let you pay for Hilde yourself.

REDL: Of course. Please.

TAUSSIG: Unless you *would* have preferred Zoe. Sharing, I mean.

REDL: Hilde sounds just the thing.

TAUSSIG: I think she's more your type. Bit on the skinny side. No bottom, little tiny bottom, not a real roly-poly. And breasts made like our friend here. Go on, go and get that other bottle!

REDL: *[To* WAITER*]* Just a moment.

TAUSSIG: I'll round them up. *[Pause]* Don't be all night then.

REDL: Just coming.

[He goes to his wallet, trying not to be awkward. He hands a note to the WAITER*]*

WAITER: Thank you, sir.

[He lights a match for REDL, *who looks up. Then notices his cigar is out]*

REDL: Oh, yes.

WAITER: Shall I take this bottle up then, sir?

REDL: Yes. Wait a minute. *[*WAITER *pauses]* Pour me another glass.

[He does so. Picks up bucket]

WAITER: Good night, sir.

REDL: Good night.

[The WAITER *goes out.* REDL *stares into his glass, then drains it, fastens his tunic smartly and steps through the curtain into the tumult]*

FADE

SCENE 4

ANNA's. *An upstairs room. Bare save for a bed. Lying on it are* HILDE *and* REDL. *Only the outline of their bodies is visible. In the darkness* REDL's *cigar glows. Silence. Then there is an occasional noise from one of the other rooms.*

HILDE: *[Whispers]* Hullo. *[Pause]* Hullo.

REDL: Yes.

HILDE: Alfred! Can't you sleep?

REDL: No. I'm not tired.

HILDE: You slept a little. Oh, not for long. Can I get you anything?

REDL: No, thank you.

HILDE: You clench your teeth. Did you know that?

REDL: No.

HILDE: When you're asleep. It makes quite a noise. Scraping together.

REDL: I'm sorry.

HILDE: Oh, please. I didn't mean that. But it'll wear your teeth
down. And you've got such nice teeth. You smell of peppermints. Can I put the light on?

REDL: It's your room.

HILDE: It's yours tonight. [She lights the lamp] Some men's
mouths are disgusting.

REDL: I'm sure.

HILDE: You look better. You almost fainted. Can't I get you anything? [Pause] Is there any champagne left? [He pours her
some from beside the bed] Don't often get champagne
bought me. Well, here's to Vienna. Wish I was going.

REDL: Why don't you?

HILDE: I shall, I'm saving up.

REDL: What will you do—the same thing—when you get there?

HILDE: I suppose so. Do you know, your eyes are like mine?

REDL: Are they?

HILDE: I've never seen a man faint before.

REDL: You should be in the army. Do you want to get married?

HILDE: [Softly] Yes. Of course. Why? Are you proposing?

REDL: I've seen what you've got to offer.

HILDE: Only just. I'm sorry.

REDL: What about?

HLDE: You don't like me.

REDL: What *are* you on about?

HILDE: Never mind. More warm champagne, please.

[He pours]

REDL: What do you mean? Eh?

HILDE: Nothing. Thank you. God bless. And I hope you'll, you'll
be happy in Vienna.

REDL: I'm sorry. Those exams and things have taken it out of me. Perhaps I'll come back tomorrow.

HILDE: Was Lieutenant Siczynski a friend of yours?

REDL: No. Why, did you know him?

HILDE: I used to see him.

REDL: Did he——

HILDE: No. Not with anyone. He usually sat on his own in a corner, reading the foreign papers or just drinking. I used to look at his eyes. But he never looked at me. *[*REDL *leans over the bed and kisses her lingeringly. She returns the embrace abstractedly. He looks down at her]* Peppermints!

REDL: Damn it! I apologized, didn't I?

[She puts her finger to his mouth to calm him]

HILDE: *And* cigars. That's what you smell of, and horses and saddles. What could be nicer, and more manly?

REDL: You're very, very pretty, Hilde. I love your red hair.

HILDE: You don't have to make love to me, Alfred. I'm only a whore.

REDL: But I mean it.

HILDE: Hired by your friend.

REDL: Pretty, little, brittle bones.

HILDE: Lieutenant Taussig.

REDL: Is that him, next door?

HILDE: *[Listens]* At this moment, I should say. *[They listen]* Is he a good friend of yours?

REDL: I can't say I'd call anyone I know a good friend.

HILDE: Are you sure you can't sleep?

REDL: Yes . . . But why don't you?

HILDE: May I put my head on your arm?

REDL: If you wish . . .

HILDE: No, I'll finish my champagne. Do you like children?

REDL: Yes. Why?

HILDE: Would you like some of your own?

REDL: Very much. Wouldn't you?

HILDE: Yes, I would.

REDL: Then what's stopping you?

HILDE: One would like to be loved, if it's possible.

REDL: Love's hardly ever possible.

HILDE: Do you believe that?

REDL: Yes. Anyway, there are always too many babies being born.
So——

HILDE: You may be right. Perhaps that's why you're in the army.

REDL: What's the matter with you? I'm in the army because it
suits *me* and I'm suited to *it*. I can make my own future. I
can style it my own way.

HILDE: What about Siczynski?

REDL: He wasn't suited to it. Who's in that other room, there?

HILDE: Albrecht . . . Would you like to go?

REDL: No. I just asked you a question, that's all. Albrecht who?

HILDE: The waiter you were talking to while I was with the young
lieutenant.

[Pause]

REDL: He's a noisy fellow.

HILDE: Or whoever's with him. *[They listen. She watches* REDL's
face] Your cigar's gone out. Here. He always gets the pick,
Albrecht. Anything he wants. Anyone. *[She moves over to
the wall and pulls back a flap and looks through]* Come
here.

REDL: What for?

[But he joins her]

HILDE: Do you want to look? *[He hesitates, then does so. She returns to the bed, empties the champagne into her glass, and
watches him. Presently, he turns away and sits on the bed.
She puts her arm round his shoulder. Offers him drink]* Have
some? *[He shakes his head]* Sad?

REDL: No. Not sad. One always just wishes that a congenial
evening had been—even more congenial.

HILDE: Think I'll go to bed. It's made me sleepy again. *[*REDL
listens] Shall I turn the light out? *[He nods. She does so. He
goes to the window and looks out. Presently——]* Good
night, Alfred.

REDL: Good night, Hilde.

HILDE: Sorry. I can't keep awake. But you don't mind . . .

[He looks across at her, puts on his tunic, takes out a bank note, picks up his cap]

REDL: Good night, Hilde. Thank you.

[He presses the note into her hand]

HILDE: I'll tell your friend you left in time for reveille. *[He turns]* Alfred . . . *[She sits up and kisses him lightly]* You have the most beautiful mouth that ever, ever kissed me. Good night, Lieutenant.

REDL: Good night.

HILDE: *[Sleepily]* You'll be a colonel one day. On the General Staff. Or even a general.

[He gazes down at her, relights his cigar. The noise from the adjoining room has subsided. He slips out]

FADE

SCENE 5

Warsaw. A darkened office. The light from a magic lantern shines white on a blank screen which faces the audience. A figure is seen to be operating it. Another, seated in front of it, is watching the screen. The first figure is LIEUTENANT STANITSIN. *The second* COLONEL OBLENSKY.

OBLENSKY: Next!

STANITSIN: Redl. *[REDL's photograph in uniform on the screen]* Alfred Von Redl. Captain. Seventh Galician Infantry Regiment. Lemberg. Born Lemberg March 4, 1864. Family background: parents Leopold and Marthe Redl. Eighth of eleven children. Father ex-horse trooper, now second-grade clerical worker Royal and Imperial Railway. Religion: Catholic. Education: Cadet School, passed out with honours. Equitation school.

OBLENSKY: Oh, do get to the meat, Stanitsin. I want my dinner.

STANITSIN: *[Flustered slightly]* Oh—just——

OBLENSKY: If there is any. They're not a very promising lot this time, are they?

STANITSIN: Passed out of War College May of last year, number twenty-three of his entry, recommended particularly, on pink paper, recommended.

OBLENSKY: *[Turns head]* So it is. Meticulous.

STANITSIN: For appointment on General Staff.

OBLENSKY: Yes.

STANITSIN: Health: periodic asthma while at Cadet School, twice almost leading to his discharge. However, in the past ten years, this complaint seems to have been almost completely overcome. Contracted syphilis two and a half years ago, underwent treatment and discharged Lemberg Military Hospital. One serious breach of discipline, involved in duel when fellow officer was killed. Acted as one of the officer's seconds. Affair hushed up and Redl reprimanded. Otherwise unblemished record sheet. Present duty: shortly returned from nine months on staff of Military Attaché in St. Petersburg, ostensibly learning Russian language.

OBLENSKY: Probably all he did do. That's all *ours* do in Vienna. Pick up German in that atrocious, affected accent. I don't know why either of us bothers to observe—just young officers going to diplomatic functions, learning the language painstakingly, like an English governess, and about as well, and not a secret in sight. Most of them just come back like Redl, with the clap at least, or someone else's crabs. Well?

STANITSIN: Waiting for new posting. Financial affairs: No source of income apart from army pay. Although he seems to have invented a fond uncle who occasionally gives him fancy presents or gratuities, of whom there is no trace. Debts, not exactly serious, are considerable. They include: tailor, the biggest trade debt, outstanding accounts at various cafés, restaurants, bootmakers, livery, wine merchants and cigar——

OBLENSKY: Oh, come along, friend. What else?

STANITSIN: Not much. Two moneylenders, small, Fink, Miklas also.

OBLENSKY: Oh—Miklas. I know him. How much?

STANITSIN: Together, some twenty-two hundred kronen.

OBLENSKY: Yes?

STANITSIN: He is also negotiating the lease of a third-floor apartment in the Eighth District.

OBLENSKY: Yes?

STANITSIN: That's about it.

OBLENSKY: Personal?

STANITSIN: Studious. Popular with fellow officers.

OBLENSKY: Oh, come along: women?

STANITSIN: Occasionally. Nothing sustained.

OBLENSKY: Spare time?

STANITSIN: Work mostly. Otherwise cafés, reading foreign newspapers, drinking with friends.

OBLENSKY: All army?

STANITSIN: Mostly.

OBLENSKY: Languages?

STANITSIN: Ruthenian native. Polish, German, some French.

OBLENSKY: And Russian. Some. Yes?

STANITSIN: I'm sorry?

OBLENSKY: What else? If anything.

STANITSIN: That's all, sir.

OBLENSKY: All right. Clever, brilliant officer, unpromising background. Ambitious. Bit extravagant. Popular. Diligent. What do you want to do?

STANITSIN: Continue surveillance, sir?

OBLENSKY: Unpromising lot. Very well. Get me a drink. Ah—good. Redl. Yes. All right. Background: nil. Prospects of brilliant military career exceptional. What he needs now, at this exact stage, is a good, advantageous marriage. An heiress is the ideal. But a rich widow would do even better. He probably needs someone specially adroit socially, a good listener, sympathetic, a woman other men are pleased to call a friend and mean it. Experienced. He knows what he wants, I dare say. He just needs someone to unobtrusively provide the

right elements. . . . Perhaps we should think about it. . . .
Anyway, remind me—sometime next week. Right. Come on
then. Next!

STANITSIN: Kupfer. [REDL's *photograph is switched abruptly from
the screen and replaced by* KUPFER's] Kupfer. Ludwig Max
von Kupfer. Major.

FADE

SCENE 6

*A terrace in the Hofburg, the Emperor's residence in Vienna.
Through the french windows, naturally, is where the court
ball is going on, with the aristocracy, diplomatic corps, officers of the Royal and Imperial Army, flunkeys, etc. Talking
to* VON MÖHL *is Chief of the General Staff, General* CONRAD
VON HÖTZENDORF.

MÖHL: Haven't been here for years.
HÖTZENDORF: Oh?
MÖHL: It's good to be back.
HÖTZENDORF: I'm sure.
MÖHL: There's nowhere quite like it, really, is there?
HÖTZENDORF: No. There's not.
MÖHL: Not where I've been, anyway. What about you, General?
HÖTZENDORF: No, no, I don't think so.
MÖHL: I haven't been here since, oh, well, when was it, well, I
was a young captain, and I was in the Railway Bureau.
HÖTZENDORF: Were you?
MÖHL: Wiry. I could bend, do anything. Like a willow. Where's
your wife, General? Would you like me——
HÖTZENDORF: No. She's all right. She's somewhere . . . Paris, that's
the nearest to it, I suppose.
MÖHL: Yes.
HÖTZENDORF: But really, altogether different.
MÖHL: Entirely.
HÖTZENDORF: In Vienna, well, everyone is bourgeois, or whatever

it is, and a good thing, too, everyone, the beggars in the street, kitchen maids, the aristocracy and, let's be honest, the emperor.

MÖHL: Yes.

HÖTZENDORF: And they all of them enjoy themselves. In Paris, well, in my experience, they're all pretending to be bohemians, from top to bottom, and all the time, every one of them are tradesmen. Well, I don't think you're a real bohemian if you've one eye—or *both* eyes in the case of Paris—on the cash box.

MÖHL: Quite.

HÖTZENDORF: Yes. That's Paris. That's the French. Trouble with Vienna: seems to have old age built into it.

MÖHL: Still, that's better than moving on to God knows what, *and* in such an ugly way, like Prussia, for instance.

HÖTZENDORF: Yes. Or England. Even more. They'll soon wreck it. Prussians *are* efficient. English wilful. There *is* a difference. Still, all *we* do is celebrate and congratulate ourselves on saving Europe from the infidel.

MÖHL: I know. . . . There's little credit for it.

HÖTZENDORF: Still. It *was* a long time ago.

MÖHL: Redl! *[He hails* REDL *from the ballroom, who appears]* Redl, my dear boy! What a pleasant surprise. General, may I? Captain Alfred Redl: General von Hötzendorf. *[They acknowledge]* Since I last saw you, Redl, I now have the honour of working on the General's staff.

REDL: Indeed, sir. Congratulations.

MÖHL: Redl was just about the finest young officer, all round, when I was commandant in Lemberg, for eleven years.

HÖTZENDORF: So you told me. Who was the very pretty young lady you were dancing with?

REDL: I'm sorry, sir, which one?

MÖHL: Hah! Which *one!*

HÖTZENDORF: Small-boned, dark, brown eyes.

REDL: Miss Ursula Kunz, sir.

HÖTZENDORF: Kunz?

MÖHL: Ah, Kunz. Miss Kunz, youngest daughter of Judge Advocate Jaroslav Kunz.

HÖTZENDORF: Ah.

MÖHL: Good man. Very.

HÖTZENDORF: Is he?

MÖHL: Seems to be.

HÖTZENDORF: Would you agree, Redl?

REDL: I, sir? From the little I know, and have been able to observe reliably, he is very competent indeed.

HÖTZENDORF: No more?

REDL: Accomplished, too . . . Unpopular.

HÖTZENDORF: Why?

REDL: I don't know, sir.

HÖTZENDORF: I believe it. Something odd, don't know what.

MÖHL: Well—yes . . . But how useful.

HÖTZENDORF: Oh, yes. Useful. Remember what Radetsky said about General Haynau? He said about Haynau, let's see: "He's my best general all right, but he's like a razor. When you've used him, put him back in his case."

MÖHL: The general was talking about Vienna, Redl. Well—— How are *you* enjoying it?

REDL: Very much, sir.

MÖHL: Better than St. Petersburg?

REDL: The Russians find it very difficult to enjoy life. Although they *do* manage occasionally.

HÖTZENDORF: Yes. Yes, but, you know, this is a great place to do *nothing*, sit in a café, and dream, listen to the city, *do nothing* and not even anticipate regretting it.

MÖHL: Ah, there's friend Kunz.

HÖTZENDORF: Who? Where?

MÖHL: With the Countess Delyanoff.

HÖTZENDORF: So he is.

MÖHL: You know her?

HÖTZENDORF: Just.

MÖHL: I think they're coming out here.

HÖTZENDORF: [*To* REDL] . . . sort of woman, know her——? [REDL *shakes his head*] Well, the sort of woman who looks at you for five minutes without a word and then says "What do you think about Shakespeare?" Or, something like that. Unbelievable.

MÖHL: Ah, Kunz! Countess. *[Enter* MAJOR JAROSLAV KUNZ *and the* COUNTESS SOPHIA DELYANOFF*]* We were just watching you.

*[*MÖHL *makes the introductions, leaving* REDL *till last]*

COUNTESS: We've met before.

REDL: Forgive me——

COUNTESS: Oh, yes. Not once, but at least three times. You were on General Hauser's staff in St. Petersburg, and a short spell in Prague, were you not?

REDL: I'm sorry.

COUNTESS: Please. I'm sure you had no eye——

MÖHL: Oh, come, Countess, I can't think of anyone more likely to get his eye fixed on someone like you. You're being unfair.

COUNTESS: No. I think not. But I forgive him.

[A FLUNKEY *presents glasses of champagne]*

MÖHL: The general and I were just talking about Vienna.

KUNZ: Yes.

MÖHL: We were just saying—there's nowhere quite like it.

KUNZ: No. You've been away some time, I believe, Colonel. Where was it?

MÖHL: Przemysl.

KUNZ: Przemysl. Ah yes, with all the fortifications.

MÖHL: Four twelve-inch howitzers, some nine- and some six-inch, forty battalions, four squadrons, forty-three artillery companies, eight sapper companies—oh, please forgive me.

KUNZ: Yes. Nowhere quite like Przemysl, in fact.

COUNTESS: I'm afraid I simply can't understand the army, or why any man is ever in it.

HÖTZENDORF: Nor should you. The army's like nothing else. It goes beyond religion. It serves everyone and everyone serves it, even Hungarians and Jews. It conscripts, but it calls the best men out, men who'd never otherwise have been called on.

KUNZ: I think perhaps it's a little like living in the eighteenth century; the army. Apart from Przemysl, that is. Still that *is* a Viennese speciality? Don't you think, General?

HÖTZENDORF: I see nothing about the eighteenth century that makes me believe the nineteenth was any better. And what makes *you* think that the twentieth will be an improvement?

KUNZ: But why do you assume *I* should think it would be?

COUNTESS: I don't think I could ever have been a soldier. I'd want to be a stranger in a street, a key on a concierge's board, inaccessible if I wanted.

MÖHL: But that's what a *soldier* is.

COUNTESS: Only at the cost of his identity. *[To* REDL*]* Wouldn't you say, Captain?

REDL: I think the general's right. The army creates an elite.

COUNTESS: No. I believe *it* is created. The army. It can't change. And it is changed from outside.

MÖHL: Nothing else trains a man——

KUNZ: Aptitudes, aptitudes at the expense of character.

COUNTESS: But it can, in its own way, provide a context of expression for people who wouldn't otherwise have it.

KUNZ: I can only say, Countess, you can have met very few soldiers.

COUNTESS: You're quite wrong, Major. Why, look at me now. Several hundred guests and who am I with? The chief of the General Staff himself, a distinguished colonel from Przemysl, a judge advocate major from Vienna and a splendid young captain. And how different you all are, each one of you. I must say: I can't think of anything more admirable than not having to play a part.

KUNZ: I'm sorry, Countess, but nonsense! We all play parts, *are* doing so now, *will* continue to do so, and as long as we are playing at being Austrian, Viennese, or whatever we think we are, cosmopolitan and nondescript, a position palmed on us by history, by the accident of having held back the Muslim horde at the gates of Europe. For which no one is grateful, after all; it was two centuries ago, and we resent it, feel ill-used and pretend we're something we're not, instead of recognizing that we're the provincial droppings of Europe. The army, all of *us,* and the Church, sustain the empire, which is what, a convenience to other nations, an international utility for the use of whoever, Russia, England, or Francis Joseph, which again, is what? Crown Imperial of nonintellect. Which is why, for the moment, it survives. Like this evening, the Hofball, perspiring gaiety and pointlessness.

[Pause]

HÖTZENDORF: Countess, please excuse me.

KUNZ: Plus a rather heavy odour of charm.

*[*HÖTZENDORF *clicks his heels and goes out]*

COUNTESS: *[To* MÖHL*]* I'm sorry if I've offended the general.

KUNZ: *I* offended, not you, Countess.

MÖHL: Correct. He's not accustomed to your kind of young banter, Kunz.

KUNZ: I didn't expect him to take me so seriously.

COUNTESS: *[Smiles]* Of course you did.

MÖHL: He is still the finest officer in the Royal and Imperial Army.

KUNZ: Very probably.

MÖHL: He is an old friend. He may not be as clever as you, Major, but his heart is in the right place.

KUNZ: Where it can be seen by everyone.

MÖHL: And I will not stand by and allow him to be sneered at and insulted.

KUNZ: I quite agree. Please excuse me, Countess. Gentlemen.

COUNTESS: Well. What tempers you men do have! What about you, Captain, we've not heard much out of you yet? I've a feeling you're full of shocking things.

REDL: What about?

COUNTESS: Why, what we've been talking about.

REDL: Like the army, you mean? I'm afraid I don't agree with the major.

COUNTESS: No?

REDL: No. I mean, for myself, I didn't want to be, or mean to be: rigid or fixed.

COUNTESS: But you're not.

REDL: No. At the same time, there must be bonds, some bonds that have more meaning than others.

COUNTESS: I don't follow.

MÖHL: Now you're baiting, Countess. Of course he's right. No officer should be allowed to speak in the way of Major Kunz.

COUNTESS: He offends against blood. He——

MÖHL: Against himself; it's like being a Pole or a Slovak or a Jew, I suppose. All these things have more meaning than being, say, a civil servant, or a watchmaker. And all these things are brought together in the army like nowhere else. It's the same experience as friendship or loving a woman, speaking the same tongue, that is a *proper* bond, it's *human*, you can see it and experience it, more than "all men are brothers" or some such nonsense.

COUNTESS: And do *you* agree with that, Captain Redl?

REDL: I don't agree that all men are brothers, like Colonel Möhl. We are clearly not. Nor should be, or ever want to be.

COUNTESS: Spoken like a true aristocrat.

REDL: Which, as you must know, I am not——

COUNTESS: Oh, but I believe you are. Don't you, Colonel?

REDL: We're meant to clash. And often and violently. I am proud to be despised by some men, no perhaps most men. Others are to be tolerated or ignored. And if they do the same for me, I am gratified, or, at least, relieved.

MÖHL: I agree with the countess about you, Redl. He has style, always had it, must have had it as a tiny boy.

COUNTESS: Your pride in the captain is quite fierce, Colonel. It's quite touching.

MÖHL: I don't know about touching, as you call it . . . it's *real*, anyhow.

COUNTESS: But that's only too clear, and why not? It's quite obviously justified.

MÖHL: Some men have a style of living like bad skins. Coarse grained, erupting, spotty. Let me put it this way: I don't have to tell you that, even in this modern age of what they call democracy, the army is still a place of privilege. Redl is the rare type that redeems that privilege. And why? Because he overpowers it, overpowers it by force, not mob-trained force, but natural, disciplined character, ability, and honour. And that's all I've got to say on the subject.

COUNTESS: My dear Colonel, I don't know who is the most embarrassed—you or Captain Redl.

REDL: Myself, Countess. A truly honest man is never embarrassed.

COUNTESS: You mean: *you* are not honest?

MÖHL: The boy's an open book. He should be in Intelligence. No one would believe him!

COUNTESS: But not tolerant.

REDL: I don't think so.

COUNTESS: Oh, indeed, I think you ignore what doesn't interest you. Which is why you didn't remember me in spite of the fact of our having met on three separate occasions.

REDL: Pardon me, Countess. I remembered immediately after.

COUNTESS: You think I am a snob because I accused you of trumpeting like an aristocrat just now. *You* are the snob, Captain Redl, not I. As Colonel von Möhl here will tell you, my husband was a petty landowner from Cracow and *I* am the daughter of a veterinary surgeon.

MÖHL: *[Laughs]* Well, don't take that too seriously, Redl.

COUNTESS: Colonel: I appeal to you!

MÖHL: Well, let me say you would say there was only *some* truth in it.

[He chuckles again. A FLUNKEY *approaches* REDL *with a salver with a card on it]*

FLUNKEY: Captain Redl, sir?

REDL: Please excuse me.

[He takes the card out of the envelope, reads it, hands it to MÖHL*]*

MÖHL: Archduke Ferdinand . . . Ah, well, you'd better get along! Quickly. Here, you! *[Grabs more champagne glasses from passing* FLUNKEY*]* Get this down you first. Very beautiful, if I may say so. Redl! Countess, your health. The archduke's the man now. Ferdinand's the one to watch, and I think he's probably all right. Knows what he's doing. Knows what's going on in the empire, Hungary, for instance, Serbia. You see, the Belvedere, that's going to be the centre of things, not the Hofburg any more. Pity that, about all that, what do you call it, morganatic marriage business.

COUNTESS: Yes, indeed. Poor woman. Having to trail behind countesses, a hundred yards behind him.

MÖHL: Why do you think he married her?

COUNTESS: Why does any man get married?

REDL: Children, property.

COUNTESS: But one sees all that, but it couldn't have operated in this case. He could have had her as his mistress like his uncle. But then, when you think of the men one knows who *are* married, and who they're married *to*, and what their real, snotty little longings are underneath their proud watch and chains, their constant broken, sidelong glances. Oh, I know all about it, even if it's difficult to understand sometimes. Captain, you mustn't keep His Imperial Highness waiting. Not while *I* lecture you on marriage.

[REDL *clicks his heels and leaves them*]

MÖHL: Well!

COUNTESS: Yes, Colonel.

MÖHL: I was just thinking, what you were saying about marriage then.

COUNTESS: And——?

MÖHL: It really is the most *lamentable* thing for most of us, isn't it? I mean, as you say, it doesn't work really. Only the appearances function. Eh? Everyone knows the *feelings*, but what's the answer, what's the answer do you think?

COUNTESS: The only answer is not to be drawn into it, like the Captain.

MÖHL: No, I think you're wrong there. Redl would make a first-class husband.

COUNTESS: You think so?

MÖHL: Absolutely. He's steadfast, sober, industrious, orderly, he likes orderly things, hates chaos. That's why marriage would suit him so well. That's what marriage represents, I suppose. I say, I *am* enjoying talking to you.

COUNTESS: And I am enjoying talking to you. Do you think Captain Redl will come back to us?

MÖHL: Oh, I should think so. Order out of chaos. I know, we'll keep an eye out for him, learn what the Archduke had to say to him. You wouldn't care to dance with such an old man, would you?

COUNTESS: But, of course, delighted. Major Kunz is a very uninspired dancer.

MÖHL: That's because he doesn't like it. Now *I* love it. I'm so glad Redl got that invitation. Good boy! Oh, I say, I *am* having a good time.

[He beams boyishly, offers his arm to her, and they leave the terrace to join the dancers in the ballroom]

FADE

SCENE 7

The drawing room of COUNTESS DELYANOFF'*s house. One oil lamp burns on a desk. On a chair are* REDL'*s tunic, sword, and cap and gloves. A sharp, clear, moaning cry is heard. Once, quickly. Then again, longer, more violent. Then silence. Fumbling footsteps outside the door.* REDL *enters in his breeches, putting on his vest, carrying his boots. He slumps into a chair, dropping the boots beside him. A voice outside calls softly: "Alfred, Alfred!"*

The COUNTESS *enters swiftly, anxious, her hair down to her waist, very beautiful in her nightgown. She looks across at* REDL *as if this had happened before, goes to a decanter and pours a brandy. With it, she crosses to* REDL'*s armchair and looks down at him.*

REDL: Sophia?

COUNTESS: My dear?

REDL: Sorry I woke you.

COUNTESS: I should think you woke the entire street.

REDL: Sorry. So sorry.

COUNTESS: Don't be silly. Here.

[She hands him the brandy. He takes some. Stares at his boots]

REDL: I think I'd better go.

COUNTESS: It's early yet. Why, it's only, I can't see, look, it's only half-past one.

REDL: Still . . .

COUNTESS: You left me *last* night at three. And when you're gone I can't sleep. I wake the moment you've gone. All I can do is think about you.

REDL: I know. Please forgive me. . . . Better put these on.

[Takes one of the boots]

COUNTESS: Alfred. Please come back to bed. . . . I know you hate me asking you, but I do beg you. . . . Just for an hour. You *can't* go out now.

REDL: I need some air.

COUNTESS: *[Softly]* Darling——

REDL: Need my orderly on these occasions. Can't get my boots on.

[She grasps his knee and kneels]

COUNTESS: Why did you wake?

REDL: Oh. Usual.

COUNTESS: And you're crying again.

REDL: I know. . . . *[His face is stony. His voice firm]* Why do you always have to look at me?

COUNTESS: Because I love you.

REDL: You'd look away . . .

COUNTESS: That's why. What can I do, my darling?

REDL: Nothing. . . . I must get these damned things . . . *[Struggles with boots]* I'd love another brandy. *[She rises and gets it]* It's like a disease.

COUNTESS: What is?

REDL: Oh, all this incessant, *silly* weeping. It only happens, it creeps up on me, when I'm asleep. No one else has ever noticed it . . . . Why do you have to wake up?

COUNTESS: Here. Alfred, don't turn away from me.

REDL: My mouth tastes sour.

COUNTESS: I didn't mean that. Anyway, what if it is? Don't turn your head away.

[She grasps his head and kisses him. He submits for a moment, then thrusts her away]

REDL: Please!

COUNTESS: What is it? Me?

REDL: No. You're—you're easily the most beautiful . . . desirable woman I've ever . . . There couldn't be . . .

COUNTESS: It's not easy to believe.

REDL: Sophia: it's *me*. It's like a disease.

COUNTESS: You must feel deeply. So do I. Why do you think you've got *me* crying as well. No one's done that to me for years!

REDL: It's like, I can't . . .

COUNTESS: *[Impatient]* But it *isn't* like the clap you got off some garrison whore. That's all over. You know it, you were cured, cured, you've got a paper to say so, and even if you weren't, do you think I would care?

REDL: It isn't that.

COUNTESS: Then what is it? Why do you dream? Why do you sweat and cry out and *leave* me in the middle of the night? Oh, God!

[She recovers]

REDL: Here, have some of this. I'll get some more.

COUNTESS: No, that's fine.

REDL: Why don't you commit yourself?

COUNTESS: Why don't *you*? My darling, try not to drink so much.

REDL: I've told you. I drink. I drink, heavily sometimes, I don't get *drunk*.

COUNTESS: Yes. So you say.

REDL: It's the truth.

COUNTESS: What are you saying? No, forget I asked. Don't take any of this as *true*, Alfred, I beg of you. It's early in the morning, everything's asleep and indifferent now—*threatening to us*, both of us, *you're* in tears, you wake up in a depression, in a panic, you're dangerous and frightened again and I'm in tears. Please, don't, please, stay, stay with me, I'll look after you, I'll make up . . . at least for something. I'll protect you, protect you . . . and love you.

REDL: I can protect myself.

COUNTESS: But you can't. Not *always*. Can you? What is it?

REDL: I must go. I can't sit here.

COUNTESS: Why can't you trust me?

REDL: I've told you . . . I *don't* mean to hurt you.

COUNTESS: And I believe you.

REDL: I just can't.

[Pause]

COUNTESS: Have you never confided in anyone?

REDL: No.

COUNTESS: Hasn't there ever been anyone? *[Pause]* What about another man? I know friendship means a lot to you. . . . What about Taussig?

REDL: No. At least . . . Only a very, a very little. I did try one evening. But he doesn't welcome confidences. He doesn't know what to do with them . . . or where to put them.

COUNTESS: You mean nobody else, not *one*, your mother, your grandfather, no one?

REDL: They might have been;——

COUNTESS: Um?

REDL: But I never did.

COUNTESS: Why?

REDL: I suppose I . . . they, *I* waited too long, and then . . . they were killed. An accident. You're shivering.

COUNTESS: Please try. Everyone owes something to someone. You *are* in love with me, Alfred, I know you are, and you've told me yourself. That must be something.

REDL: Put this on.

[He places his tunic round her shoulders]

COUNTESS: What about you? *[He shrugs]* You look better. *Are* you?

REDL: Yes. At least they go quickly. Just at a bad time. In the night. Or when I'm having to force myself to do something as an exercise, or a duty, like working late.

COUNTESS: I tell you: you work too hard.

REDL: Or sometimes I get caught in some relaxation. Sitting in a café, listening to gossip, and I enjoy that after a long day, and I'm curious. But if I listen to a conversation that's got serious, say, about politics, the Magyars, or merging with Germany, or something like that, I feel myself, almost as if I were falling away and disappearing. I want to run. . . . But, I've felt I should take a serious, applied interest in this sort, in, ours is a complicated age, and I'm some small part of it, and I should devote as much attention and interest to it as I can muster. I should be giving up time——

COUNTESS: What time, for heaven's sake? You already——

REDL: Much more than I do, *much* more. I used not even to try.

COUNTESS: You mean *I* waste it?

REDL: But I can't relax or be at ease.

COUNTESS: Why are you so watchful? You always seem to be at the ready in some way, listening for something . . . some stray chance thing.

REDL: I don't know what that means.

[He goes to the decanter]

COUNTESS: Please, Alfred. You've an early train in the morning . . .

REDL: Do you know: the only time I drink heavily is when I'm with you? No, I didn't mean that. But when you're badgering me and sitting on my head and, and I can't breathe.

COUNTESS: Why do you always have to make love to me with the——

REDL: There you go!

COUNTESS: Why? Why do you insist? Before we even begin?

REDL: I might ask you why *you* insist on turning the light on.

COUNTESS: Because I want to look at your face. Is that so strange?

REDL: You must know, *you* must know, we're not all the same.
COUNTESS: Why do you never kiss me?
REDL: But I do.
COUNTESS: But never in bed.
REDL: Oh, let's go back. We're tired.
COUNTESS: And turn your head away?
REDL: Damn your eyes, I *won't* be catechized!
COUNTESS: Why do you never speak?
REDL: What do you want out of me? Well, I tell you, whatever it is, I *can't* give it. Can't and won't.

   [Pause]

COUNTESS: I thought it was only whores you didn't kiss or speak to.
REDL: You would know more about that. *[She looks up at him miserably, shivering. He feels outmanoeuvred. Takes his tunic from her and puts it on]* Excuse me.
COUNTESS: If you leave me, you'll be alone.
REDL: That's what I want, to be left alone.
COUNTESS: You'll always be alone.
REDL: Good. Splendid.
COUNTESS: No, it isn't. You know it isn't. That's why you're so frightened. You'll fall alone.
REDL: So does everyone. Even if they don't know it.
COUNTESS: You can't be *saved* alone.
REDL: I don't expect to be saved, as you put it. Not by you.
COUNTESS: Or any other woman?
REDL: Or anyone at all. *[He picks up his cap and gloves]*
COUNTESS: What have I done?
REDL: *I* am the guilty one. Not you. Please forgive me.
COUNTESS: Don't, don't go. *[Pause]* One feels very old at this time of night. *[She goes to the window. He watches her, distressed]* It's the time of night when people die. People give up. *[He goes behind her, hesitates, puts his head against hers for comfort. Pause]* You can't have your kind of competitive success *and* seclusion.

[He sighs, draws away and goes to the door]

REDL: Good night, Sophia.
COUNTESS: Good night.

[Pause]

REDL: Would you like to have tea?
COUNTESS: When?
REDL: Tuesday?
COUNTESS: I can't.
REDL: Wednesday?
COUNTESS: Please. *[He turns]* Yes, please.

[He goes out]

FADE

SCENE 8

OBLENSKY's *office. He is reading a letter to* STANITSIN.

OBLENSKY: "In haste. Enroute for Prague. Wherever I am, my
dearest, you will trouble my heart. I can say no more, I can-
not think. The work here will do me good I expect. Try to
do something yourself. This is a difficult time. I seem to:
seem to——" can't read it—"speak . . . speak out of nowhere.
You deserve only the best, not the worst. Forgive me: Alfred." Where's hers? Ah: "My dearest love, why are you
writing to me like this? You seem to have forgotten everything. It was not all like those short times during the night.
The rest *was* different"—underlined. "Don't, I beg you, *don't*
deceive yourself. Why don't you answer my letters? I wait
for them. Give me a word, or something that will do. At least
something I can go over. I can do nothing. Now *I* am helpless. Loved one, don't something this. Forever, your Sophia.
P.S. Did you never intend coming that Wednesday? I can't
believe it." Hum. What do you suppose he means, where is
it—"this is a difficult time"?

STANITSIN: Well, the moneylenders are pressing pretty hard. He's sold his gold cigarette case and fancy watch.

OBLENSKY: Has he? "You deserve only the best, not the worst." Odd sentiment for a distinguished officer, don't you think? He can't feel *that* sensitive about his extravagance, he's too reckless. Besides, as far as *he* knows, she's quite rich.

STANITSIN: Maybe he's just bored with her.

OBLENSKY: I don't think so, I'd say he's a passionate man, a bit callous too, and selfish, very, but there's something *in* all this.

STANITSIN: Come to that, the Countess sounds pretty convincing.

OBLENSKY: I hope not. All right. [*He nods to* STANITSIN, *who opens the office door, and admits the* COUNTESS] Sit down. You seem to have lost your man.

COUNTESS: For the moment.

OBLENSKY: You mean you think you can get him back?

COUNTESS: Possibly.

OBLENSKY: Do you want to?

COUNTESS: What do you mean? I do what you tell me.

OBLENSKY: What's your assessment of REDL?

COUNTESS: Ambitious. Secretive. Violent. Vain. Extravagant. I expect you know as much as I do. You don't have to sleep with him to find that out.

OBLENSKY: Precisely. It doesn't seem to have added much to our total knowledge. However, patience. We're in no hurry. Captain Redl will be with us for a long time yet. Years and years. He'll probably improve with keeping. What's he doing with himself?

STANITSIN: What he says, working. Of course, he's hard up for the moment, but he'll——

OBLENSKY: Have you offered him money?

COUNTESS: Twice. He refused.

OBLENSKY: Won't take money from a woman. And I suppose you told him it didn't count between lovers?

COUNTESS: Naturally.

OBLENSKY: And there's no woman in Prague, nowhere, anyone? No one-night stands or twopenny stand-ups?

STANITSIN: Nothing. He leaves his office in the War Building every
    day at 4:15, goes down to the café, has a coffee or two, reads
    all the foreign newspapers, has an early dinner, then goes
    back to his office and works till about ten, even eleven or
    twelve sometimes.

OBLENSKY: He *is* telling the truth.

STANITSIN: Occasionally he'll drop in for a drink somewhere on
    his way home or meets his friend Taussig for half an hour.
    More often than not he justs sits alone.

OBLENSKY: Doing nothing?

STANITSIN: Just sitting. Looking.

OBLENSKY: Looking at what?

STANITSIN: I don't know. What *can* you look at from a café win-
    dow? Other people, I suppose. Watch.

OBLENSKY: The Passing Show.

COUNTESS: Is there anything else?

OBLENSKY: No, my dear. Stanitsin will brief you.

[She rises]

COUNTESS: Is it—may I have my letter?

OBLENSKY: I don't see why not. *[Hands one to her]*

COUNTESS: No, I meant his, to me.

OBLENSKY: I'm afraid that's for the file. Sorry. I can send you a
    copy. I wonder if he *will* write again. Don't forget to report,
    will you?

[STANITSIN sees her out. OBLENSKY lights a cigarette]

FADE

SCENE 9

*A café. REDL sits alone at a table. Sitting a few tables away is
a young man. REDL reads a paper. Throws away his cigar butt.
Enter TAUSSIG.*

TAUSSIG: Ah, Redl, there you are. Sorry I'm late.

REDL: What will you have?

TAUSSIG: Don't think I'll bother. I promised to meet someone in ten minutes.

REDL: The one in the chorus at the Opera House?

TAUSSIG: That's the one.

REDL: Where?

TAUSSIG: She's taking me to her lodgings.

REDL: Before the performance? I hope it doesn't affect her voice. What's she like?

TAUSSIG: She rattles. Nice big girl.

REDL: They always are.

TAUSSIG: She's got a girl friend.

REDL: Thank you, no.

TAUSSIG: You seem awfully snobbish sometimes, Alfred.

REDL: Do I? I'm sorry. It's just that I'm not too keen on the opera. Are you going—afterwards?

TAUSSIG: What?

REDL: To the performance?

TAUSSIG: Oh, yes, I suppose so. Your head must be hardened by all those ciphers. Löhengrin, I think. What's it like?

REDL: Boring.

TAUSSIG: So I believe. Oh, well. Sure you won't have supper after? She really is quite nice. They both are.

REDL: No, thank you, really.

TAUSSIG: Not going to Madame Heyse's do, are you?

REDL: No.

[Pause]

TAUSSIG: Does that young man over there know you?

REDL: What young man?

TAUSSIG: Well, there's only one.

REDL: No. Why?

TAUSSIG: He's done nothing but stare at you. Oh, he's turned away now. Knows we're talking about him.

REDL: Prague's as bad as Vienna.

TAUSSIG: Keeps giggling to himself, as far as I can see.

REDL: Probably a cretin. Or a Czech who hates Austrian army officers. I can't face another of those evenings or dinners, here or anywhere. They all talk about each other. They're all clever and they're afraid of each other's cleverness. They're like beautiful, schooled, performing dogs. Scrutinizing and listening for an unsteady foot. It's like hunting without the pig. Everyone sweats and whoops and rides together, and, at any time, at any moment, the pig may turn out to be *you*. Stick!

TAUSSIG: Well, if I can't tempt you . . . Can I have one of your cigarettes? I say, the old case back, eh?

REDL: And the watch. Everything in fact.

TAUSSIG: Good for you. Make a killing?

REDL: I tipped my mare against Steinbauer's new gelding. Want a loan?

TAUSSIG: No thanks. The countess isn't bothering you, is she?

REDL: I told you—no. We never got on. She was prickly and we were always awkward together. It was like talking to my sister. Who died, last week incidentally, consumption, and I can't say I thought about it more than ten minutes.

TAUSSIG: What will you do?

REDL: Now? Oh, have a quiet dinner. Go for a walk.

TAUSSIG: A walk? I don't know—well, if I can't persuade you. 'Bye.

[REDL nods. TAUSSIG strides off. He picks up a paper, lights a new cigar. Presently the YOUNG MAN comes up to him]

YOUNG MAN: Excuse me, sir.

REDL: Well?

YOUNG MAN: May I glance at your paper?

REDL: If you wish. *[Irritated]* The waiter will bring you one if you ask.

YOUNG MAN: I only want to see what's on at the Opera.

REDL: Löhengrin.

YOUNG MAN: Oh, thank you. No. I don't think I like Wagner much. Do you?

REDL: No. Now please go away.

[The YOUNG MAN grins at him, and leans across to him, saying softly]

YOUNG MAN: I know what *you're* looking for.

[REDL *looks stricken. The* YOUNG MAN *walks away. He is almost out of sight when* REDL *runs after him*]

REDL: You! [REDL *grabs him with ferocious power by the neck*] What do you mean?
YOUNG MAN: Nothing! Let me go!
REDL: You pig, you little upstart pig. What did you mean?
YOUNG MAN: [*Yells*] Let me go!

[*Heads turn.* REDL's *anger subsides into embarrassment. The* YOUNG MAN *walks away.* REDL *returns to his seat, lights his cigar, orders a drink from the* WAITER. *A Gipsy Band strikes up*]

FADE

SCENE 10

A bare, darkened room. In it is a bed. On it two figures, not yet identifiable. A light is struck. A cigar end glows.

REDL'S VOICE: Why wouldn't you keep the light on? [*A figure leaves the bed and goes to a wash basin. Sound of water*] Um? Oh! Why did I wait—so long. [REDL *lights a lamp beside the bed. By the washstand is the handsome form of a young* PRIVATE SOLDIER] Paul?
PAUL: Yes?
REDL: Why?
PAUL: I don't know. I just prefer the dark.
REDL: But why? My darling. You're so exquisite to look on—— You mean it's me?
PAUL: No. You look all right.
REDL: What is it, then? What are you dressing for?
PAUL: Got to get back to barracks, haven't I?
REDL: What's your unit?
PAUL: That'd be telling, wouldn't it?
REDL: Oh, come on, I can find out.

PAUL: Yes. General Staff and all that, isn't it?

REDL: Paul. What is it? What have I done? What are you opening the door for?

[PAUL *has opened the door. Four young* SOLDIERS *come in. They look at* REDL, *who knows instantly what will happen. He struggles violently at first, and for a while it looks as if they might have taken on too much. The young* SOLDIERS *in turn become amazed by* REDL's *vicious defence of himself, which is like an attack. All the while* PAUL *dresses, pockets* REDL's *gold cigarette case, cigar case, watch and chain, gold crucifix, notes and change.* REDL *becomes a kicked, bloody heap on the floor. The* SOLDIERS *leave.* PAUL, *having dressed fully by now, helps* REDL *sit up against the bed, looks down at his bloody face*]

PAUL: Don't be too upset, love. You'll get used to it.

[*Exit*]

CURTAIN

ACT TWO

{*decorative rule*}

SCENE 1

*A ballroom, Vienna. A winter evening in 1902. In the back-
ground a small, eccentrically dressed* ORCHESTRA *plays. The
light is not bright when the curtain goes up, except on the*
SINGERS. *Concentrated silently, at first, anyway, are the
GUESTS, among whom is* REDL, *one of the few not in fancy
dress of some kind. However, he looks magnificent in his uniform and has put on his few decorations. He sprawls, listening thoughtfully to the* SINGER, *smoking one of his long black
cigars. The* SINGER *is dressed in an eighteenth-century dress
which might allow the wearer to play* SUSANNA *in* Figaro *or
one of Mozart's ladies like* ZERLINA. *The* ORCHESTRA *plays very
softly, the* SINGER *is restrained at this time, which is as well,
because the voice is not adequate. However, it has enough
sweetness in feeling to immediately invoke the pang of Mozart. Perhaps "Vedrai Carino" or "Batti, Batti" from* Don
Giovanni. *It ends quickly. Applause. Then a* MAN *dressed to
play* FIGARO *appears, the lights become brighter, and the two
go into the duet in the first scene of* Figaro. *This should take
no more than three minutes. It should be accepted at the
beginning as the indifferent effort of a court opera house cast
with amateurs, but not without charm and aplomb.*

The FIGARO *in this case is a straight man. Presently, the
SUSANNA begins straight, then gradually cavorting, camping,*

and sending up the character, the audience, and *Mozart as only someone in drag has the licence. The ballroom audience has been waiting for this, and is in ecstasy by the time it is over. Some call out "do the Mad Scene." Or "Come Scoglio." The* SUSANNA, *egged on, does a short parody of something like "Come Scoglio," or "Lucia" done in the headlong, take-it-on-the-chin manner.*

This only takes a couple of minutes and should be quite funny. Anyhow, the ballroom audience apparently think so. Obviously, most of them have seen the performance before. There is a lot of giggling and even one scream during the ARIA, *which* SUSANNA-LUCIA *freezes with mock fury, and ends to great applause.* SUSANNA *curtsies graciously. The lights in the room come up, the* ORCHESTRA *strikes up and most of the guests dance. It is essential that it should only gradually be revealed to the audience that all the dancers and guests are men. The costumes, from all periods, should be in exquisite taste, both men's and women's, and those wearing them should look exotic and reasonably attractive, apart from an occasional grotesque. The music is gay, everyone chatters happily like a lot of birds, and the atmosphere is generally relaxed and informal, in contrast to the somewhat stiff atmosphere at the ball in Act I. Among those dancing at present are* KUPFER, *dressed rather dashingly as* SCARAMOUCHE. KUNZ, *dancing one handed, with* MARIE ANTOINETTE, *looks rather good as* LORD NELSON. *The* WAITER ALBRECHT *from Scene 3, dressed as* COLUMBINE *with* KUPFER. FIGARO *dances with a* LADY GODIVA *in gold lamé jockstrap.* DOWNSTAGE, *holding court, is the host,* BARON VON EPP. *He is an imposing man with a rich flexible voice which he uses to effect. At present, he looks astonishingly striking with upswept hair, ospreys in pompadour feathers, a pearl and diamond dog collar at his neck, and a beautiful fan, as* QUEEN ALEXANDRA. *Again, it is essential that the costume should be in meticulous taste and worn elegantly and with natural confidence. Sitting beside him is someone dressed as a whimpled mediaeval lady, to be identified as* STEINBAUER. *Like* REDL *now, some years older.*

REDL *is accompanied by* LIEUTENANT STEFAN KOVACS, *who is fixed in a mixture of amusement and embarrassment.* REDL *himself is quite cool, looking extremely dashing in his Colonel's uniform and decorations and close-cropped hair, staring very carefully around at all the guests, his eyes missing no one. He lights one of his long black cigars and joins the* BARON's *group, which includes* STEINBAUER, SUSANNA *and a ravishing* TSARINA.

NOTE: At any drag ball as stylish and private as this one, the guests can be seen to belong to entirely different and very distinct categories.

1. The paid bum boys whose annual occasion it is—they wait for it from one year to the next and spend between three and six months preparing an elaborate and possibly bizarre costume. This is the marketplace where in all probability they will manage to acquire a meal ticket for months ahead. They tend to either tremendously careful, totally feminine clothes—or the ultimate in revelation—e.g., Lady Godiva, except that he/she might think, instead of a gold lamé jockstrap, that a gold chastity belt with a large and obvious gold key on a chain round her/his neck would be better.

2. The discreet drag queens. Like the Baron/Queen Alexandra, and the Tsarina—their clothes, specially made for the occasion by a trusted dressmaker, as the night becomes wilder are usually found to have a removable skirt revealing stockings, suspenders, jewelled garters and diamond buckles on their shoes. But even despite this mild striptease, they still remain in absolutely perfect taste.

3. The more self-conscious rich queens, who, though in drag, tend to masculine drag, and end up looking like lesbians. Someone tells me they saw one once in marvellously cut black riding habit —frilled white jabot and cuffs, long skirt and boots, top hat with veil. Also in this category are the ones who go out of their way to turn themselves into absolute grotesques, and quite often arrive in a gaggle. They make a regal entry, enjoying having their disguise penetrated or not as the case may be. If, for instance, the theme of the ball were theatrical, they would probably chose to come as the witches from *Macbeth*. But marvellously theatrically thought out in every detail.

4. Another category of rich, discreet queens, who don't want to offend their host by making no effort at all but who balk at dressing up; for them full and impeccable evening dress with sash orders and neck decorations and elaborately overmade-up faces. They usually look more frightening than any of the others—with middle-aged, decadent faces, painted like whores.

5. There are the men who positively dislike women and only put on drag in order to traduce them and make them appear as odious, immoral, and unattractive as possible.

6. Finally, the ones who don't even make that effort but wear, like Redl, full-dress uniform and decorations—or evening dress.

It's not inconceivable that some of the bum boys would dress as pampered children.

Remember when they dance you don't find the male ones dancing only with the female ones, but possibly a hussar with a man in evening dress, or two men in evening dress together—or two shepherdesses together.

In category 4 you would also be likely to find the made-up face—the impeccable tails and white tie plus ropes of pearls and blazing diamonds.

BARON: Ah, Redl! How good to see you. Where have you been? You're always so busy. Everyone says you're in Counter Intelligence or something and you're frightfully grand now. I hope you're not spying on anyone here, Colonel. You know I won't have that sort of thing. I only give this ball once a year, and everyone invited is under the obligation of strictest confidence. No gossiping after. Otherwise you can all do as you like. Who's this?

REDL: May I introduce Lieutenant Stefan Kovacs—Baron von Epp.

BARON: Very nice. Why are you both in mufti? You know my rule.

REDL: I wouldn't call the dress uniform of the Royal Imperial Army exactly mufti.

BARON: I'm surprised they let you in. I expect you know everyone, or will do.

REDL: It's rather astonishing. Almost everyone.

BARON: It's not astonishing at all. Colonel Redl, this is Captain Steinbauer—aren't you? Yes. She is.

REDL: [To STEINBAUER] Lemberg. Seventh Galician.

STEINBAUER: That's right. Siczynski.
REDL: Yes.

[They look at each other. Sudden gratitude for the remembrance. And weariness, sadness. The BARON *quickly dismisses the cloud]*

BARON: And that's the Tsarina there. I don't know *who* she is exactly. A Russian spy I should think. Watch yourself, my dear, the colonel eats a spy in bed every morning, don't you, Alfred? That's what they all tell me. It's even in the papers. And this is Ferdy. *[He indicates* SUSANNA*]* Didn't you think he was divine?
REDL: Superb.
STEFAN: He really has a fine voice. I thought he was a real soprano at first.

[They all look at him with some suspicion]

SUSANNA: What do you mean? I *am* a real soprano!

[They all laugh. STEFAN *feels he has blundered more than he has in fact.* REDL *chips in]*

REDL: Isn't that Major Advocate Kunz?
BARON: Where? Oh, yes, I see. Nelson, you mean. Doesn't he look marvellous. One arm and all! Wonder where he keeps it? He's my insurance.
REDL: What?
BARON: If there's ever any trouble, Kunz is my legal insurance. *Very* influential that one! She'll deal with anything that ever comes up—secret police, anything, spies. No, spies is you, isn't it, Alfred, *you're* the spy-catcher, we'll leave any lovely little spies to you. *[To* TSARINA*]* Wait till he catches *you*. I daren't think *what* he'll do to you!

[The TSARINA *giggles]*

Eh, Alfred? What do you do to naughty little spies?
REDL: *[Bends down and grasps the* TSARINA's *earlobe]* I tie them over the back of my mare, Kristina, on a leading rein, and beat them with my crop at a slow canter.

BARON: How delicious! Now, her earring's fallen off, you've excited her so!

[*The* TSARINA *retrieves her earring and smiles up in a sweet, friendly, curious way at* REDL, *who smiles back, touched by an instant, simple, affectionate spirit. He turns to* STEFAN, *who has looked away. Quickly noted by the* BARON]

BARON: I haven't seen your Lieutenant Kovacs before, Alfred.

REDL: He's only just graduated from the War School.

BARON: All that studying and hardening the body and noontide heat and sweating, and horses! You all look quite beautiful, well, some of you, but I hate to think of you in a war. A real war. [*A* SHEPHERDESS *serves champagne*] Oh, come along, come along. No one's drinking half enough yet. Alfred! [REDL *downs a glass. He looks flushed and suddenly relaxed*] And another! You're behind the rest of us. And a good place for you, said someone. [REDL *takes another. Hands one to* STEFAN] And Ferdy, you have some more. Good for the voice. Bit strained tonight, dear. I want you to do "Una Donna A Quindici Anna."

FERDY: Don't think I can.

BARON: You can do *anything*. Practically. [*To* REDL] He has hair on his instep—like a goat. Show them. Oh, well . . . Where have you two come from? The Lieutenant looks rather glum.

REDL: We were at the Hofburg for an hour or two.

BARON: No wonder he looks glum. Come along! Drink up, Lieutenant. I can't have anyone sober at my party. [*To* REDL] I suppose you *had* to go, being so powerful now and impressive.

REDL: Oh, come along.

BARON: No, I hear it's quite true. [*To* STEINBAUER] You remember the colonel then?

STEINBAUER: Years ago. I always knew he'd make a brilliant officer. We all did. Congratulations, Colonel!

[*Raises glass—talks to* TSARINA]

BARON: Mind your wimple. She gets drunk too easily, that one.

Which is probably why she's still only a humble captain in number seventy-seven. *[Out of* STEFAN's *hearing]* Are you sure your friend wouldn't rather be back at the Hofburg?

REDL: He'll be all right. Try and leave him alone.

BARON: I can't leave anyone *that* pretty alone. Do you want the Tsarina? She's Kunz's really, but she's pretty available. *[Pause.* REDL *considers]* And Kunz isn't the kind who makes scenes. He doesn't care . . . He's a bit cold too.

*[*STEFAN *hears the last of this]*

STEFAN: Did you say Kunz? Isn't a man like that taking a bit of a risk?

BARON: Aren't we all?

STEFAN: Yes, but for someone . . .

BARON: We are none of us safe. This——*[He sweeps his fan round the ballroom]* is the celebration of the individual against the rest, the us's and the them's, the free and the constricted, the gay and the dreary, the lonely and the mob, the little Tsarina there and the Emperor Francis Joseph. *[They laugh]* Tell your friend it's so, Alfred.

REDL: Oh, I agree.

STEFAN: *[To* REDL*]* Forgive me, I feel I'm unwanted.

BARON: Nonsense. You're *wanted.* Tell him not to be a silly, solemn boy, Alfred. *[*REDL *squeezes the boy's arm and laughs. The* BARON *refills* STEFAN's *glass]* Actually, Kunz is an odd one. He seems to take appalling risks, but he knows the right people everywhere and anywhere, and he'd sell anyone, and I know him. He's my first cousin. He'd do it to me.

STEFAN: Blood not thicker than water?

BARON: His blood is thinner than anything, my dear.

FERDY: Darling! She wants to know——

BARON: What is it? I'm talking.

FERDY: Are you really a Baron?

[The TSARINA *giggles]*

BARON: Tell her she'll find out if she's not careful.

TSARINA: *[To* FERDY*]* Are you the Baroness then?

FERDY: *[Nods]* Oh. I let him. He fancies himself chasing the ladies, but he's just the same as I am. Nothing more at all.

TSARINA: What about the lieutenant?

FERDY: Oh, I should think so. Either too stupid to know it, or hasn't woken up to it yet.

TSARINA: Or doesn't want to wake up to it. Looks a bit dreary.

FERDY: Do you fancy him? You'll have the colonel after you. You'll be shot down.

[While this duet has gone on, the BARON, STEFAN, and REDL have drawn away from the GIRLS into their own conversation. Some class division here too]

BARON: Vienna is so dull! All that Spanish gloom at the Hofburg gets in everywhere, like the moth.

FERDY: *[Calls out] You* need moth balls!

[Collapse]

BARON: The Viennese gull themselves they're gay, but they're just stiff-jointed aristocrats like puppets, grubbing little tradesmen or Jews and chambermaids making a lot of one-two-three noises all the time. Secretly, they're feeling utterly thwarted and empty. The bourgeoisie daren't enjoy themselves except at someone else's expense or misfortune. And all those cavorting, clever Jews are even more depressing, pretending to be generous—and *entirely* unspontaneous. Hungarians, they're gay, perhaps that's because they're quite selfish and pig-headed. Kovacs: oh, dear, are you Hungarian? Well, never mind, that's me again, I'm afraid, speak first, think afterwards——

REDL: No, Baron, you're ahead of everyone.

BARON: Only wish I were. Poles are fairly gay. You're Polish or something, aren't you, Alfred? And somehow they're less *common* than Russians. Serbs are impossible, of course, savage, untrustworthy, worse than Hungarians, infidels in every sense. I think your friend despises me because I'm such a snob. What is your father, Lieutenant?

STEFAN: A chef at the Volksgarten Restaurant.

BARON: And do you think I'm a snob?

STEFAN: You appear to be.

BARON: Well, of course, I am. Alfred will tell you how much. However, I'm also a gentleman, which is preferable to being one of our dear Burgomaster Lueger's mob. Taste, a silk shirt, a perfumed hand, an ancient Greek ring are things that come from a way not only of thinking but of being. They can add up to a man. [To STEFAN] Would you like to walk on the terrace? The view is rather remarkable on an evening like this.

STEFAN: Alfred?

BARON: We'll join you. Or come back soon. I want to ask the Colonel's advice. About some espionage. [STEFAN bows and leaves through the high, central glass doors] Well, my dear friend. And how are you? You're prosperous I hear.

REDL: I had a small legacy.

BARON: Good. A man like you knows what money's for. And you look so well. Forgive me for sending the boy away for a moment.

REDL: That's all right. He'll find something to amuse him.

BARON: Would it be impertinent to ask: you're not wasting your time there, are you?

REDL: It would.

BARON: What? Oh, I see. Quite right. Only I admire you, Redl. So does everyone else. You're a credit to—everyone. I just want you to succeed in everything you undertake.

REDL: Thank you.

[KUNZ comes over with his partner, MARIE ANTOINETTE]

BARON: Jaroslav! Have some champagne.

KUNZ: Thank you.

BARON: And let me introduce Colonel Redl—Major Advocate Kunz.

[They salute each other appropriately]

FERDY: Colonel! Would you come over here a minute. The Tsarina wants to give herself up. [TSARINA screams] She says, she says she wants to confess!

[The TSARINA *pulls off* FERDY's *wig and smacks him with it.* REDL *smiles and excuses himself to* KUNZ]

BARON: Ferdy! That's naughty! The Colonel was talking to Major Kunz.

FERDY: No, he wasn't. Here! *[He places* REDL *beside him and the* TSARINA] We've been talking to you. *[To* BARON] *You* don't listen! It's secret.

[The BARON *smiles happily]*

BARON: Alfred *knows* all the secrets. It's his job. *[*FERDY *and the* TSARINA *conduct a whispered conversation with* REDL *for a while. He is drinking freely now, and is excited and enjoying himself. The* BARON *turns to* KUNZ] Don't you think my little Ferdy's brilliant? He'd make an adorable "Cherubino."

KUNZ: I think he's prettier as "Susanna."

BARON: Perhaps. He made that costume himself. Up half the night.

KUNZ: Did you see who I came with?

BARON: No. Why?

KUNZ: Good. I thought I'd spice your party a bit this year.

BARON: What have you done?

KUNZ: I brought a woman.

[The BARON *looks astonished. Then yelps with laughter]*

BARON: Oh, *what* a good idea! What a *stroke!* Where is she? *[He looks around]*

KUNZ: That's the point. Later on, we'll all have to guess.

BARON: And find out! Marvellous! We'll unmask her. I'll offer a prize to the man who strips her.

KUNZ: And, I think, a punishment for anyone who is mistaken.

BARON: Exactly. What fun! I do enjoy these things. I wish we could have one every month. I'm so glad you liked Ferdy.

KUNZ: How long is it now?

BARON: Three years.

KUNZ: Long time.

BARON: For me. Let's be honest, for nearly all of us. *And* women. No, three years is a big bite out of a lifetime when you never know when it may come to an end, or what you may have missed. But he's very kind. He's still young. But his growing old gnaws at me a bit, you know. Not that he still doesn't look pretty good in the raw. Oh, he does. But about me, he doesn't mind at all.

KUNZ: Who's the little flower with Redl?

BARON: No idea. *Something's* made her wilt. They've both just come from the Hofball.

KUNZ: So have I.

BARON: Of course. Poor you. And with your lady escort. I wonder if I'll spot her. *[He stares around]* That's her!

KUNZ: That is the doorman at the Klomser Hotel.

BARON: Oh! I see I'm not going to. What on earth made you go to the Hofball?

KUNZ: I thought it might be amusing to go there first. *[KUNZ nods at REDL, who is being captivated by FERDY, and starting to get recurring fits of giggles]* Look at the colonel.

BARON: *[Pleased]* He's enjoying himself.

KUNZ: I've never seen him like that before.

BARON: How many people have seen *you?* He's letting his hair down. What's left of it. It's starting to go. I noticed just now. He's a handsome devil.

KUNZ: Very.

BARON: And a brilliant officer, they say. Suppose you should be if you're at the top in counter espionage.

KUNZ: Preferably. He works morning and night.

BARON: He's only a railway clerk's son, did you know? So I suppose he's had to. Work, I mean. But he plays too. Look at him. *[REDL and FERDY are swopping stories and giggling intermittently and furiously. REDL tries to light another cigar, but he can scarcely get it going. The TSARINA watches blankly and happily]* He told me once how hard he'd tried to change.

KUNZ: Hey, you! Little Shepherdess! *[He takes a drink from a blushing SHEPHERDESS]* Beautiful. Yes?

BARON: Tried everything, apparently. Resolutions, vows, religion, medical advice, self-exhaustion. Used to flog a dozen horses into the ground in a day. And then gardening, if you please,

fencing and all those studies they do, you do, of course—
military history, ciphers, telegraphy, campaigns, he knows
hundreds of them by heart. He knows his German literature,
speaks superb French and Russian, Italian, Polish, Czech,
and Turkish if you please.

KUNZ: Not bad for a Ruthenian railway clerk.

BARON: As you say. Oh, take your eye off Redl. He's not after the
Tsarina. Or Ferdy. Is he? No, I don't think so. He's just being
himself for once. Don't you think we should all form an empire of our own?

KUNZ: What's that?

BARON: Well, instead of all joining together, you know, one empire of sixty million Germans, like they're always going on
about. What about an empire of *us*. Ex million queens.

KUNZ: Who would there be?

BARON: Well, you and me for a start. I'd be minister of culture,
I think. REDL could catch any spies, *women* spies. And you
could do what you liked.

KUNZ: And who else?

BARON: Not Jews I think. They're the least queer, in my opinion.
Their mothers won't let them. Germans, Prussians, they're
very queer. All that duelling. Poles, not so much.

KUNZ: Italians?

BARON: No, they're like women, only better, women *con brio*.
Hungarians are just goats, of course, but some are quite nice.
French: too spry to let life play a trick on *them*.

KUNZ: What about the English?

BARON: Next, after the Germans.

KUNZ: I agree with that. Queen Victoria was quite clearly a man.

BARON: But *she* was a German, wasn't she?

KUNZ: Ah, yes. Still, you're right about the English.

BARON: I believe Redl has an Eton straw boater hanging over his
bed as a trophy. They say it belongs to the younger son of
the British Ambassador. *[Pause]* How's that son of yours?
[KUNZ looks immediately on guard] I was only asking.

KUNZ: He's well.

BARON: I'm sorry. It must be difficult. If people *will* get married.

KUNZ: Well, *I* did.

BARON: The boy knows nothing?

KUNZ: Nothing.

BARON: His mother hasn't——

KUNZ: No. And she won't.

BARON: Why not? *Doesn't* she——

KUNZ: She pretends.

BARON: Ah! They *do*. And the boy?

KUNZ: *He's* all right, if that's what you mean.

BARON: You mean you're *not* all right?

KUNZ: Who knows? Is this Redl's flower?

[STEFAN approaches]

BARON: Yes. My dear boy, you must meet the Major Advocate Kunz. Lieutenant—I'm sorry——?

STEFAN: Kovacs.

[They salute]

BARON: Hungarian. Did you enjoy the terrace? I knew you would. Oh, thank heaven the music's stopped. Alfred's been having the giggles with little Ferdy while you've been away. Do have another glass, dear boy.

[REDL and FERDY stand up, giggling helplessly. The others listen]

FERDY: And the manager said, he said to me: we don't allow ladies in here, in here without male escorts. *[REDL doubles up]* And, so I pointed at the Baron and said, what do you think *he* is!

[REDL falls on the TSARINA, who squeals]

KUNZ: *[To STEFAN]* Is this your first visit to this kind of thing?

STEFAN: Yes, sir.

BARON: Oh, don't call him sir. Just because he's dressed as Nelson. He's only an old army lawyer. I must say you look very fine with that black patch. We must find a Lady Hamilton for him before the evening's out, mustn't we? I was saying, where do you keep your arm? *[KUNZ leaves it out of his tunic, and stretches it]* Ah, there it is, you see?

KUNZ: That's better.

BARON: You danced very well, all the same.

KUNZ: [To STEFAN] Would you care to?

[STEFAN *is slightly confused for a moment*]

STEFAN: Thank you, I'm a bit hot.

BARON: Must be cold on that terrace.

KUNZ: You see, this is a place for people to come together. People who are very often, in their everyday lives, rather lonely and even miserable and feel hunted. As if they had a spy catcher like the colonel on their heels.

STEFAN: Of course. I understand that.

KUNZ: And, because of the Baron's panache and generosity—and, let's be frank, recklessness——

BARON: Look who's talking——

KUNZ: They come together and become something else. Like sinners in a church.

[FERDY *stands up*]

LADY GODIVA: Two monks in the street.

TSARINA: I *like* monks.

LADY GODIVA: Two monks. Walking in the street. One's saying his rosary to himself. The other passes by as he's saying "Hail Mary." And the other stops and says: "Hullo, Ursula."

[REDL *collapses. So does* FERDY. *Then recovers professionally. The others watch, and some of the dancers too, including* KUPFER *and* ALBRECHT-COLUMBINE, *and* FIGARO *and* LADY GODIVA. *General laughter. The* BARON *is pleased.* FERDY *sits back next to* REDL *and they both drink and giggle together, mostly at nothing, until later in the scene when* REDL *takes in* KUPFER *and becomes hostile: to* KUPFER, *drunkenness, and himself*]

KUNZ: You're not enjoying yourself much. [Small pause] Are you?

[STEFAN *blushes*]

STEFAN: Not at all.

KUNZ: You mustn't judge the world at carnival time. There is such a thing, such a contract, such a bond as marriage——

BARON: You should know, poor soul.

KUNZ: And there is friendship, comradeship. In the midst of all this, I ask you not to sneer, or I will beat your sanctimonious head in——

BARON: Jaroslav——

KUNZ: Aristotle, if you've heard of him.

STEFAN: I have——

BARON: Please; take no notice . . .

KUNZ: I'm glad to hear it. Says it can be either good, or pleasant, or useful. Which is true, but not always. But he also says it lasts in such men only, only as long as they keep their goodness. And goodness, unfortunately, Lieutenant, does not last.

STEFAN: No?

KUNZ: No. And don't be insolent.

STEFAN: Then don't be offensive.

BARON: Tempers, darlings, tempers!

KUNZ: It seldom lasts, shall we say? But then such men are rare, anyway.

[*The other guests gather round, and listen, and begin to take part. During this sequence,* REDL *sobers up and stiffens*]

KUPFER: Good evening, Colonel Redl.

REDL: I don't . . .

KUPFER: *Now* you do . . .

BARON: *Everyone!* [*To* ALBRECHT] Met *everyone* before.

KUPFER: Kupfer. Major Kupfer, sir. General Staff. Ninth Corps. Prague.

REDL: Prague, Prague . . . This is Vienna. What are you doing here?

KUPFER: Same as you, sir. On leave.

REDL: *I'm* not on leave.

KUPFER: I didn't necessarily mean literally——

REDL: You'll remember Steinbauer then?

KUPFER: Of course. [*He greets the wimpled* STEINBAUR *casually*] It was a blow about Siczynski. [*Pause*] Wasn't it?

REDL: Was it?

KUPFER: Wasn't he a particular friend of yours?

REDL: I scarcely knew him. We neither of us did . . .

KUPFER: Why did you agree to be his second? It wasn't a very correct thing for such a correct officer as you to be doing.

REDL: I thought he should have support . . . No one liked him.

KUPFER: But *you've* always been popular, Colonel.

REDL: Are you being . . . because if so . . .

KUPFER: You only have my admiration, Colonel. With all the advantages I was born with, I only wish I—could—ever go—so far. You seemed to be having an entertaining time just there, Colonel. Please don't let me——

FERDY: Don't you think he's beautiful? I adore it when he screws his monocle in his eye.

[REDL doesn't think this at all funny, though the BARON and KUNZ are pleased, and, of course, KUPFER. REDL stands more erect than ever, and lights up a fresh cigar, grabbing a glass from the passing SHEPHERDESS]

REDL: Hey, you! Fräulein!

FERDY: Have you heard about that extraordinary Dr. Schoepfer?

KUPFER: No. Who is he?

FERDY: Don't you know? My dear, he sounds divine! The Tsarina went there last night.

STEINBAUER: What does he do?

FERDY: Just talks, my dear, for *hours*. Not a smile. Medical do's and all that, but, if you say you're a student, you can get in.

KUPFER: What's he talk about?

FERDY: Why, *us*. He sounds an absolute scream. Can't stop talking about it.

REDL: Us? Speak for yourself.

BARON: What's he say then, Ferdy?

FERDY: Oh, that we're all demented something, something cox on the end, darling.

[Laughter]

LADY GODIVA: Well, he's right, of course.

FERDY: That we're all potential criminals, and some of us should even be castrated. *[Screams]* And that we're a warning symptom of the crisis in, oh, civilization, and the decline in Christian whatnots.

BARON: Oh, and he goes on about marriage and the family being the basis of the empire, and *we* must be rooted out. *She* says he's a scream.

[They look at the TSARINA, *who nods, giggles, and goes crimson]*

MARIE ANTOINETTE: Is he a Jew?

FERDY: But, of course, darling! She says he looks like Shylock's mother.

KUPFER: But who is he?

KUNZ: A neurologist, I believe. Nerves.

BARON: Well, I'm sure he'd get on mine.

KUNZ: I think he's one of those people who insist they can penetrate the inner secrets of your own nature.

BARON: I understand the inner secrets of my nature perfectly well. I don't admire them, but I do know them, anyway better than this Dr. Schoepfer.

FERDY: Silly mare!

BARON: And I'm quite happy as I am, I'm no criminal, thank you, and I don't corrupt anything that isn't already quite clearly corrupt, like this ghastly city. On the contrary, I bring style, wit, pleasure, energy, and good humour to it that it wouldn't otherwise have.

KUPFER: Well said, Baron.

BARON: More drinks, everyone! *[To* MUSICIANS*]* And music!

ALBRECHT: I went to a doctor once, and he just said "pull your socks up." Do you know what he told me to do? Go into the army! *[Shrieks]* And find yourself a nice girl. Get married. So: naturally, I went into the army. Artillery. In the second week I'd been seduced by the corporal of horse *and* a sublieutenant.

BARON: Oh, I went to a doctor like a silly thing when I was a student. He just looked very agitated and told me there was nothing he could do and to go away. A few years later I heard he'd cut his throat . . .

MARIE ANTOINETTE: I plucked up courage to tell *our* family doctor, and I said I'd like to be sent away to some special clinic in Vienna . . . Well, I thought he was going to go raving mad. Vienna, he said, Vienna, *you* want to go to Vienna. I'll send you to hell. You'll find all you want *there,* you quivering, scheming little sissy!

ALBRECHT: When I first came to Vienna, it seemed like paradise, but now I do get a bit bored. Not here, of course, Baron. But you know what I mean. Same tired old exhibits. Nothing new ever seems to come in.

TSARINA: *[Now sitting on the* BARON's *knee, shyly]* I remember the first time a man tickled the palm of my hand with his middle finger, when we shook hands, and then later he told me what he was. I was very religious then, and I thought he was wicked. I really did at the time.

KUNZ: Perhaps you were right.

LADY GODIVA: *I* went to our priest. He quoted Aquinas and said anything that was against nature was against God . . . He always kept an eye on me afterwards, always pulling me up and asking me questions.

STEINBAUER: *My* priest said: you *can't* be like that. You're a soldier, a man of courage and honour and virtue. Your uniform itself embodies the glory of the empire and the Church. I worshipped Radetzky at the time, and he knew it. So he said, do you think someone like Radetzky could have ever been like that? I didn't know about Julius Caesar and Alexander then.

FIGARO: *[To* REDL, *who is like a frozen ox]* I hate these screamers, don't you?

LADY GODIVA: I used to go to the priest after I'd confessed I was in love with Fritz. Then I used to lie like crazy about it, and say nothing was happening, although we were having sex regularly. And he'd give me absolution and say, "It may not take on immediately——."

[Laughter]

LADY GODIVA: If Fritz just moved his little finger at me, I'd go back. Then he went with a girl suddenly and got married. When she was pregnant, we had beers together, and he pinched my arm and kissed me. Then he laughed and said: "You know what you are, find someone else the same.". . . But he laughed . . .

FERDY: I should think so, you soppy little thing. [FERDY *is bored with all this and wants attention*] I only went to a doctor once and he just said take more exercise, dear. So I did.

[*He executes a skilful entrechat to general amusement till* REDL *strikes him hard across the face, knocking him down right into the other guests. The boy is stunned by the force of it. Silence*]

REDL: Baron—forgive me.

[*He clicks his heels and goes, followed presently by* STEFAN *in silence. Then the* BARON *booms out over a few* "Wells!," etc.]

BARON: Someone pick up poor Ferdy. You silly boy! I knew you shouldn't have flirted with Colonel Redl. He's a dangerous man. Are you better? There now! Come along, everybody, that's quite enough melodrama. On with the ball—I sup-pose——

[*They reassemble. Lights lower. And they hear the spirit of Mozart as* FERDY *sings, not without some sweetness,* "Vedrai Carino" *or* "Batti, Batti." *Or something similar which is tolerably within his range*]

FADE

SCENE 2

Lecture Room. Rostrum. A glass of water. DR. SCHOEPFER *is speaking.*

SCHOEPFER: The *evasion*, naturally, of responsibility . . . For instance, in enjoying the physical sensations of the body without any reference to the responsibilities involved in the relationship. Or, indeed, to society or any beliefs, such as a belief in God. They can never, in their ignorance, some men say folly, in their infirmity, never attain that complete love, the love that only is possible between men and women, whose shared interests . . . *[There is a suppressed giggle]* . . . whose shared interests include the blessed gift of children and grandchildren which alone, I think, most people would agree, even today, which alone gives a grand and enduring purpose to sexual congress. *[He drinks from the glass of water]* Now, gentlemen: these traits are caused by regression to the phallic stage of libido development, and can be traced to what is in fact a flight from incest . . .

FADE

SCENE 3

A hill clearing outside Dresden, surrounded by fir trees. Cold winter. OBLENSKY *is warmly wrapped up in his great coat, sitting on a tree trunk smoking a cigarette.* STANITSIN *stands beside him.*

STANITSIN: Here he comes.

OBLENSKY: To the minute. As you'd expect. You'd better give me the file. Oh, just a minute, have you got the parcel I asked for? *[*STANITSIN *nods]* It wasn't easy this week getting in. The boy Kovacs is staying there while he's commanding this exercise.

*[*REDL *enters, smoking a cigar. He looks cool and sure of himself]*

REDL: Mr. Smith?

OBLENSKY: Yes, indeed. Rather *this* is Mr. Smith.

REDL: Look, I haven't time to waste fooling about——

OBLENSKY: Quite. You got our message, and, blessedly, you are here, Colonel Redl.

REDL: And who the devil are you?

OBLENSKY: Colonel Oblensky.

REDL: Oblensky . . .

[OBLENSKY *waits for the effect to take, and goes on*]

OBLENSKY: It won't take you long, Colonel. I know your regiment is waiting for you . . . loosely speaking. I have a file here, which I would like to acquaint you with briefly. Would you care to sit down? [REDL *doesn't move*] Just a matter of minutes. I have no anxiety about you reaching for your revolver to shoot either of us. I know you will realize that all this file is duplicated both in Warsaw *and* St. Petersburg. What I do beg of you is to pause before you think of turning it on yourself. I think we can find a satisfactory, and probably long-term, arrangement which will work out quite well for all of us, and no trouble.

REDL: [*Recovering, coldly*] May I see?

OBLENSKY: Naturally, oh, this is Lieutenant Stanitsin.

[STANITSIN *bows*]

REDL: Mr. Smith?

STANITSIN: My pen name, sir.

[REDL *puts out his hand impatiently for the file.* OBLENSKY *hands him the contents in batches. They watch* REDL *flip through, stone faced*]

REDL: Mess bills in Lemberg! Eighteen eighty-nine! Tailors' bills, jeweller's, stables', coachbuilders', tobacconists'. What *is* all this? They're just bills.

OBLENSKY: Rather unusual bills for a young officer of no independent means.

REDL: I have an uncle——

OBLENSKY: You have no uncle, Colonel. Two brothers only. Both happily married—and penniless. [*Hands him another bill*] Cartiers. One gold cigarette case inscribed "To dearest Stefan with love, Alfred."

REDL: My nephew.

[OBLENSKY hasn't the heart to smile at this. REDL's immediate humiliation is so evident]

OBLENSKY: Your bank statements from the Austro-Hungarian Bank in both Vienna and Prague for the month of February.

[REDL hardly looks at them. Pause]

REDL: Well?

OBLENSKY: I'm sorry, Colonel. We'll soon get this over. One letter, date, Feburary 17, 1901. "My darling, don't be angry. When I make no sign, you know or should know, that I love you. Please see me again. All I long for is to lie beside you, nothing else. I don't know what to do to kill the time before I see you again, and watch you, how I can do something to pass the time."

REDL: It is no crime to write a love letter, Colonel, even if it isn't in the style of Pushkin.

OBLENSKY: The style's tolerable enough for a man in love. . . . But this letter is not addressed to a woman.

REDL: There's no name on it.

OBLENSKY: There is on the envelope.

REDL: *Not* very convincing, Colonel.

OBLENSKY: Very well. Those—if you'd just glance through them quickly—are signed affidavits from——

[REDL won't look at them. He has mustered himself wonderfully. He feels the chance of a small hope]

[Politely, casually] The page at the Grand Hotel, a musician at the Volksgarten—this is only the last six weeks, you understand—a waiter at Sacher's, a corporal in the Seventh Corps in Prague, a boatman in Vienna, a pastry cook, a compositor on the *Deutsches Volksblatt* and a *reporter* on the *Neue Freie Presse*. *[Pause]* One right-wing paper, one liberal, eh?

[REDL puffs on his cigar]

REDL: *[Slowly]* Whores. Bribed, perjuring whores.

OBLENSKY: Yes. Against the word of a distinguished officer in the Royal Imperial Army. . . . Oh, dear . . . Stanitsin. Photographs . . . [STANITSIN *hands a bundle of large photographs to* REDL *who looks at the first four or five. Then he hands them back. Pause. He sits on another trunk and slowly puts his face in his hands*] Offer the colonel some brandy. [STANITSIN *offers him a flask, which he drinks from*] I think *I'll* have some, Stanitsin. Now that's all over, let us all have some. Forgive me, Colonel. Now: time is short for us. What you decide to do is up to you. There are three courses open to you. One we have mentioned. The second is to leave the army. The third is to remain in the army and continue with your brilliant career. Do you know what Russia spent on espionage last year, Colonel? Nine million roubles. Nine. This year it will be even more. What do your people spend? Half? No, I've watched you for more than ten years, and you'd be surprised probably, or perhaps I'm wrong, about how much I know about the kind of man you are. What can you do? Change your way of life? It's getting desperate already, isn't it? You don't know which way to turn, you're up to your eyeballs in debts. What could you do? Get thrown out, exposed for everything you are, or what the world would say you are. Would you, do you think, *could* you change your way of life, what else do you want after all these years, what would you do at your age, go back to base and become a waiter or a washer up, sit all alone in cafés again constantly *watching*? What are you fit for? [*His tone relaxes*] The same as me, my dear friend, the same as me, and very good indeed you are at it, soldiering, war and treachery, or the treachery that leads to wars. The game. It's a fine one. And no one's better at it in Europe than me—at the moment. [*Smiles*] Heavy turnover sometimes. Tell me, do none of your brother officers know or suspect?

REDL: Kovacs, Kupfer, Steinbauer . . . No.

OBLENSKY: And Kunz? Kunz's only real indiscretion is the Baron's annual ball, and he could always say he went as a relation or even as a tourist, even though it's hardly respectable. We've never caught him out in all these years, have we, Stanitsin? He does . . . doesn't he . . . ?

REDL: I assume so.

OBLENSKY: The other two, Steinbauer and Kupfer, well, they
seem to have left wormcasts all over Europe, so they're no
threat to you. And Kovacs, he's only—been—with *you*, hasn't
he?

REDL: Yes.

OBLENSKY: Sure?

REDL: [*Wryly*] Colonel Oblensky, I may find myself here before
you, in this position, but I remind you that I *am* an officer in
the Austrian Chief of Staff's Counter Espionage Department.
I know how to interrogate myself. The answer's yes.

[OBLENSKY *smiles*]

OBLENSKY: Oh, I'm the last to underestimate you, Colonel. Last
report from General Staff Headquarters January 5: "su-
premely capable, learned, intuitive and precise in command,
tactful, excellent manners." And now your handling of the
corps exercise on Monday: "He is uncommonly striking.
Both as a battalion and regimental commander." And there's
your Regiment, the Seventy-seventh Infantry. Didn't the emperor call it "my beautiful Seventy-seventh"? Oh, you certainly chose the right career, Colonel. Cigarette? I think the
really interesting thing about you, Redl, is that you yourself
are really properly aware of your own distinction—as you
should be. If you ever do feel any shame for what you are,
you don't accept it like a simpleton, you heave it off, like a
horse that's fallen on you. And the result is, I suppose, what
they mean by that splendid Viennese style. Ah, the time, yes,
we must be going. Give the Colonel his package.

[STANITSIN *does so*]

REDL: Is that all?

OBLENSKY: You must be returning to the regiment, Colonel.

REDL: What's this?

OBLENSKY: Mr. Smith will contact you when you've had a few
days to rest and recover generally. The package contains
seven thousand kronen in notes. . . . Far more than *you* pay,
Colonel. [REDL *puts it in his pocket slowly, collects himself,*

and bows] Good-bye, Colonel. I don't suppose we shall meet again for a long time—if ever . . . It *is* a little risky, even for you, isn't it? *[He laughs, full of good humour]* Oh, Stanitsin, the parcel. *[He hands a paper bag to* REDL, *who, puzzled, takes from it an Etonian straw boater]* Perhaps you should return it to the British Ambassador. *[He laughs heartily]* Forgive me, Colonel, but I do have a very clumsy, clumsy sense of humour sometimes. No, always!

*[*STANITSIN *smiles and goes out. The two men watch him. Presently they hear his laughter floating back through the woods]*

CURTAIN

ACT THREE

REDL's *apartment in Vienna. Baroque, luxurious. It is late afternoon, the curtains are drawn, the light comes through them and two figures can just be seen in bed. One is* REDL, *who appears to be asleep. The other, the figure of a* YOUNG MAN, *is getting up very quietly, almost stealthily, and dressing. There is a rattle of coins and jewellery.*

REDL: Don't take my cigarette case, will you. *Or* my watch. *[The boy hesitates]* There's plenty of change. Take that. Go on. Now you'd better . . . hurry back. *[The boy slips out quickly, expertly.* REDL *sits up and lights a cigar. He gets up and puts on a beautiful dressing gown. Presently* KUPFER *comes in]* Who's that? Oh, you? Why don't you knock?

KUPFER: I knew you were alone.

REDL: What's the time?

KUPFER: Four. Shall I open the shutters?

[He does so. REDL *shrinks a little]*

REDL: That's enough.

KUPFER: The sun's quite hot. *[He sits in an armchair by the window]* I waited. Till your little friend left.

REDL: Very courteous. Well?

KUPFER: I've news.

REDL: Bad, no doubt.

KUPFER: Afraid so.

REDL: Out with it.

KUPFER: Stefan was married secretly this morning. *[Pause]* To the Countess Delyanoff.

[Pause]

REDL: Naturally. The bitch . . . Does she want to see me?

KUPFER: Why, yes—she's waiting.

REDL: Well, go and get her. And then go away. *[KUPFER turns]* No. Wait outside. *[KUPFER goes and REDL smokes his cigar, looking out of the window. Soon the COUNTESS enters]*

COUNTESS: Alfred?

REDL: So: you pulled it off.

COUNTESS: Alfred. We've endured all of that. Can't we——

REDL: No. What's he doing, marrying *you?*

COUNTESS: He loves me. No more . . .

REDL: I suppose you're calving.

COUNTESS: I'm having his child, Alfred.

REDL: I knew it! Knew it!

COUNTESS: He *would* have married me. He was disgusted by your behaviour.

REDL: Oh?

COUNTESS: You must admit, Alfred, telling him I was Jewish wasn't very subtle—for *you.*

REDL: Well, you are, aren't you? And I don't believe you'd told him.

COUNTESS: No, I hadn't. But my *not* telling him was cowardly, not vulgar, like yours *was.* You surprise me, Alfred.

REDL: And he'll have to resign his commission as he's no means?

COUNTESS: He wants to go into journalism.

REDL: And become a politician.

COUNTESS: Alfred, we had such feeling for each other once.

REDL: I didn't, you Jewish prig, you whited sepulchre, does he know what you really are, apart from a whore, a whoring spy?

COUNTESS: No. He doesn't. No one knows. Except you. It's extraordinary you should have kept it a secret, but I don't expect you to behave differently now.

REDL: Don't count on it. . . . You little Jewish spy——

COUNTESS: I'm not, not now, Alfred, you know . . . it was my husband, when he was alive——

REDL: Don't snivel. You took *me* in.

COUNTESS: I didn't. I loved you . . .

REDL: Well, I didn't love you. I love Stefan. *We* just fooled one
another. Oh, I tried to hoax myself too, but not really often.
So: tonight's your wedding night. *[Pause]* I tell you this:
you'll never know that body like I know it. The lines beneath
his eyes. Do you know how many there are, do you know
one has less than the other? And the scar behind his ear, and
the hairs in his nostrils, which has the most, what colour
they are in what light? The mole on where? Where, Sophia?
I know the place here, between the eyes, the dark patches
like slate—like blue when he's tired, really tired, the place
for a blow or a kiss or a bullet. You'll never know like I
know, you can't. The backs of his knees, the pattern on the
soles of his feet. Which trouble him, and so I used to wash
them and bathe them for hours. His thick waist, and how
long are his thighs, compared to his calves, you've not
looked at him, you never will.

COUNTESS: Stop it!

[Pause]

REDL: You don't know what to do with that. And now *you've* got
it.

COUNTESS: God, I'm weary of your self-righteousness and all your
superior railing and your glib cant about friendship and the
army and the way you all roll out your little parade: Michel-
angelo and Socrates, and Alexander and Leonardo. God,
you're like a guild of housewives pointing out Catherine the
Great.

REDL: So, you'll turn Stefan into another portly, middle-aged
father with—what did you say once—snotty little longings
under their watch chains and glances at big, unruptured bot-
toms.

COUNTESS: Alfred: every one of *you* ends up, as you well know, with a bottom quite different, much plumper and far wider than any ordinary man.

REDL: You think, people like you, you've got a formula for me. You think I'm hobbled, as you say. But I'm free of you, anyway. You, what about you, I can resist you!

COUNTESS: Do you know, remember, what you once said to me. "I can never blame you. You are my heart."

REDL: I do blame you. I was lying. And Stefan is my heart.

[Pause]

COUNTESS: He said you told him I was Jewish. And what I looked like, what I *would* look like, drooping hairy skin and flab, and so on——

REDL: And now you're going to be a mother. You think you're a river or something, I suppose.

COUNTESS: That's right, Alfred. A sewer. Your old temple built over a sewer.

REDL: Sophia, why don't we . . .?

COUNTESS: No, Alfred. I'm in your grip. But I'll make no bargains. Do as you wish.

REDL: I bought him a beautiful new gelding last week.

COUNTESS: It should be back in your stables by now. And your groom's got all the other——

REDL: Get out.

COUNTESS: I'm going, Alfred. Do as you wish. You may think a trick was played on you once, but you've repaid and re-played it a thousand times over. I pity you: really——

REDL: Don't then. I'm really doing quite well.

[She goes out. KUPFER comes in]

KUPFER: Well?

REDL: Well? Nothing. . . . I suppose you think you're moving in?

KUPFER: Do you want me to draw up a full report on your file on the countess?

REDL: That file is *my* property. And *you'll* do as you're told. I'm going to sleep. Close the shutters.

[KUPFER *does so.* REDL *falls asleep almost immediately on the bed. Soon little moaning noises are heard from him.* KUPFER *smokes a cigarette in the early evening light*]

FADE

SCENE 2

The Red Lounge of the Sacher Hotel, Vienna. A string orchestra plays. REDL *and* KUPFER *are drinking together.* KUPFER *is in a sour, watching mood.* REDL *is even cooler than usual and is smoking and appraising the other occupants of the lounge. He hails a* WAITER.

REDL: *[To* KUPFER*]* Another?

KUPFER: No. I'm going.

REDL: *[To the* WAITER*]* Just one then. So soon?

[Pause]

KUPFER: Why St. Petersburg, for heaven's sake?

REDL: Because I've signed the order, and General Staff is not equipped to countermand orders. It works on the sweet Viennese roundabout method. Anyway, there's no one else.

KUPFER: But a whole year. I don't even speak Russian. It's nonsense.

REDL: Not to the Bureau. And now you *can* learn Russian, as I did. You should pick it up in half that time. It's the vowels that'll bring *you* down.

KUPFER: Thank you.

REDL: I'll get you back before the year's out. Don't worry.

KUPFER: You *are* sure of yourself, aren't you?

REDL: I have to be, don't I? And why not? *[He takes his drink from* WAITER*]* No one is interested in doubts. This is an age of iron certainties, that's what they want to know about, run by money-makers, large armies, munitions men, money-makers for money-makers. *You* were born with a silver sabre up your whatnot. *[Lifts his glass]* St. Petersburg! I'll give you some names and addresses.

KUPFER: If only you'd at least admit it's because of Mischa. Why can't you be honest?

REDL: Because honesty is no use to you. People who don't want it are always yelling the place down for it like some grizzling kid. When they get it they're always miserable. . . . Besides, Mischa is getting married, as you know.

KUPFER: I thought you'd put the stopper on that.

REDL: I didn't think we should tie him to a girl in a confectionery shop, a broad-faced, big-hipped little housefrau who can hardly read and write, and, what's more, doesn't care, all chocolates and childbirth. Still, if he wants that, he shall have it. It's a poor reward. Sad, too . . .

KUPFER: You do pick them, don't you?

REDL: Yes . . . But that is the nature of it. Marriage has never occurred to *you* for instance, has it? *[Pause]* Since Stefan I've let them go their own ways. If that's all, if that's the sum of it, if that's what they want. . . .

KUPFER: At least be honest with your*self*. The girl came round again last night.

REDL: Did she then? I told Max to throw her out. Next time he'll throw her down the stairs.

KUPFER: Then *she'll* end up in hospital as well.

REDL: Damn it, he's only got a nervous breakdown, or whatever they call it nowadays.

KUPFER: She says he's off his head.

REDL: Nonsense. He's always been overstrung. Maybe a bit unbalanced. He'll recover. And then he can marry her.

KUPFER: And he calls *me* cruel!

REDL: *You* were born like it. All your sort of people are. It's expected of you.

KUPFER: And what about *your* sort of people then?

REDL: Sometimes it's inescapable. I'm still nicer than you, Kupfer.

KUPFER: Why do you hate me, Alfred? *[Pause]* Why then?

REDL: I've said often enough no one, and not you, is to call me Alfred in public . . . *[Hesitates]*

KUPFER: Then why do you let me live with you?

REDL: You don't. I allow you a room in my apartment.

KUPFER: Exactly. You know, better than anyone, about jealousy.

REDL: It's a discipline, like Russian. You master it, or you don't. It's up to you, isn't it? Ah, here's Hötzendorf and Möhl.

KUPFER: Who's the boy?

REDL: Try and restrain your curiosity a little.

> [*They rise and greet* GENERAL HÖTZENDORF, GENERAL MÖHL *and* SUBLIEUTENANT VIKTOR JERZABEK. *All salute stiffly, aware of their own presence in the lounge*]

HÖTZENDORF: Ah, Colonel, the lieutenant tells me that great automobile and chauffeur outside belong to you.

REDL: Yes, sir. New toy, I'm afraid.

HÖTZENDORF: Expensive toy. Don't see many like that. Thought it must belong to some fat Jew. [REDL *is discomfited*] Oh, don't misunderstand me, the vehicle itself is in impeccable taste, Redl, like everything to do with you.

REDL: Will you join us, sir?

HÖTZENDORF: Just having a quick dinner. Brought some work with us, then back to the office.

MÖHL: The lieutenant is the only one who seems able to take down the general's notes fast enough.

HÖTZENDORF: Well, quickly then. I wanted a word with you.

REDL: Waiter! I was just celebrating some good fortune. My uncle in Galicia has just left me a legacy.

> [*Chairs are feverishly placed round the table for the arrivals. Everyone sits and orders*]

HÖTZENDORF: Well done. Good. Yes, very good taste. Though I still prefer a good pair of horses, can't run an army with automobiles. No, but you know it's not that the Jews themselves are specially rotten. It's what they represent. For instance, no belief in service, and how can the Empire survive without the idea of service? Look at the Jews in Galicia, you must know, Redl, getting them into the army—quite impossible.

REDL: Indeed. *And* the high percentage of desertion.

MÖHL: Really? I didn't know that.

REDL: Nineteen percent.

HÖTZENDORF: There you are. They're outsiders, they feel outsiders, so their whole creed of life must be based on duplicity—by necessity.

REDL: I agree, sir. Even their religion seems to be little more than a series of rather pious fads.

HÖTZENDORF: Quite. We're all Germans, all of us, and that's the way of it. At least: Jews, when they get on, remind us of it.

REDL: Which I suppose is a useful function.

HÖTZENDORF: Talking of that, Redl, I want to congratulate you on your handling of that Cracow spy affair. Everyone, absolutely everyone's most impressed and highly delighted, including the emperor himself.

REDL: I'm deeply honoured, sir.

HÖTZENDORF: Well. You do honour to us. I see you already have the order of the Iron Crown Second Class. Möhl here is recommending you for the Military Service Medal.

REDL: I don't know what——

HÖTZENDORF: You know your stuff, Redl. You've an extraordinary understanding and intuition as far as the criminal intelligence is concerned. And, there it is, spies are criminals like any other. We all just use them like any thief or murderer.

MÖHL: That's right, he's right.

HÖTZENDORF: Cracow is our first bastion against Russia. If war breaks out, it's imperative those fortresses don't crack. They'll go for them first. If that little ring you rounded up had succeeded, we could have lost a war the day it started. From April I am proposing that you take over the Prague Bureau. Rumpler will direct Vienna.

REDL: I'm overwhelmed, sir.

MÖHL: To be confirmed of course.

REDL: Of course.

[HÖTZENDORF *raises his glass*]

HÖTZENDORF: Congratulations, Colonel. To your continued success in Prague. [*They drink the toast. The three arrivals rise at a signal]* Well, gentlemen. Good-bye, Redl. Oh, this young man tells me he's your nephew.

REDL: That's right, sir.

HÖTZENDORF: Good. Well, the General Staff can do with all the Redls there are around.

[Salute. They pass through the lounge. REDL *sits.* KUPFER *is dumbfounded]*

REDL: Rumpler *would* stay in Vienna, naturally, with his coat of arms. Still, Prague . . .

KUPFER: Nephew!

REDL: Not yet. But I can't let an unknown lieutenant from no-where ride about Vienna in my new Austro-Daimler phaeton. And I promised him faithfully the other day he could drive it himself sometime. He's quite clever mechanically. *[*KUPFER *turns on his heel, and goes out.* REDL *lights a cigar and nods to the* HEAD WAITER*]* Send me the waiter over. I want the bill.

WAITER: Yes, sir.

REDL: No, not him. The young one.

FADE

SCENE 3

Hospital Ward. High, bare, and chill. In an iron bed, sitting up, is a young man, MISCHA LIPSCHUTZ. *Beside him is a young girl,* MITZI HEIGEL. *The sound of boots striking smartly on the cold floor of a hospital corridor.* REDL *enters briskly. In greatcoat, gloves, carrying cane. An* ORDERLY *comes up to him respectfully.*

ORDERLY: Colonel, sir.

REDL: Colonel von Redl. To see Mischa Lipschutz.

ORDERLY: At once, Colonel, sir.

[He leads him to MISCHA's *bed.* MISCHA *hardly takes him in.* MITZI *looks up, then down again, as if she has become numbed by sitting in the same cold position so long]*

ORDERLY: Shall I tell the young lady to go?

REDL: No. Mischa. How are you? I've brought you a hamper. *[No response. He hands it to the* ORDERLY*]* See that he gets all of it. Are you feeling any better? When do you think you'll be out then, eh? You look quite well, you know. . . . Perhaps you're still not rested enough. . . . Mischa . . . *[To* ORDERLY*]* Can't he hear me? He looks all right.

ORDERLY: Perhaps your voice sounds strange, just a fraction, sir? Mischa: Colonel Redl is here.

MISCHA: Mischa.

ORDERLY: How are you, the colonel's asking?

MISCHA: I've been here quite a long time. I don't quite know how long, because we're absorbed into the air at night, and then, of course they can do anything they like with you at will. But that's why I keep rather quiet.

REDL: Who, Mischa?

MISCHA: They do it with rays, I believe, and atoms and they can send them from anywhere, right across the world, and fill you up with them and germs and all sorts of things.

REDL: Mischa, do you know where you are?

MISCHA: On a star, sir, on a star. Just like you. I expect you were sent to Vienna too, sir, because you are the same kind of element as me. The same dual body functioning.

*[*REDL *stands back. The* ORDERLY *shrugs, the* GIRL *doesn't look up.* REDL *walks out quickly]*

FADE

SCENE 4

A hotel room near the Polish border in Galicia. It is cheap, filled with smoke but quite cosy. OBLENSKY *is sprawled on a low sofa, his tunic open, relaxed, hot with much vodka.* REDL *is slightly drunk too, though less cheerful.*

OBLENSKY: Come here, over here, have some more. Where are you, Redl, you're always disappearing? Why are you so restless always? All the time limping home with scars, and now you've got a bitten lip, I see. Tell me now, about this new boy, what's it—Viktor——

REDL: He's not new.

OBLENSKY: I thought it was last February.

REDL: December.

OBLENSKY: Five months! Oh, I suppose that is a long time for you.

REDL: How often are you unfaithful to your wife?

OBLENSKY: When I'm not working too hard, and if I can arrange it, daily.

REDL: You seem to arrange most things.

OBLENSKY: Don't say it in that tone of voice. I was looking it up the other day. You've had eighty thousand kronen out of me over the years.

REDL: Out of Mother Russia.

OBLENSKY: Quite so. And she can ill afford your way of life.

REDL: She's had her money's worth.

OBLENSKY: Not over Cracow.

REDL: Oh, not again.

OBLENSKY: Well, later. Tell me about what's it, Viktor? Is he handsome?

REDL: Extremely.

OBLENSKY: Yes, but how handsome, in what way?

REDL: Tall, fair, eyes pale . . .

OBLENSKY: Is that what you like? Watery?

REDL: Tell me what *you* like.

OBLENSKY: My dear friend, ha! *[He roars with laughter]* Nothing has the enduring, unremitting crudity of what I like. And *no* interest. I like nothing exotic. Now, the countess, you know, Delyanoff, you used to write those strained love letters to, I could have had her at any time, naturally. But, nothing, no interest, here, whatsoever. *[He crosses himself]* Too exotic. And I suppose intelligent. I can understand *you* trying her out very well. All I want is a lump, a rump, a big, jolly roaring and boring, let us have no illusion, heaving lovely, wet and friendly, large and breasty lump! *[He roars, jumps up laughing, and fills their glasses]* What I wouldn't do for one now! Yes, with you here too, Redl! Would that disgust you?

REDL: No.

OBLENSKY: Flicker of interest?

REDL: Very little. I *have* watched.

OBLENSKY: Oh, dear. You make me feel cruder than ever. Tears of Christ! I'd make her jump and giggle and give her fun. All girls like fun. Even if they're educated. Do you give fun? Much?

REDL: Some, I imagine. Perhaps not too much. If I liked anyone it was because they were beautiful, to me, anyway.

OBLENSKY: Yes, I see. That's quite different. I don't see very much beauty. I mean don't need it. You're a romantic. You lust after the indescribable, describe it, to yourself at least, and it becomes unspeakable.

REDL: You sound like a drunken Russian Oscar Wilde.

OBLENSKY: Me? Oscar Wilde! *[He splutters with pleasure, and pours them out more vodka]* Perhaps there's a cosy chambermaid here, if they have such a thing in this hole. I'll ask Stanitsin. Do you get afraid very often?

REDL: Yes.

OBLENSKY: *[Switching]* I'll tell you some things that stick in my throat about you people. Do you mind?

REDL: If you wish.

OBLENSKY: Well, one: you all assume you're the only ones who can understand anything about yourselves.

REDL: *[Politely]* Yes?

OBLENSKY: Well, two: frankly you go on about beauty and lyricize away about naked bodies as if we were all gods.

REDL: Some of us.

OBLENSKY: Or else you carry on like—rutting pigs. *[They both address each other in a friendly way across the barrier they both recognize immediately]* It isn't any fun having no clear idea of the future, is it? And you can't remake your past. And then when one of you writes a book about yourselves, you pretend it's something else, that it's about married people and not two men together. . . . That is not honest, Alfred.

REDL: Don't be maudlin, Colonel.

OBLENSKY: Redl; you are one of those depressing people whom you always know you are bound to disappoint. And yet one tries. *[He looks quite jolly all the same]* Well, you must be used to dancing at two weddings by this time. You've been doing it long enough.

REDL: You do enjoy despising me, don't you? Can we finish now?

OBLENSKY: Not till Cracow is settled. I don't despise you at all. Why should I? I don't care. I'm only curious.

REDL: My confessions are almost as entertaining as the Cracow fortifications.

OBLENSKY: You're quite wrong, quite, quite . . . I listen to you, I enjoy your company, see how much vodka we've drunk together, I don't drink with many people, Alfred. May I? I don't know anyone quite like you. It's taken a long time, hasn't it? You're giving nothing away this time.

REDL: What about Cracow?

OBLENSKY: Well, my dear friend, it was most embarrassing. Suddenly, my whole organization pounced on—*poum!* And who did it! You!

REDL: It was unavoidable. I felt there were suspicions . . .

OBLENSKY: But no warnings . . .

REDL: I tried, but it had to be.

OBLENSKY: Hauser was about my best agent.

REDL: I'm sorry. But you might have lost *me* otherwise.

OBLENSKY: Maybe. But if *I* don't turn up with something, something *now*, I'll be roasted. You've got to *give* me someone. And someone significant I can parade at a big trial, like your affair. Well?

[Pause]

REDL: Very well. I have someone.

OBLENSKY: Who?

REDL: Kupfer.

OBLENSKY: Isn't he on your staff? St. Petersburg?

REDL: Yes.

OBLENSKY: Governments don't usually pounce on the diplomatic or military missions of other governments.

REDL: If it were outrageous enough.

OBLENSKY: Well, if you can fix it, and it's really scandalous.

REDL: I can.

OBLENSKY: Very well then, fix it, Redl. *[He hurls his glass into the fireplace where it smashes]* Fix it. Now: We've hardly started yet.

FADE

SCENE 5

REDL's *apartment in Prague. A beautiful baroque room, dominated by a huge porcelain fireplace and double Central European windows.* VIKTOR *is in bed, naked from the waist up.* REDL *is staring out of the window angrily.*
[Pause]

VIKTOR: I think *I'll* get up. . . .

REDL: Why do you make such disgusting scenes with me? If you had the insight to imagine what you look like.

VIKTOR: Oh, don't. *[He flings his blonde head across the pillow]*

REDL: Oh, stop screaming, you stupid little queen! You don't want to get married, you whore, you urchin! You just want to bleed me to death. You want more. Dear God, if ever there was a ludicrous threat, you don't want the girl or any girl, you couldn't. I've seen her too, remember. *I* could, mark you, and *have*. But not you. When I think . . . How do you imagine you would ever have got a commission in a cavalry regiment, you, who would have bought you three full-blooded horses, and paid your groom and mess bills, *and* taught you to shoot like a gentleman, to behave properly as a fire leader and be a damned piss-elegant horseman in the field? You couldn't open your mouth and make an acceptable noise of any sort at all. *[*VIKTOR *weeps softly]* You're so stupid you thought you could catch me with a shoddy ruse like that. You'll get no bills paid, nor your automobile, that's the bottom of it, you're so avaricious, you'll get nothing. You're so worthless you can't even recognize the shred of petty virtues in others, some of which I have still. Which is why you

have nothing but contempt for anyone, like me, who admires
you, or loves you, or wants and misses you and has to beg
for you at least one day a fortnight. Yesterday, yesterday, I
spent two excruciating hours at the most boring party at
Möhl's I've ever been to, talking to endless people, couldn't
see or hear, hoping you—God knows where you were—that
you'd possibly, if I was lucky, might turn up. Just hoping
you might look in, so I could light your cigarette, and watch
you talking and even touch your hand briefly out of sight.

VIKTOR: I *do* love you.

REDL: In your way, yes. Like a squalling, ravenous, raging child.
You want my style, my box at the opera instead of standing
with the other officers. You're incapable of initiating anything yourself. If the world depended on the Viktors, on people like you, there would be no first moves made, no inex-
pedient overtures, no serving, no invention, no spontaneity,
no stirring whatsoever in you that doesn't come from elsewhere . . . Dear Mother of God, you're like a woman! [VIK-
TOR *howls.* REDL *pulls him out of bed by the leg and he falls
heavily to the ground with a thump]* You've no memory, no
grace, you keep nothing. [REDL *bends over him]* You are
thick, thick, a sponge soaking up. No recall, no fear. You're
a few blots . . . All you are is young. There's no soft fat up
here in the shoulder and belly and buttocks yet. But it will.
Nobody loves an old, squeezed, wrinkled pip of a boy who
was gay once. Least of all people like me or yourself. You'll
be a vulgar fake, someone even toothless housewives in the
marketplace can bait. *[Grabs his hair and drags him]* You
little painted toy, you puppet, you poor duffer, you'll be,
with your disease and paunch and silliness and curlers and
dyed wispy hair and long legs and varicose veins like
bunches of grapes and prostate and thick waist and rolling
thighs and big bottom, that's where we all go. *[Slaps his
own]* In the bottom, that's where we all go and you can't
mistake it. *Everyone'll see it!* [He pauses, exhausted. His
dressing gown has flown open. VIKTOR is sobbing very softly
and genuinely. REDL stands breathless, then takes the boy's

head in his arms. He rocks him. And whispers]: It's not true.
Not true. You *are* beautiful. . . . You always will be. . . .
There, baby, there. . . . Baby. . . . It won't last . . . All over,
baby. . . .

FADE

SCENE 6

Office of GENERAL VON MÖHL, TAUSSIG *is handing papers to
the dazed* GENERAL.

TAUSSIG: This is the envelope, sir. As you see, it's addressed to
Nicolai Strach, c/o General Postal Delivery, Vienna. It lay
there for several weeks before it was opened by the Secret
Police, who found it contained five thousand kronen and the
names of two well-known espionage cut-outs, one in Dresden and another in Paris. The letter was resealed. Rumpler
was informed immediately and we waited.

MÖHL: And?

TAUSSIG: Redl took three days' leave and motored in his automobile to Vienna where he picked up the letter. On Thursday
evening.

[Pause]

MÖHL: Redl?

[He might almost have burst into tears]

TAUSSIG: Sir. Then. His account at the Austro-Hungarian Bank,
unpaid bills for stabling, furniture, tailoring, *objets d'art,* and
so on. Automobile maintenance, totalling some fifty thousand
crowns. Assets: a little over five, plus valuable personal
properties as yet unvalued. Some securities worth perhaps
eight thousand kronen. His servant Max is owed a year's
wages, but doesn't seem to mind. A trunk full of photographs, women's clothes, underwear, etc., love letters to various identified and unidentified men, a signed oath from

Lieutenant Jerzabek, swearing not to marry during Redl's
lifetime and only afterwards by way of certain complicated
financial losses in Redl's will. Redl's will . . .

MÖHL: All right. General von Hötzendorf must be informed at
once. No: I must do it. He'll go out of his mind. Redl! How
people will enjoy this, they'll enjoy this. The *élite* caught
out! Right at the centre of the empire. You know what they'll
say, of course? About the *élite*.

TAUSSIG: Perhaps it can be kept a secret, sir. Do you think? It's
still possible.

MÖHL: Yes. We must do it now. Where is Redl?

TAUSSIG: The Hotel Klomser.

MÖHL: We'll see Hötzendorf, get his permission, and then we'll
go there, together, you and I. We'll need a legal officer, Kunz
I'd say. But he *must* be sworn to outright secrecy. Those
damned newspapers . . .

TAUSSIG: Kunz is the man for that, sir.

MÖHL: Very well. Let's break the news to General Hötzendorf.

FADE

SCENE 7

REDL's *bedroom at the Hotel Klomser. Above his bed the
black, double-headed eagle of Austria and a portrait of
Francis Joseph.* REDL *is seated at a bureau. In front of him
stand* MÖHL, TAUSSIG, *and* KUNZ. REDL *signs a document, gives
it to* KUNZ, *who examines it, then puts it into his briefcase
which he straps up briskly.*

KUNZ: That's all, General Möhl. . . .

REDL: You know, General, I know you'll be offended if I say this
because I know you're a deeply religious man, and I . . .
well, I've always felt there was a nasty, bad smell about the
Church. Worse than the Jews, certainly. As you know, I'm a
Catholic myself. Who isn't? Born, I mean. [*He takes the champagne bottle out of the bucket and pours a glass*] Born. But

I think I hate the Spaniards most of all. Perhaps that's the flaw . . . of my character . . . they *are* Catholics. Those damned Spaniards were the worst marriage bargain the Habsburgs ever made. Inventing bridal lace to line coffins with. They really are the worst. They stink of death, I mean. It's in their clothes and their armpits, quite stained with it, and the worst is they're so proud of it, insufferably. Like people with stinking breath always puff and blow and bellow an inch away from your face. No, the Spaniards are, you must admit, a musty lot, the entire nation from top to bottom smells of old clothes in the bottom of trunks.

[MÖHL *motions to* TAUSSIG, *who hands him a revolver.* MÖHL *places it on the bureau in front of* REDL. *Pause*]

TAUSSIG: Are you acquainted with the Browning pistol, Redl?
REDL: No. I am not. [TAUSSIG *takes out the Browning Manual and hands it to* REDL] Thank you, Taussig. Gentlemen . . .

[*They salute and go out.* REDL *pours another glass of champagne and settles down to read the manual*]

FADE

SCENE 8

A street outside the Klomser Hotel. Early morning. MÖHL, TAUSSIG, *and* KUNZ *wait in the cold.* REDL's *light is visible.*

TAUSSIG: [*Looks at watch*] Five hours, General. Should we go up?
MÖHL: No.
KUNZ: Forgive me, gentlemen. I'm going home. My wife is waiting for me. My work seems to be done.
MÖHL: Of course.
KUNZ: Good night.

[*A shot rings out. They stare.* KUNZ *moves off*]

MÖHL: Well . . .

[*They light a cigarette*]

FADE

SCENE 9

A *Chamber of Deputies. Vienna. Deputies. In the back-
ground blow-ups of* The Times *for May 30, 1913, headed*
"SUICIDE OF AN AUSTRIAN OFFICER [FROM A CORRESPONDENT]
VIENNA. MAY 29." [*Facsimiles available from British Museum
Newspaper Library*]

DEPUTY: The autopsy showed the bullet had penetrated the oral
cavity, passing obliquely through the brain from left to right.
Death must have been practically instantaneous due to haem-
orrhage. The question is, not who gave this officer the manual, but who allowed him to be given a revolver for this
purpose at all?

MINISTER: There will be no concealment of any irregularities.

DEPUTY: Is it not true that this officer was exposed by reason of
his official contacts with certain confidential elements in the
military-political sphere for a period of some years, with special duties in connection with the frontier protection and the
order of armament?

DEPUTY: Was not this same officer in the confidence of von Moltke,
the chief of the Imperial German High Command?

DEPUTY: Surely someone must have been around with the wit or
perception to have suspected something . . .

DEPUTY: Are we all asleep or what!

[*Roar*]

DEPUTY: *What's become of us?*

[*Roars*]

DEPUTY: Is it not true that he was, in fact, the son of one Marthe
Stein, a Galician Jewess? [*Uproar*] Why was this fact not
taken note of?

MINISTER: The high treason which General Staff Colonel Redl was able to practise with impunity for a period of many years is an occasion of the gravest possible public disquiet, which is far from being allayed, if not actually increasing. This is due not only to the abominable crime committed by this officer—but more by the way in which the case has been managed by the authorities of the Royal and Imperial Army.

DEPUTY: Yes, but what do you *do* about it? What do you *do?*

MINISTER: We must not alarm the public more than is necessary. It is true that the crime committed by Colonel Redl against his country and the uniform he wore is felt in the most sensitive way by the whole population. However, the only adequate protection of the honour of officers lies in rigid standards, and if individuals act against the honour of that class, the only helpful thing is the expulsion from it of those individuals by all the forms prescribed by law. . . .

FADE

SCENE 10

OBLENSKY'S *office. Lights dimmed.* STANITSIN *working the magic lantern.*

OBLENSKY: Next!

[A photograph is snapped on to the screen]

STANITSIN: Schoepfer. Julius Gerhard. M.D., Ph.D., F.R.C.S., Member Institute Neuro Pathology, Vienna. Member Vienna Institute. Hon. Fellow of the Royal Society of London. Born Prague March 25, 1871. Family Jewish. Distinguished patients. List follows. Political and Military. In 1897, at the age of twenty-five, he delivered a brilliant lecture on the origins of nervous diseases. . . .

FADE

CUTS AND ALTERATIONS
REQUESTED BY THE LORD CHAMBERLAIN

Act I–1   "His spine cracked in between those thighs. Snapped. . . . All the way up."

I–4   This scene must not be played with the couple both in bed.

I–4   From: Stage direction – She moves over to the wall. . . .
      To: . . . . Presently, he turns away and sits on the bed.

I–5   Reference to "clap" and "crabs."

I–7   Reference to "clap."

I–10   Omit the whole of this scene.

II–1   Omit the whole of this scene.

III–1 The two men must not be in bed together.

III–1 From: "You'll never know that body like I know it. . . ."
      To: ". . . you've not looked at him, you never will."

III–1 From: "So: you'll turn Stefan . . ."
      To: ". . . than any ordinary man."

III–2 "You were born with a silver sabre up your whatnot."

III–4 "Tears of Christ!"

III–5 Omit the whole of this scene.

TIME PRESENT

A time to embrace and a time to refrain from embracing. A time to get and a time to lose: a time to keep, and a time to cast away.

ECCLESIASTES

CAST

EDITH
PAULINE
CONSTANCE
PAMELA
MURRAY
EDWARD
BERNARD
ABIGAIL

ACT ONE

〰〰〰〰〰〰〰〰〰〰〰

CONSTANCE'S *flat in Pimlico. For the present she is sharing it with* PAMELA. *There is some evidence that it is lived in by two people with different temperaments and interests. On the whole, the impression is rather severe, more a working area than a place to lounge around. The influence of* CON-STANCE *is in the Scandinavian furniture and abstracts. There is also the evidence of her profession of M.P. There is a wall of books, reports, white papers, volumes of* Hansard, *year-books, filing cabinets, and hundreds of back numbers of political weeklies, all very neatly arranged for reference. There is a prominent, large Swedish desk covered with still more books, newspapers, reports, galley proofs, and a type-writer with paper in it. A glass table with a large selection of drinks, a record player, a television set. Records on the floor* [PAMELA'S *untidiness*]. *A couple of modish, uncomfortable, steel and leather chairs. Two doors leading to bedrooms. A partitioned kitchen full of jars for exotic herbs, chopping boards, wine racks, businesslike knives, strings of garlic, and so on. In the less severe part of the room there are Japanese lampshades, a daybed, and a pile of expensive-looking clothes wrapped in plastic covers, clearly just back from the cleaners. On one wall on this side is an old poster. It says simply* "NEW THEATRE, HULL. GIDEON ORME—MACBETH—WITH FULL LONDON CAST *etc*." *On the table is a rather faded production photograph of an ageing but powerful-looking actor in Shake-*

spearian costume. It is late at night and when the curtain rises EDITH, PAMELA's *mother, is sitting on one of the uncomfortable chairs with a cup of tea and reading a copy of Hansard. She is in her late fifties and looks tired but alert. The doorbell rings. She goes to it and calls out firmly before opening.*

EDITH: Who is it?

VOICE: Mummy? It's Pauline.

[She admits PAULINE, *her youngest daughter, who is about eighteen and pretty]*

EDITH: I thought Pamela gave you a spare key.

PAULINE: She wouldn't.

EDITH: Wouldn't?

PAULINE: No.

EDITH: Well, why not? She gives them around to all sorts of peculiar people.

PAULINE: Don't know. Thinks I'm going to have a rave up while she and Connie are out I expect. Any news?

EDITH: I rang about twenty minutes ago. Pamela's been with him since eight o'clock. She said he was a bit quieter. Whatever that means. He always seems to chatter whenever she's there. She lets him go on and on then gets more exhausted than ever. By the time I get there, he complains all the time about how tired he is and can't sleep. Why am I so tired, Edith? I haven't done any work for years. Not since I was at the Shaftesbury. He even got that wrong last night. That was long before the war. He complained all the time just before *I* left. Are you sure you want to come? It's not much fun, darling. You know, sitting up all night in a hospital room.

PAULINE: No, I'll come.

EDITH: Want some tea before we go?

PAULINE: No, thanks.

EDITH: I've got a flask for us. That night sister, not the other one, she's not very concerned for your comfort.

PAULINE: Glad I'm not a patient. I've never been ill in bed. It must be a bit odd.

EDITH: Yes, you have. You've had measles and tonsilitis. And very badly.

PAULINE: Yes, but I don't remember that. I mean being ill, like a, like an experience, lying there. Wondering what they're going to do to you if you're going to get up. So he complains?

EDITH: Nurses, the doctors, the food, the bed, oh, everything.

PAULINE: He never says anything to me much. Oh, he looked at me a long time Tuesday night and then just asked me if I took drugs.

EDITH: Oh, he asks me silly questions.

PAULINE: He said would I get some for him. What'd he ask you?

EDITH: Oh, nothing. I think he often doesn't know what year it is. He thinks he's still on the stage or that we're still married. You really needn't come, you know.

PAULINE: I know.

EDITH: Pamela's *his* daughter. He's made that *very* clear. And besides it's different with him and her.

PAULINE: Hello, reading the old *Hansard?*

EDITH: Yes.

PAULINE: Daddy?

EDITH: No, Constance.

PAULINE: Ah. Any good?

EDITH: I should think so. Not exactly my subject. "New Humber and Fisheries Development Act." Second reading.

PAULINE: I should think not.

EDITH: One of the brightest of the last batch. So Daddy says. Perhaps we should ask her to dinner one evening. When all this is over.

PAULINE: Odd fish for Pamela to shack up with.

EDITH: How do you mean?

PAULINE: Oh, I don't know but I suppose she's frightfully intellectual and an M.P. and all that. And—well, I mean, Pamela's an actress.

EDITH: She's not exactly unintelligent, darling. Even if she does get her life in a bit of a mess. And I think Constance has been kind to her and after that last affair bust up and all.

PAULINE: What? Oh, Alec. But that was for years. Like marriage. Worse.

EDITH: And I think she genuinely admires Pamela. As an actress. And *she* says Constance is the only person who's really encouraged her in her work. Which is true. I used to take an interest. But I had two younger children. And your father's impossible to get to a theatre.

PAULINE: Didn't the old man encourage her?

EDITH: Well, with her own father it was complicated of course. I could never make out what he really wanted for Pamela, being such a famous actor. But then when I said she ought to get a good degree and a profession, he wasn't too keen on that either. Still, she might have spent fifteen years or so, like I did, training her mind to end up washing nappies and getting up coal.

PAULINE: Did you mind much?

EDITH: Of course I minded. Well, I had three children. But of course, I minded. One always minds waste. And the worst waste I can think of is training a woman to the top of her potential and then just off-loading her into marriage when she's probably at her most useful. Probably at the height of her powers.

PAULINE: Well, you can't say Pam's done that.

EDITH: No, but then she's an actress. I meant someone like, well, like Constance is a good example.

PAULINE: Do you think she'll end up first woman prime minister?

EDITH: She's got a very good chance of being a Cabinet minister. Well, so Daddy says, and she's always in the papers. Still, Pamela hasn't done too badly. Having a famous father may not have always helped her. It's hard to tell. They either expect too much of you or compare you unfavourably. She should have done better.

PAULINE: Perhaps they don't write the parts. I mean Pamela's a bit special too, isn't she?

EDITH: How do you mean?

PAULINE: Well, she's not a raving beauty exactly but she's not ugly but you don't quite know what to *do* with her. I suppose it doesn't matter these days. But she's been at it a long time. I mean years.

EDITH: I wonder if she'll want some tea.

PAULINE: I mean I remember coming up to London to see her play Titania *years* ago. I was a little kid. I'd just started school.

EDITH: I don't remember.

PAULINE: She wasn't very good.

EDITH: If you were so young, you wouldn't have known. I thought she was excellent. And a beautiful costume.

PAULINE: You just said you didn't remember.

EDITH: Well, I do now. I'm tired. It's these long waiting sessions with Gideon. And that place is so freezing.

PAULINE: Would you like me to go for you tonight? I don't mind.

EDITH: That's very sweet of you, darling. But I think it has to be me. Me or Pamela. I think it's all right for you and Andrew to help out in the daytime.

PAULINE: I don't think he likes me all that much.

EDITH: I don't know if he really wants anyone with him. He's certainly not particularly pleased to see me. He usually just grunts when I go in or makes me do something for him. Make him comfortable or change his pillows. Or sometimes he just looks away as if he's not seen me . . . Pamela, I suppose. He must want her with him. But he's harsh with her too sometimes, I've heard him.

PAULINE: He's jolly old.

EDITH: He's only seventy-two for heaven's sake, Pauline.

PAULINE: Well, if you don't think that's old——

EDITH: Well, I'm fifty-eight. I suppose you think I'm half in the grave.

PAULINE: No. But the old boy really seems different somehow. Different scene altogether. What else did he ask about?

EDITH: Gideon? Oh, oh, he rambled. I think he thought I was some actor-manager he used to know. Kept talking about seeing the returns, and the week—and then he asked, well, if Daddy and I still made love to each other.

PAULINE: What did you say?

EDITH: Asked me in front of the nurse. Anyway, he didn't really want to know.

PAULINE: No?

EDITH: He was never a jealous man. Sexually, I mean. They said that's why he was no good as Othello. He simply couldn't understand. I'd say he was pretty free of all jealousy. But then he's rather a simple man in many ways.

PAULINE: And do you?

EDITH: What?

PAULINE: What he asked you. You know, Daddy?

EDITH: Good heavens, Pauline, I've told you, I'm not a zombie just because I'm not *your* age any longer.

PAULINE: Sorry.

[CONSTANCE *lets herself in. She is in her early thirties. Bulging briefcase*]

EDITH: Hello, Constance. I'm sorry we're still here.

CONSTANCE: Please. You're welcome. Did you get yourself anything? Hello, Pauline.

PAULINE: Hi.

EDITH: All I wanted, thanks. I usually have something in the waiting room—just a sandwich or something—and either Andrew or Pauline go in with him for a few minutes. Just to give me a break. But it's very good of them. Hospital rooms aren't places for young people to hang about.

CONSTANCE: There are worse places.

EDITH: But it's such a help being able to come over here and put my feet up while Pamela's taking over. Otherwise it takes me an age to get home.

CONSTANCE: How is he?

EDITH: All right. I spoke to Pamela about half an hour ago. She should be back now.

CONSTANCE: Who'll be there in the meantime?

EDITH: Andrew. It'll only be for ten minutes.

CONSTANCE: Isn't there a night nurse?

EDITH: Yes, but she's not there all the time. I mean they can't be of course. And he panics if he's left alone. Especially if he nods off and there's no one there when he wakes up.

CONSTANCE: It must be frightening, especially at this time of night.

EDITH: He won't trust anyone, I'm afraid. He's convinced he's going to be alone.

CONSTANCE: Not even Pamela?

EDITH: Yes. I suppose he *does* trust her?

CONSTANCE: And no improvement?

EDITH: There's always hope I suppose.

CONSTANCE: I wish that were true.

EDITH: One has to carry on, on that basis. You look tired yourself.

CONSTANCE: Looked like being an all-night sitting for an awful moment.

PAULINE: Did you speak to Daddy?

CONSTANCE: We had a coffee together. He said he'd pick up Andrew from the hospital.

EDITH: We'd better go. He'll be tired too. Where's Pamela got to!

CONSTANCE: Perhaps I'd better get her some scrambled eggs or something. How did she sound?

EDITH: Um?

CONSTANCE: On the phone.

EDITH: Oh, all right. Not very communicative. Old men can be very wearing indeed. Especially in these circumstances. I know what he's like with me. But with Pamela it's even worse. [*Pause*] I don't think he's really afraid.

CONSTANCE: No?

EDITH: No.

CONSTANCE: Isn't everyone?

EDITH: No, I don't think so.

CONSTANCE: Especially when you're in full possession of all your faculties. It isn't as if he's drugged stupid.

PAULINE: He wishes he was.

CONSTANCE: Pamela tells me he talks endlessly. And makes jokes.

EDITH: He doesn't know who I am half the time. I know it. He's *very* difficult to understand.

CONSTANCE: Really? He sounded rather coherent from what Pamela said to me.

EDITH: Well, I don't know about that. I only know what I see.

CONSTANCE: He is, he is dying, isn't he?

EDITH: I suppose so.

CONSTANCE: Does anyone know?

EDITH: You know what they're like. They're not interested. Especially if you're what they call "the relatives." They make it pretty clear what a nuisance you are—just the fact that you exist.

CONSTANCE: Can *I* do anything at all?

EDITH: I don't think so, thank you, Constance. My husband's as well placed as——

CONSTANCE: I know. Of course. But, well, you know what I feel for Pamela, and I hate to feel there's so little I can do to help her.

EDITH: You're her friend. That's enough. She needs friends. Without her father. Well, she'll find it harder still. *[Pause] We're* not friends. She and I, I mean. Well, certainly not like Pauline and Andrew and I are friends. In an odd way, we three seem to be more like the same generation. We understand each other. Perhaps it's just the old problem of remarrying and having more children. Something happens. It's different with the other child. It must be. However intelligent you try to be. I think that's true isn't it, Pauline? Or am I deceiving myself? Pamela seems in the middle somewhere.

PAULINE: No. That's right I guess.

CONSTANCE: Can I ask you?

EDITH: Well?

CONSTANCE: About Sir Gideon. What are your feelings about him?

EDITH: Gideon hasn't been my husband for over twenty years.

CONSTANCE: It seems strange when you put it like that.

EDITH: It's the fact. We went separate ways long ago. Not that our ways were ever joined particularly. He was a lot older than me, you see.

CONSTANCE: Yes.

EDITH: And he was also famous long before I met him, I never even saw him play very much I suppose. . . . I had a degree in English and French and . . . oh, well, all long past history. Where do you suppose she's got to? We'll go, I think.

CONSTANCE: She probably walked.

[Enter PAMELA. *She is in her early thirties too]*

PAMELA: Hello. Hello, Edith. I walked.

EDITH: Are you all right, darling?

PAMELA: Oh, all right.

CONSTANCE: Sure? Something to eat? I'm getting some. Scrambled eggs? *[She shakes her head]* Tea?

PAMELA: No, thanks. I'll have a glass of champagne.

CONSTANCE: *[To others]* Are you sure you won't have something. You've got a long night.

EDITH: We must be going.

[But she doesn't move. The attention of all of them is on PAMELA, *as if she had brought danger or ill fortune with her. She waits. Sees her clothes]*

PAMELA: Ah, the old plunder's back from the cleaners. At last. What's left of it.

EDITH: How is he?

PAMELA: Chatty.

EDITH: Still?

PAMELA: Don't worry. Andrew's boring him to death quite literally. About being turned on and dropping out and all.

EDITH: I don't know what I'd have done without Andrew in that place.

PAMELA: Constance, would you open it? I'm too exhausted. That bog-faced night nurse hadn't put any in the fridge. You have some, Mother. It'll get you through.

EDITH: No. Thank you. We must go.

[Pause]

PAMELA: Rested?

EDITH: Not much.

PAMELA: You should take a pill. I do. Don't look so glum. I tell you, he'll have quietened down by the time you get there.

EDITH: He'll wake. He always does. How is he *really?*

PAMELA: How do I know? Sometimes I think he'll live forever. He'll last tonight. Why pretend?

[CONSTANCE *pours champagne*]

PAMELA: That's what I want. That's what he wanted, poor darling. Constance?

CONSTANCE: No, I'm making tea.

PAMELA: Oh, go on. For my sake if not yours.

CONSTANCE: All right then, I will.

PAMELA: Mother? [EDITH *hesitates*] Andrew's all right. He's having a bedside happening all to himself. Papa's pretending to be asleep. He might even drop off with the effort. I won't offer you any, Pauline. She doesn't approve of alcohol, do you? Haven't got any L.S.D. to offer you.

PAULINE: Thanks, Pamela. I think I will have a glass.

PAMELA: Oh, good. Unless Constance has got some pot upstairs. Didn't your lover leave his tin behind the last time? There! Nothing vulgar. Just good trusty old Moet. Her lover drinks nothing but Dom Perignon. Very vulgar. Oh, that's better. [*To* CONSTANCE] Did you vote or divide or whatever? [*She nods*] Don't tell me—you won. What were the figures.

CONSTANCE: 245–129.

PAMELA: Surprise. Like playing for matches really, isn't it? [*To* PAULINE] I suppose that hippie outside belongs to you?

EDITH: Who?

PAMELA: Does he have a name or is he a group? It was a bit difficult to tell if he was one or several.

PAULINE: You know perfectly well.

EDITH: Did you bring Dave, darling?

PAULINE: He doesn't mind waiting.

EDITH: You should have brought him up.

PAMELA: No, she was quite right.

PAULINE: He's O.K., mummy. He said he'd come with us.

EDITH: You know Pamela.

PAMELA: Well enough. Anyway, Constance has just had her nice carpet cleaned.

PAULINE: So what are you supposed to be proving?

PAMELA: I'm just enjoying my first drink of the evening.

PAULINE: Just bitchy and you know it.

PAMELA: You see, you really don't know me. But no loss. For either of us.

EDITH: Are you sure you haven't had a drink?

PAMELA: I told you.

EDITH: You do seem—a bit exhilarated.

PAMELA: I walked through the side streets. No Andrew.

EDITH: I shouldn't stay up, Pamela.

PAMELA: *You've* never been an actor. One needs to wind down.

PAULINE: Have you been performing then?

PAMELA: No, but my papa has. You don't think someone will tow Dave away if you leave him?

PAULINE: Oh, you're a drag——

PAMELA: Looks pretty high to me.

EDITH: What's the matter with him?

PAMELA: He's on what your children call a trip, mama. Having unmemorable visions in a psychedelic, sort of holiday camp shirt and a racoon coat in my doorway. Trip clothes, right, Pauline?

PAULINE: You just hate any sort of fun or anything.

PAMELA: Give him the trip home, will you, darling? And I don't think it's such fun taking Dave, Dave for an all-night rave in hospital, so just get your skates on will you and get rid of him?

PAULINE: No. I'm not going to.

PAMELA: Don't look at your mother. Do as *I* tell you. I'm bigger than you.

PAULINE: And he's bigger than you. So *you* get rid of him.

CONSTANCE: Shall I go down?

EDITH: It's not necessary. We're going.

PAMELA: Not with him you're not. My Father was always very particular about who visited him. Whether it was at home or at work. Getting into his dressing room was like going into Fort Knox. And I don't see why he should be invaded by Dave the Rave. Hippie Andrew's bad enough.

CONSTANCE: I'll speak to him.

PAMELA: No, you won't. He'll be back in the doorway tomorrow night if you chat him up. Pauline——

PAULINE: You kill me. You're a provincial.

PAMELA: Very likely. As your mother will remember, I was born in India. It's where a lot of us come from. Just as you like then. I'll call the law.

PAULINE: Oh, come off it. *[To* EDITH*]* I'll have a word with him.

EDITH: Well, do hurry then. Pamela may be right. Perhaps just the two of us.

PAMELA: Just send him back where you found him. Where was it? The Sidcup Rave Cave. Yes?

PAULINE: Get lost, draggy.

PAMELA: I'll get the law, if you don't move, darling.

EDITH: Oh, stop sniping at the girl, Pamela.

PAULINE: We just do fun things, so what's the matter with *you,* then?

EDITH: But do tell him, darling. Or else let me go on my own. Perhaps that's the best idea.

PAULINE: No, you can't stay up on your own.

PAMELA: Well?

EDITH: I don't think I even remember Dave.

PAMELA: Why should you? He's an American. You met him, Constance. He's been here before. He writes a regular column—when he's not too high—for the farthest out paper. The *Village What.* Sorry, that's just what it's called. Don't you remember: thought London was on the way to being the leadingest place, round-the-clock city, oh, and for freak-outs, cats, chicks, soul groups, and pushing things, like the senses as far as they will go.

CONSTANCE: Oh, that one.

PAMELA: Has a very bad skin.

PAULINE: So what about it? What's so wrong about a bad skin? Why should we change what we really are for you? What are *you,* anyway?

PAMELA: Just a gipsy, dear, that's all. And I don't think blackheads or spots are exactly an aesthetic, what'sit imperative.

PAULINE: All that's finished.

PAMELA: I forgot. He also plays the finger-cymbals. Seven thousand people came to hear him accompany his fellow poets at the Albert Hall.

PAULINE: You wouldn't know a clarinet if you saw one.

PAMELA: Where did seven thousand beautiful people come from, he said. Did he say that to you?

CONSTANCE: Repeatedly.

PAMELA: They were all hideously self-conscious and ugly, I'm afraid. Just like Dave.

PAULINE: You don't know it yet, Pamela, but you'll wake up to it, all your scene is really out, and it'll be out for good and you with it.

PAMELA: I think you're right.

PAULINE: Those draggy plays. Who wants them?

PAMELA: Who's arguing?

PAULINE: Oh—you're just camp.

PAMELA: So I've been told. Just like my father. I wish I could say the same for you. It's impossible to argue with someone wearing such cheap clothes. Take a glass of champagne down to Dave. He doesn't *need* to look quite so ugly, you know. I suppose he thinks *he's* beautiful, of course.

CONSTANCE: Do you want me to come with you?

PAMELA: Why not? You're a party authority on education or about to be or something. You could, let's see, you could try to apply the problems of relating poetry, freak-outs, crazy slides, happenings, action painting, and so on to the comprehensive school. Or the grammar school. Or trip clothes. She actually sells those things she's wearing. What's the name of the shop? Switched Off or Knocked Off or something. Oh, no, I forgot, that's finished now, isn't it? The shoddy clothes scene. It's the bookshop, she sells books and records and dope, I shouldn't wonder. "Ecstatic," that's the name of that one. "Ecstatic." And there's an art gallery attached. Quite a scene, isn't it, Pauline. And then there's her pad in the evenings.

EDITH: She's helping me through a very difficult time, darling.

PAMELA: Is she? What time is that?

EDITH: What's the matter with you?

PAMELA: What difficult time?

EDITH: Gideon's illness, you stupid girl, what else?

PAMELA: You're doing all right. It's nearly over. Her pad, where she raves in the evening, whatever you might wonder that is, getting laid, I suppose, well, now and then, lying about mostly, getting high in her pad, which is just a bed-sitter full of unappealing modish junk and old laundry.

EDITH: I'll ring you at the usual time. Try and get some sleep. You've been too long in that little room.

CONSTANCE: Perhaps I could go. Tomorrow?

PAMELA: She could take over from you.

EDITH: That's not necessary. Poor Andrew—he'll be wondering. Goodnight, Constance. Do go to bed, Pamela.

PAMELA: I'm not tired. Good night, mama. I'll see you in the morning . . . you'll ring me?

EDITH: Yes, I've told you.

PAMELA: No, I don't mean leave it to Pauline or Andrew. You'll get straight through yourself. You will? [EDITH *nods*] Anyway, I don't think anything'll happen tonight. Good night, Pauline.

PAULINE: Good night.

PAMELA: Wave to Dave for me.

EDITH: Why don't you take your own advice and have a pill?

PAMELA: I probably shall. Good night, mama. [*Pause. They go out.* CONSTANCE *closes the door on them*] Thank God! They've gone! We must be *going*. Why didn't she *go?* Instead of drinking champagne and going on about it, being so busy looking tired and distressed. She's Madam Distress Fund, my mama. Calling her mama is better than Edith. Edith almost makes her sound dignified.

CONSTANCE: I suppose she hasn't had much sleep for quite a while. None of you have.

PAMELA: They don't need it. My mother's a bat, and, as for the kids, they're only half conscious most of the day or night so, as they'd say, who needs sleep. *I* need sleep. Lots of it. I sleep my life away. Or I would if I could. Now *we* can talk. Have some more. How are *you?*

CONSTANCE: I'm all right. I've been worried about you.

PAMELA: At least she didn't call you Connie. I've got her out of that. Do they call you Connie in the Party? I'll bet they do.

CONSTANCE: Some of them.

PAMELA: Does lover?

CONSTANCE: No. I thought it was test number one.

PAMELA: Yes. I should say, I should say it probably was. They don't bring out the best in me. If there's a best nailed down under somewhere. Not even you, not much.

CONSTANCE: Your worst can be pretty attractive.

PAMELA: I can't think that's true. I think you believe it though.

CONSTANCE: I don't want to sound like your mother, sorry—mama, Edith, or whatever you like, but I think you *should* get some sleep.

PAMELA: Yes. In a minute.

CONSTANCE: I suppose they've dealt with Dave?

PAMELA: Oh, he's harmless.

CONSTANCE: How was it?

PAMELA: How was what?

CONSTANCE: Your Father?

PAMELA: Oh, all right.

CONSTANCE: Was he chatty?

PAMELA: Not very.

CONSTANCE: Darling, you're exhausted. Why don't you let me go first thing? Just at the beginning. You could have an extra couple of hours. Your Mother wouldn't mind.

PAMELA: Why should she? *He* might.

CONSTANCE: I see.

PAMELA: I told you. He's particular.

CONSTANCE: No. Well, I suppose I don't really know him.

PAMELA: He'll grumble at her a bit. If he's able.

CONSTANCE: You look afraid.

PAMELA: Do I? I'm not panicky, if that's what you mean.

CONSTANCE: No, I didn't. . . .

PAMELA: I held his hand mostly. I brought him some caviare but he didn't want it . . . I just couldn't stay any longer. I knew I couldn't get rid of her once her turn came. He won't like it if it's tonight. She can make the "arrangements" anyway. What do you do? Ring that place in Ken. High Street. Well, she'll enjoy all that. Great organizer, mama. Great, sloppy-minded organizer. She'll be telling young Pauline that I'm overtired and strained. What she means is venomous and evil tongued and selfish.

CONSTANCE: Well, you're not. So do shut up.

PAMELA: Oh, I *am* selfish. I won't give money to take full-page ads about Vietnam or organize them like mama. I certainly wouldn't give money. I'm too mean. Too mean and too poor. Just because I share a bath and an inside lavatory doesn't mean I'm not poor. Well, does it? I'm even unemployed. Oh, you think it's funny, but I am, I'm unemployed. My father will leave nothing but debts, as mama will tell you. He's left me what's left of his wine cellar, all his junk that nobody wants and he asked, yes, he asked me last night, to leave all his empty champagne bottles to the Inland Revenue. Don't think he's got many of those even. I'll send mine for him. The kitchen's full.

CONSTANCE: I got the dustmen to take them away.

PAMELA: Well, please don't. They're for father's area inspector. I promised him. Oh, I think about Vietnam. Not as much as you do. But I'm not giving my money away. Thank you. And then I think of myself. Don't you?

CONSTANCE: Yes. Pamela——

PAMELA: What? More?

CONSTANCE: Let me, let me try and help.

PAMELA: Help?

CONSTANCE: Yes.

PAMELA: What had you in mind?

CONSTANCE: You believe in friendship, don't you?

PAMELA: Yes.

CONSTANCE: Well. Let me do something. Was tonight bad?

PAMELA: Worse than yesterday. Oh, the same. The same. Could you close that window? I know you like fresh air, but this is ridiculous.

CONSTANCE: Sorry, I think your mother——

PAMELA: Oh, of course. Yes, I believe in friendship, I believe in friendship, I believe in love. Just because I don't know how to doesn't mean I don't. I don't or can't. I wish she wouldn't call him Gideon. Oh, I suppose he doesn't mind. I do though. No, it's right for her to call him Gideon.

CONSTANCE: Isn't that what she always called him?

PAMELA: Yes. Well, it's his Christian name. Or one of his Christian names. His names are a bit of a mess, really. Well, his father was a bit dotty and called him Tristram. Tristram, Gideon. Yes, well, you see, sort those out if you're a lovely, struggling boy. And papa thought of Gideon and the Midianites, being brought up on the Bible and not much else, and liking earrings, I think it was the earrings did it. He gave all his wives and mistresses and girls, gave them all earrings. He gave me some. What do I mean *some*? Have you seen my jewel-case? Oh, you must see it. He was very good at women's jewellery. Well, what was I saying? Oh, Gideon. Then, then there was his name, his professional name. Prosser, Tristram Prosser, the old boy must have been out of his mind, well, I think he was a bit. He didn't want the old boy's name because he didn't want to, to use the name even if it was a rotten one, *and* Welsh one, mark. Because the old boy, *his* father was a big deal in the provinces. I mean he was so big in the provinces he'd never come to London. Never came to London in his life. Wasn't good enough for him. Conceited old devil. So, anyway, papa, when he started out of regard for his mother's agony in producing him—called himself Orme. Passed the Square one day, small but dignified he thought, that's it: Gideon Orme. Of course, he was mad. But whoever knows about names? Gideon Orme. Good God. I mean you couldn't get on the epilogue with a name like that now. But then, well. . . . But people tried to talk him out of it. I think it was trying to get away from the Welsh and his father and he got somehow stuck with the Orme. He'd a Jewish grandmother. Always said that was the best part of him. I doubt it but it might have helped. But he used to say, I mean he never wanted *anyone* to know about the *Prosser,* he'd say when the woodnotes go really wild, my dear, it's just that keening old Welsh self-regard. *Do* tell me. When I let it out. Pamela, if you ever hear me put the PEW into PURE, call out something and something English and derisive or something, because then I'm being bad. And if I'm being bad. I'll go on because no one will notice. They'll think it's just

me. So everyone called him Orme. I never called him anything else. Not after mama left. She *always* called him Gideon. But in the profession he was just Orme. The Welsh are
like the Irish, he'd say they're too immodest to be really
good actors. I don't want to be mistaken for one of these. Not
that they'd know the difference. Except the Irish are a bit
worse. Well, they invented the stage Irishman and blamed
it on the English like everything else just to cover up. Dear
Orme. He should be rescued from Andrew by now. He
doesn't know how to abuse Andrew.

CONSTANCE: Haven't you told him?

PAMELA: He knows his ground with Edith. But with Andrew, he
just doesn't know what he's about. You haven't met Andy,
well, he's got none of Pauline's instinct to please, which is
at least something, though not much. Mama thinks he's saint-
like, and he probably is, except he's earth bound, he's saint-
like, he's an opportunist, indulged, enclosed and supported
by your colleague, his father. What's *he* like?

CONSTANCE: I should say he's pretty able. Persuasive . . . quite
attractive in some ways.

PAMELA: No, not him. Oh, then daddy's brother saint character.
Too good for politics. That's his badge.

CONSTANCE: Well——

PAMELA: He's too good to be true. That's why mummy fell for
him. He's not tough enough. For politics. And he's not good
enough. Now, you're nearly tough enough but probably too
good.

CONSTANCE: Thank you.

PAMELA: No, Andrew. Well, he started off as a wine snob.

CONSTANCE: Are you sure you won't?

PAMELA: Yes, thanks.

CONSTANCE: I wish you'd talk to me.

PAMELA: What do you mean? I never stop talking to you. Why
don't you tell me to shut up. I can go to bed, as you say.

CONSTANCE: No. Let's stay up a bit longer. I could do with an
unwind myself.

PAMELA: What was *your* day like?

CONSTANCE: Busy. Bit end of term atmosphere.

PAMELA: Bit like a girls' school, isn't it?

CONSTANCE: More like a boys' school where a few day-girls are tolerated.

PAMELA: I shouldn't have said you were ever tolerated. The place needs a bit of pash and glamour. You looked frightfully sexy in that pink dress, in the paper, you know, meeting that delegation thing.

CONSTANCE: I don't think my constituents were too enthusiastic about it. They probably thought I didn't look serious enough.

PAMELA: You looked as if the entire Cabinet was lining up for you. They should be grateful you don't look like that woman— what is she, in the Treasury—the one with the teeth?

CONSTANCE: I wouldn't mind being as bright as she is.

PAMELA: I wouldn't mind if she were as pretty as you.

CONSTANCE: I don't think you should judge by externals so much.

PAMELA: I've just a superficial manner, often saying serious things. Which is the other way round to people like her. Just because she's got a double first in P.P.E. or I.T.V., there's no reason why she shouldn't get her teeth fixed. That's arrogance and self-deception. Perhaps that's why she's a big wheel in the Party.

CONSTANCE: I think she's a nice woman, really, shy and, yes, well, a bit serious, but a first-rate mind.

PAMELA: Um. Well, you know her. I find it hard to believe she's really wise to inflict those green teeth on people. Sort of autumnal teeth, aren't they? That should make her shy but she's not. I think someone must have told her once she looked like a tiger and she's been flashing them at you behind that crimped-up seaweed she thinks is a serious politician's hairdo ever since. Is it a wig?

CONSTANCE: No. Poor woman. We can't all look like film stars.

PAMELA: Well, perhaps she should, poor dear. How can you be really intelligent and be satisfied with that? It's obviously all a great production number. Even if she does feel she's got unfair competition with the men.

CONSTANCE: It isn't easy, Pamela. It's easier in your line.

PAMELA: Nonsense. Why do you have to strive? Besides, I don't look like a film star.

CONSTANCE: Yes, you do.

PAMELA: Yes, which one? It sure ain't Garbo. How old is she?

CONSTANCE: Garbo?

PAMELA: No, your lady.

CONSTANCE: Oh, thirty-seven, eight.

PAMELA: Well, she looks eighty-eight of course. Thirty-eight! You must be joking. Perhaps she should have the jabs, or a face job, or the lot. Perhaps she has already. Constance!

CONSTANCE: What?

PAMELA: Well—poor woman! Think! No wonder she's so solemn. Why, she's got tits like old ski-socks filled with sand. And a pre-form bra *no* one could make a wedge in. Is she married?

CONSTANCE: Oh, to some academic, I think.

PAMELA: Marriage must be pretty academic, too. Just as well.

CONSTANCE: I don't think you'd mind her so much if you met her. She's quite harmless.

PAMELA: You *can't* bring her back here—can you? To one of your parties? I know these brainy girls, they get terribly girlish and all frilly when you're not expecting it. They turn up at things like your Annual Conference Ball looking like Americans in cashmere sweaters with sequins on. And rhinestone spectacles. She's not harmless, she's not harmless at all. She's spending my money, and I haven't got any, you sit up there all hours of the night debating about how to spend my money. How to get hold of my money. What have you been doing with my money today? Give me those things, what'sit, Order Paper thing. What's this? Humber and Anglia Fisheries and Redevelopment Act. *[Pause]* And you won? Why don't you introduce the Lady Politicians' Teeth Filling Development Act? What's this?

CONSTANCE: Something I'm working on during the recess. Can I have it back, please? It's not interesting.

PAMELA: Then why are you working on it? "Striding into the Seventies with Labour!" You're really joking!

CONSTANCE: Please, Pamela.

[Pause]

PAMELA: Bit like school, isn't it? Please can I have my satchel back? And then they throw it over the hedge for you. *[She gives it back]* Striding into the seventies. I haven't got used to hobbling about in the sixties yet. Give us a chance.

CONSTANCE: Time is in short supply in the present.

PAMELA: Then we should keep it in its place. Whenever we can. Just because we can't win.

CONSTANCE: It's very easy to poke at people who are trying to cope realistically with the future. And glib.

PAMELA: But what about the meantime? We've got to get through that, haven't we? I don't know about striding off anywhere. I seem to be stuck here for the moment . . . that's not being glib. We have to wait up . . . not be able to get to sleep . . . it's strange how easily men seem to get off to sleep . . . always before you . . . off . . . and you wake up tired . . . but not in the seventies . . . Tomorrow . . . that's early this morning, *this* morning. . . .

CONSTANCE: Why are you so scornful to me?

PAMELA: I'm not.

CONSTANCE: It's as if you hate what I do, what I am, everything about me. I know a lot of it seems funny and wasted effort but a lot of effort *is* funny and wasted.

PAMELA: I don't mind effort. I'm not so keen on strain.

CONSTANCE: You make me feel very shabby and inept and all thumbs sometimes.

PAMELA: *I* do! But, Constance, I don't . . . I don't know anything I'm ever talking about except for odd things. I'm almost totally ignorant, you know that.

CONSTANCE: No, you're not. You're very perceptive.

PAMELA: I'm not perceptive. I'm just full of bias. *And* I'm uneducated. I went to about twenty expensive schools and I never learnt anything in any of them. Except to play tennis.

CONSTANCE: You know how I admire you and what you do.

PAMELA: But I've never done anything very memorable. How can you?

CONSTANCE: I know you have formidable qualities . . .

PAMELA: Even if they haven't been exploited yet?

CONSTANCE: I respect and admire you for what you are.

PAMELA: I respect and admire you.

CONSTANCE: I don't think so. I wish you did.

PAMELA: It shouldn't matter to you.

CONSTANCE: Well, it does. Your good opinion is important to me. More so than most of the people I deal with. I know we inhabit different worlds, but they're not really so different always. And, also, I thought that we were, were very much alike, you and I.

PAMELA: Yes. I always did too.

CONSTANCE: I couldn't believe it when you agreed to come and stay here.

PAMELA: Well: both left behind by our chaps. It gave us something to talk about in the long unconnubial nights.

CONSTANCE: I don't think it was as simple as that.

PAMELA: It wasn't so different moving out of my house. I didn't have much affection for it.

CONSTANCE: You wouldn't rather move back?

PAMELA: No. Are you suggesting it?

CONSTANCE: You know I'd like you to stay. But only if you want to. If I bore or irritate you——

PAMELA: Of course you don't, you idiot. We get on rather well, I think. You sounded like a wife then.

CONSTANCE: Did I? Sorry. It's just that I didn't want you to feel obliged to stay. You helped me over a difficult patch.

PAMELA: So did you. If I go back there, I only keep finding bits of his things in cupboards and drawers. Each time I think I have thrown everything out or sent it back to him, there's a belt or a tie or an old cheque book. I suppose I ought to let it. I just can't bring myself to all the bother of it.

CONSTANCE: I could find someone for you. It's not difficult to arrange. We always seemed to like the same things and react similarly. Most women just seem to make me impatient.

PAMELA: You prefer men. That's because you're such a gossip.

CONSTANCE: Really—I hate it.

PAMELA: Well, men are great on it.

CONSTANCE: But you know what I mean?

PAMELA: Yes. You like crowds too. So do men mostly. The sort you know.

CONSTANCE: What sort is that?

PAMELA: Oh, clever. Successful.

CONSTANCE: Do you know any unsuccessful men?

PAMELA: Well—not many maybe. But I know some pretty stupid ones. Oh, darling, please don't look so upset. I'm only chattering and going on about that poor lady's rotten teeth. Everyone makes jokes about M.P.s, they're like honeymoon nights and mothers-in-law. Don't hold that against me. I admire what you do tremendously. Just because I haven't got the ability to do it myself.

CONSTANCE: You don't mean that.

PAMELA: But I do, my darling. It's like everyone thinks actors have got no brains and live in some world walled up from the realities everyone else is immersed in. Something . . .

CONSTANCE: Your voice sounds quite different sometimes. I suppose it's when you don't believe in the lines you're reading.

PAMELA: How can I convince you?

CONSTANCE: You have.

PAMELA: Oh, for God's sake. Have some humour.

CONSTANCE: Please don't be angry. I'm sorry.

PAMELA: Sorry for what? Sticking up for yourself?

CONSTANCE: O.K. Let's not talk about it.

PAMELA: Well, why not talk about it? I've obviously upset you.

CONSTANCE: You didn't mean to.

PAMELA: Perhaps I did . . . I don't know. Maybe we should talk about it.

CONSTANCE: Have some more of this. I'm glad you liked the pink outfit. It was horribly expensive.

PAMELA: I could see. And don't change the subject. I don't think I'm the only one who knows about clothes. I wish you wouldn't buy cheap clothes.

CONSTANCE: Thanks.

PAMELA: Oh, hell, you know what I mean.

CONSTANCE: You just said it—I buy cheap clothes.

PAMELA: Well, it's all right for kids like Pauline.

CONSTANCE: She's young, you mean.

PAMELA: Yes, if you like. Who cares if she wears badly finished day-to-day rubbish, and if her skirts are up around her fat little thighs by her crutch.

CONSTANCE: We don't all have long legs like you.

PAMELA: But I wear them down to here.

CONSTANCE: Well? You have style.

PAMELA: So do you.

CONSTANCE: You don't think so.

PAMELA: How do you know? What I think? Nobody knows. I certainly don't at all.

CONSTANCE: Don't let's quarrel.

PAMELA: I thought we were having a parliamentary style debate on skirt length. Anyway, public opinion is on your side. They're not going below the knee for fifty years. I read it last night. [Pause] Perhaps we aren't very alike after all, you and I?

CONSTANCE: Because we argue about skirt lengths?

PAMELA: I've thought about it lately. Orme was asking me about you tonight and I suppose it occurred to me then. I don't really think we are.

CONSTANCE: Probably.

PAMELA: You should be pleased. Not sad.

CONSTANCE: Perhaps I've always wanted to be someone like you. To have long legs, and style. Instead of just making efforts. But I suppose what's saddening is that you make it sound all like a rejection.

PAMELA: What?

CONSTANCE: Your attitude to me.

PAMELA: You make me sound like a selection committee that's turned you down.

CONSTANCE: I think you have.

PAMELA: Well, don't lose any sleep over it. I've turned down better people than you. [Pause] I didn't mean that in the way it came out.

CONSTANCE: It probably came out purely enough. It seemed like it.

PAMELA: Why don't you make me shut up, go home. No, well, go to bed, stop being a bitch.

CONSTANCE: I've told you: I like *you* as you are.

PAMELA: Well, you must be a pretty small club.

CONSTANCE: I really have made your teeth grate. I can see it.

PAMELA: You look so damned fragile sometimes. Someone should take you in his arms. Why doesn't that priggish, self-righteous husband come back and give you a cuddle or something. And own up he's been sleeping around himself for years and years!

CONSTANCE: He's got rigid standards. Besides, that's not what I need.

PAMELA: Oh, come off it, Constance, that's what we all need—love and friendship and a hot cuddle. And they really *are* on short supply.

CONSTANCE: It's very clear what your true opinion of me is. It's like the way some men look at one. Patting you on the head if you show signs of being bright, and picking you up and putting you down in *their* way——

PAMELA: Listen. You're far more likely to be bored by what you think of as my green-room banter.

CONSTANCE: No. I think you're a very serious person. And I pay you the respect due to a serious person and what they do.

PAMELA: And what they do! That's it. You get this thing because you think I don't respect what you do. What you do, what you do, what you do, what's it matter? I don't care what anyone thinks.

CONSTANCE: I think you're lucky. At least you appear to. I'm afraid I *am* different.

PAMELA: My opinion about you or anything isn't worth—what—any more than that great booby of a tinker bell, Abigail! Abigail: just because she's made a movie and someone's talked about the mystery behind her eyes. She's got no mystery behind her eyes, she's just myopic, which enables her to be more self-absorbed than ever and look as if she's acting when she's just staring at wrinkles on your forehead.

CONSTANCE: Thank heavens! Oh—come, there's more to her than that.

PAMELA: I'll tell you just what there is. And this I do know about. She moons about on street corners in a French movie, looks listless and beautiful in her own big, beady way while you hear a Mozart Requiem in the background. She plays with herself, gets the giggles while she's doing it, and they say she's a cross between Garbo and Buster Keaton. Abigail—who's never seen a joke in her life when it was chalked on a blackboard for her, who was the only person in the entire world who didn't know the truth about her daddy until she found him tucked up with a Greek cabin steward and the family's pet bulldog! And that was before she got engaged to the biggest poove in the business. She was *twenty-three*. And *twenty* already when she stood up to her nanny and told her she *would* go on dressing up as Castro if she wanted to. I hope her movies are big in Cuba. They should be. They ask *her*, that blowtorch Mary Pickford, what she thinks about the Russian and Chinese doctrinal conflict, and actually print what she says out of the hairy mystery behind her eyes.

CONSTANCE: That's better. You've stopped being cross with me.

PAMELA: Yes, I'm cross. What do you think she knows about it. She belongs to Disneyland. So do I. She doesn't even understand what's going on *there*. Except she knows she wants fat, sympathetic parts because she's dim enough to enjoy them and making sweeping, spurious gestures all over the place while she'll trample on a pussy cat or the char's baby to death while the world wonders how anyone can be so young, gifted, touching, and spirited and full of simple sorrow for the world's unloved and unwanted, while she herself is the most lovable and wanted of all starry creatures.

CONSTANCE: Hasn't she got a dress rehearsal for her play?

PAMELA: Yes. And she'll probably ring me if it's over and ask after dearest Orme. Not wondering whether or not I'm asleep. I know—I'm not. I'm talking about her. Give me some more of that. And silly actresses who don't know what they're talking about, and people like you bothering to listen to them.

CONSTANCE: Well, you're not Abigail.

PAMELA: No, I'm not. But if I were, I'd be what I'm not—a whopping, enduring, ironclad, guaranteed star!

CONSTANCE: I think I'd better open another one. After Abigail.

PAMELA: Yes. If she rings, *you* talk to her. As for—are you all right now?

CONSTANCE: Fine. We both are. We *are* rather alike.

PAMELA: Maybe. Do you miss your child very much?

CONSTANCE: Yes.

PAMELA: How often do you see him?

CONSTANCE: About twice a week.

PAMELA: Do you mind *him* having custody. And all that meeting in the zoo and stuff?

CONSTANCE: I don't often enjoy it much.

PAMELA: What is he—four? I wouldn't mind having a son. Except I couldn't possibly look after it.

CONSTANCE: Of course you could. I think you'd be a lot of fun for a child.

PAMELA: Do you? I think I'd be easily bored. You have extraordinary belief in my abilities.

CONSTANCE: I don't think so. It's a little like feeling freshly looted each time.

PAMELA: Somebody loses. Somebody's guilty, somebody else comes through. When you win your constituency, the other poor candidate loses.

CONSTANCE: That's politics. He's a Tory.

PAMELA: So am I. I don't see why you should get on at my expense.

CONSTANCE: That's just an affectation.

PAMELA: No, it's not. I mean a real one. Not the sort you sit and make faces at. I couldn't afford a child in a property-owning democracy. I'd have to have loads of nannies. It could sit in the dressing-room sometimes—if I was working. But I'd have to be always working to pay for the nannies, and that wouldn't work at all.

CONSTANCE: You could get married.

PAMELA: What for?

CONSTANCE: It works for some people.

PAMELA: Tories like me are not "some people," Constance.

CONSTANCE: Some things do work, you know.

PAMELA: You sound like Edith.

CONSTANCE: Thanks. I know what you think of her.

PAMELA: If I had a son, I wouldn't have a clue what I'd want him to be. I don't mean like an engine driver or something futile like an astronaut or a star export manager. I mean would he prefer champagne to drugs. I mean, I *wonder* about your child. Will he get stoned . . .

CONSTANCE: I believe the statistics suggest it's more likely than he's going to a university.

PAMELA: Oh, he'll go to a university. If you've got "A" levels, we're after *you!* And even if you've only got "O" levels, we're *still* interested. Fancy. Lower streams of the poor little devils, upper levels of the bigger fish. I'd be in no stream at all. All those school inspectors and examiners and seducers from industry hanging about like men in raincoats, offering prospects and excitement and increments. How awful. If a man comes up to you, darling, however friendly he might be, talking about your "A" levels, don't, repeat don't, talk to him. He's after *you,* he wants to make a University Challenger out of you. Don't talk to them, they're sick. Yes, but mummy's known it for a long time. Get back home before the park gates close or he'll take out his careers section in the *Daily Telegraph* and show it to you. Come home and you can have crumpets and champagne for tea with mummy. Did you know that's the perfect device for testing whether your gynaecologist is any good or not? Do we drink champagne at bearing down time? Or do we not?

CONSTANCE: I wish I'd known.

PAMELA: My dear, first thing to ask. No, I don't really feel like you. I know, I don't, for instance, feel that most things I do must be an improvement on what I did before. So much improvement—like sex. I don't think I'm probably particularly good at it. I don't know. It's hard to tell, isn't it?

CONSTANCE: I think one knows pretty well. Well, at our stage of the game.

PAMELA: Yes. Perhaps you do have a more accurate notion. You and Murray make it pretty big, don't you?

CONSTANCE: Very.

PAMELA: Yes. I can see you do know.

CONSTANCE: I think you don't believe I know any more than you know.

PAMELA: Do stop reproaching me. With my late gentleman, it was pretty good I should say. *He* said it was. I suppose he was being truthful—as he saw it. However he saw it. Sometimes it was amusing. Or, of course, lonely. Or sometimes something not very much at all. That's not been your experience either much, has it? Edith's always supposed to be great in the hay. Don't like to think about it. Least of all with Orme. *He* never spoke about it to me. But she's always telling me her ratty little details. She's not exactly fastidious. Now Orme. You could eat your dinner off his taste in anything. Constance: what's your other name?

CONSTANCE: Sophia. Female wisdom.

PAMELA: Oh, my God, they lumbered you, didn't they? I'm not telling you mine. My mother was really being pretentious. Pamela's bad enough. And *don't* tell me you like it. If you do, I'll tell you, you don't have any style after all. *[Pause]* Suppose it's trying to be honest to say you're not sure. *[At desk]* "Going into Europe." Sounds like getting into the Pudding Club. Public spending, the price we have to pay, private sectors, incentive and exports, both—guess—both sides of industry, productivity, exploiting our resources to the full, readjustment. I suppose they're like words you're supposed to believe in, like your Catechism, I believe in God the Father, the Holy Catholic Church, forgive us our trade gaps.

CONSTANCE: I'm sorry, Pamela, I wish you wouldn't rummage around my desk. It's arranged very carefully.

PAMELA: So I see. I don't see, I mean I don't *see* economics at all. I mean I see astrology. Fine. But, well, ever since I have been born there's been an economic crisis. We went off something called the gold standard I think when I was born, there's been no confidence in sterling, crashes, devaluing, loans, and all the star gazing and at the end of it people are better off, better fed, better housed than ever and if you never look at these forecasts, it makes no difference.

CONSTANCE: I think that's one of your simplifications, to put it mildly.

PAMELA: Would you? Say that, would you? I'd say it was one of my commonplace revealed truths. However, you're the one who knows.

CONSTANCE: Oh, do stop saying that.

PAMELA: I don't think I've said it before. Did any letters come for me this morning?

CONSTANCE: No. I don't think so. Oh, a card from a gallery, I think. Any for me?

PAMELA: Don't know why I asked. No one ever writes to me. Except for some occasional sun-questing queen who sends me a card from wherever the wog rumbo is thickest at the moment.

CONSTANCE: Was there any afternoon post, I asked you?

PAMELA: No, I don't think so. Some bills maybe.

CONSTANCE: Are you sure?

PAMELA: No. Why should you be in such a tizz about a few letters? Slow down.

CONSTANCE: I don't want to slow down if you mean come to a sort of standstill——

PAMELA: Implying?

CONSTANCE: It may seem inconsequential to you, but it *is* my work.

PAMELA: Not expecting a love letter. I thought Murray always rang.

CONSTANCE: No. He'll ring soon. I expect he's at a party.

PAMELA: Orme used to write beautiful letters. In superb handwriting, of course. He'd write to me regularly if he was on tour or in America. With little drawings, drawings of himself and what his mood was and what his performance

looked like. He drew quite well. But he hasn't written to me
for years. Not since he gave up work.

CONSTANCE: Why do people give up? I think I underrate it.

PAMELA: I don't. I'm miserable when I'm not working, which is
about half the time. You know what I'm like.

CONSTANCE: Well, then?

PAMELA: I think: excessive effort is vulgar.

CONSTANCE: Thanks again. Is that part of your high Toryism? It's
a little shopsoiled. That kind of romancing and posturing,
I mean.

PAMELA: I think there's a certain grace in detachment.

CONSTANCE: You sound like an old-style lady journalist.

PAMELA: I thought you said saying "lady" anything was conde-
scending? That men did it to belittle women they saw as
rivals.

CONSTANCE: You never sound particularly detached. Your on-
slaught on poor Abigail, for instance. Sounded just vicious
to me.

PAMELA: Ah, Constance, like so many people you don't understand the content of tone of voice. You're like an American,
you have no ear. All voices are the same to you. It's only
what is said that seems significant. Old Orme *had* to give up.
What was there left for him? He'd done everything. He said,
I can't dodder on as Lear again. It needs a younger man.
Anyway, nobody liked it before when I did it. Lost twenty
thousand pounds. Said I was too young and didn't care for
the verse. You know how they say it as if you ill-treated children. Now they'd say I was too old. Mind you, I'd still be
better than anyone else.

CONSTANCE: Must be great to have that degree of surety.

PAMELA: He just knew himself. And the others. He didn't want
to be liked particularly.

CONSTANCE: Lucky.

PAMELA: Essential if you're any good at all. He was cool. Pauline
and Dave think they're cool. But you can't be cool if your
sense of self and, well, ridicule is as numb as *theirs*.

CONSTANCE: Seems to me you're doing what you accuse me of—theorizing.

PAMELA: True. Didn't somebody say "Addison in print was not Addison in person"?

CONSTANCE: So? Miss Ignorant.

PAMELA: I think you *should* pay more attention to tones of voice. They are very concrete. You have plenty of them.

CONSTANCE: You mean I dissemble?

PAMELA: I mean you are many things to different people.

CONSTANCE: A trimmer?

PAMELA: In the House, to your constituency, in the papers, on the telephone, in bed; I don't know about that, but you're determined not to be caught out. You're determined. You've read the books the others have, the reports, the things in the air at the moment, the present codes and ciphers. It all has to be broken down. The information has to be kept flowing. Or you'll feel cut off, left behind. You keep trying.

CONSTANCE: What should I do then?

PAMELA: What your fears and desires tell you together, I imagine. As you say, it's all stuff you enjoy. I tried writing love letters to someone. For quite a long time. Then I found my handwriting was getting like his. I don't know what I can go on saying. I love you. I need you. I want you. I ache for you. I need you beside me and in my bed. Don't let's part like this again. It's more than I can bear. It's never been like this in my life before. I never thought it could be. *[Pause]* I tried writing erotica to him. But I couldn't bring myself to send it ever. I'd write it down, pages of it. I'd like to. I want you to . . . I dreamt that. . . . Then make up a dream. But it was too explicit. And then it seemed impersonal. Puritanism, I expect you'd say.

CONSTANCE: It's a pity you couldn't have gone with Murray to the party. He was frightfully sorry you couldn't go.

PAMELA: Was he? What did he think I'd do? Look in on my way from the hospital?

CONSTANCE: No, of course not. I think he just finds you very attractive. And it sounded as if there might be some interesting people there.

PAMELA: I've been meeting interesting people for years. I just wish people would stop trying to fix you up. So and so would like to meet you. Just scalps. I'm thirty-four . . . twenty-six years old, and I don't need to go to parties and meet interesting people. I can make out for myself even if the terrain *is* all married men, pooves, and tarted up heteros head over heels about themselves.

CONSTANCE: Like your friend Edward?

PAMELA: He's not my friend or my lover or anything. He just comes in and talks to me. I suppose even he gets bored with his dollies and scrubbers. Not with himself, mind, but he can't believe that there's someone who doesn't think he's the greatest knockout a woman ever laid eyes on.

CONSTANCE: Why should it bother him?

PAMELA: Good question. He's younger than I am—though not as much as he says. I know that. He's a big deal star and a new scene and all that. As for Murray, he's *your* gentleman.

CONSTANCE: He's intrigued by you.

PAMELA: Well, he shouldn't be telling you then. It's unfair and unkind. What's the matter with him?

CONSTANCE: He doesn't. I've watched him look at you. And sometimes I know he's thinking of you.

PAMELA: He hardly knows me.

CONSTANCE: He knows you through me.

PAMELA: That's scarcely the same.

CONSTANCE: It's quite potent. *[Phone rings]* I'll take it.

PAMELA: Why are you always so sure it must be for you? It's probably some man sniffing around. The moment you've been detached, they're on the doorstep seeing what the chances are.

Especially for you—married women on the shelf. Wanting to be taken down and given a bit of what they need.

CONSTANCE: It's probably Murray.

PAMELA: If it's Lady Tinker-Bell Abigail, I'm in bed.

CONSTANCE: *[Phone]* Hello . . . Oh, yes, just a minute. . . . It's Andrew.

PAMELA: Hello. . . . Yes. I *am* in bed. You've woken me up. . . . Well, your mama may send him to sleep. . . . What time? . . .

No, all right. . . . Well, I'll just have to manage, won't I?
Yes, I know you have to work. . . . What *are* you doing?
Good God. Oh, well—what's all that noise? I see. . . . Night.

CONSTANCE: Nothing wrong?

PAMELA: Oh, he wants to leave the hospital earlier to get to work.

CONSTANCE: We shouldn't bicker. Please forgive me. I know what
it must be like for you.

PAMELA: We're not quarrelling, are we?

CONSTANCE: Well, I think we're a bit out of kilter.

PAMELA: Do you know where he is? Andrew? He's just left Orme
and gone to that party. I suppose he's one of the interesting
people. What's the betting Edward isn't there too? He told
me to tell you your gentleman's just leaving.

CONSTANCE: I didn't know he knew Murray.

PAMELA: Well, they know each other now. Lucky Murray. I wonder what other celebrities he's met.

CONSTANCE: It sounded rather more a literary-political sort of do.

PAMELA: Oh, I think Andrew's got literary connections of a kind.

CONSTANCE: What's he do?

PAMELA: At present? Seems he's a waiter in one of the fag amateur restaurants in Brompton Road. Dressed as a lion tamer,
I think.

CONSTANCE: Perhaps we should go? Murray adores those sorts of
places.

PAMELA: Not if you're hungry.

CONSTANCE: Do they let girls in the place? Or just tamper with
their food?

PAMELA: The food doesn't go to much tampering. He's a poet.
I think he cuts out bits of old copies of the *Illustrated London News* and American comics and pastes them together.
Yes, they get published. He used to paint a little in the same
fashion. He'd glue bits of his levis on to strips of glass and
top them up with different coloured paints and plaster. He
told me this evening he wants his dad to put him into publishing. Perhaps that's why he went to Murray's party. He's
very keen on a lot of American plays, sort of about leaving
nude girls in plastic bags at railway stations. Nonverbal, you

understand, no old words, just the maximum in participation. I don't know whether the old boy will stump up. Perhaps Murray could help him.

CONSTANCE: Why should he?

PAMELA: I don't know. A lot of people find him "interesting."
Some weekends he runs old movies backwards on the ceiling
in an old Bethesda chapel in Holland Park.

[Door bell. CONSTANCE rushes to it. MURRAY is there. Thirty-
ish]

CONSTANCE: Darling!

MURRAY: Get my message?

CONSTANCE: Yes. Come in.

MURRAY: Am I too late?

CONSTANCE: No. We're just having some champagne.

PAMELA: Have some.

MURRAY: Thanks. How are you, Pamela?

PAMELA: Not bad.

CONSTANCE: She's exhausted, poor darling. Make her go to bed.
I can't.

MURRAY: You look remarkable for it.

CONSTANCE: [To PAMELA] See?

PAMELA: See what?

MURRAY: How's your father?

PAMELA: Oh. The same. As far as I know.

MURRAY: I'm sorry. I just met your brother.

PAMELA: Please—stepbrother.

CONSTANCE: Sit down, darling. Doesn't he look smashing?

PAMELA: Ravishing. How was the party?

MURRAY: Not bad. Heard one or two interesting things. What
does your stepbrother do?

PAMELA: Now? He's a part-time poove's waiter.

MURRAY: He told me he was going into publishing.

PAMELA: I expect he will. He started off as a wine snob, going to
vineyards and reporting on growth and so on. It was for this
City firm and he used to dress like an old Etonian then. Before that he was at one of mama's pet schools and wore levis

and wax in his ears like pearl earrings. Same at the university.

MURRAY: Which one?

PAMELA: Oh, I don't know, one of those new estates where all the furniture looks to have come from Heals' January sales. He became a probation officer for a bit. He'd a degree for that kind of service. He wanted to do something "meaningful," as my American gentleman used to say. He got accused of having relations with a boy from an approved school. Anyway, they thought he'd got the wrong meaning and I think he was bored and underpaid, so he did do Zen for a bit but I don't think he got paid for it. Then the Committee of One Hundred. He's always been pretty violent, so he enjoyed hitting his great head against brutal bobbies for a spell. Oh, and he went to Cuba. Same time as Lady Tinker-Bell, the blowtorch.

MURRAY: Lady Tinker-Bell?

CONSTANCE: She means Abigail.

MURRAY: Do I detect professional envy?

PAMELA: Professional boredom. He'd send me cards and pictures of Abigail in her Castro hat singing people's songs. But he got some Cuban girl in the pudding club and got knifed by a fellow revolutionary, so perhaps he wasn't bent, after all. Anyway, he got slung out for bourgeois carryings-on.

MURRAY: You're not exaggerating of course?

PAMELA: Murray, I *never* exaggerate. You're like your Constance. No ear for inflection.

MURRAY: He seemed pretty lively to me.

PAMELA: Did he? Yes, I suppose he did. He'd been cooped up in quite the wrong scene all the evening. What's the matter? You think I'm frivolous?

MURRAY: I don't know you.

PAMELA: Constance says you do.

CONSTANCE: She's no more frivolous than I am.

PAMELA: No? I think Murray's one of those intellectuals who thinks all actors live in a narrow, insubstantial world, cut off from the rest of you. Well, kid yourself not. You're all of you

in show business now. Everybody. Of course, Orme was
never in show business. Books, politics, journalism, you're all
banging the drum, all performers now. What are you busy-
ing yourself with these days?

MURRAY: Oh, usual stuff. Reviewing, articles, bits on the box.

CONSTANCE: He's written a play. I think it's quite extraordinary.
Tell her about it.

MURRAY: If you'd like me to.

PAMELA: No. I can't bear people describing things like that to
me. The people who do it well are usually no good anyway.
They're just critics passing as writers.

CONSTANCE: Then you must read it. Really.

PAMELA: All right, Constance. But don't sell it to me.

[Phone rings]

PAMELA: Yours, I suppose.

[CONSTANCE has got to it]

CONSTANCE: Yes . . . Abigail?

PAMELA: I'm asleep. No thanks to her.

CONSTANCE: I made her go to bed. She's worn out, poor dear . . .
Yes, nearly all day . . . No different I'm afraid.

PAMELA: As if she cares. Get rid of her.

CONSTANCE: Yes, I'll tell her . . .

PAMELA: No, don't.

CONSTANCE: How was your dress rehearsal? . . . How exciting for
you. . . .

PAMELA: I'll bet.

CONSTANCE: And now you go on tour first? Well, I hope it goes
well. . . .

PAMELA: Oh, it will. A bomb in Brighton. They should burn that
joint down. They think it's 1950.

CONSTANCE: I'll give it to her. . . .

PAMELA: Tell her to get her girdle washed.

CONSTANCE: Of course, we'll come. . . .

PAMELA: No, she doesn't wear underwear, lovely.

CONSTANCE: Yes, we'll come round after. If you'd like us to. . . .

PAMELA: Isn't there a touring date in Vietnam?

CONSTANCE: No, I was up, anyway. . . . 'Bye. . . .

PAMELA: Well done.

CONSTANCE: I could hardly be rude to her could I? I don't know her.

[Door bell]

PAMELA: Oh, God, open house! I *will* go to bed.

MURRAY: I'm sorry——

PAMELA: No. Not you.

[CONSTANCE goes to the door. EDWARD is there. Looks about twenty-eight]

PAMELA: What do you want?

CONSTANCE: Edward.

EDWARD: Sorry. I saw your light.

PAMELA: No, you didn't. You just rang. Why don't you knock up Abigail in the middle of the night. She likes pure, spontaneous gestures.

EDWARD: I just left her. I went to her dress rehearsal.

CONSTANCE: Come in then. Have a drink. You know Murray.

EDWARD: Hi.

MURRAY: How was it? The dress rehearsal.

EDWARD: Oh, O.K. I was in the bar in the middle act with some of the kids.

PAMELA: Fine.

EDWARD: I guess it was all right. I just think plays are a bit of a drag.

CONSTANCE: Didn't you do one last year?

EDWARD: Yeah. But six weeks was all I could take. And I had to fire the director and keep fighting to keep the author out and all that jazz.

PAMELA: That and never knowing his lines and getting drunk and not turning up twice a week.

EDWARD: We broke the house record.

PAMELA: You're a big star, darling. One epic in two and a half years and a nose job.

EDWARD: Am I in the way?

CONSTANCE: Not at all.

PAMELA: Would you mind?

CONSTANCE: We can't get Pamela to go to bed.

EDWARD: No. Well, it's early.

PAMELA: Why aren't you out hell raising or whatever you do in the newspapers.

EDWARD: Things are pretty quiet. Don't know where everybody is.

PAMELA: London's full of interesting people, especially for you, Edward. I don't know why you're called a hell raiser—it's only getting drunk all night—that and working at being louder and more Welsh than even you are—and you've got a very poor head. No dollies tonight?

EDWARD: Well, Sue's at home. But I thought I'd look around.

PAMELA: Sue won't take that so well. She likes to go out with you. She's like the old line about justice—not only must be done but must be seen to be done. Why don't you two go to bed?

CONSTANCE: What about you?

PAMELA: I'm coming, I'll put the lights out and get rid of Edward.

EDWARD: Any brandy in the house?

CONSTANCE: Sure. Murray? How about you?

MURRAY: All right. I'll take one to bed with me.

CONSTANCE: Please don't keep her up, Edward. She's flaked out.

EDWARD: Right. *[Helping himself]*

MURRAY: Good night, Pamela; I hope your father's better.

PAMELA: Thanks.

CONSTANCE: Don't forget. If you want *anything* tomorrow. I'm so sorry about tonight.

PAMELA: I'm sorry.

[CONSTANCE embraces her. MURRAY watches]

CONSTANCE: Good night, Edward.

EDWARD: 'Night.

[MURRAY and CONSTANCE go into bedroom]

EDWARD: Big thing going?

PAMELA: I imagine so.

EDWARD: Things same at the hospital then?

PAMELA: Yes. Sorry to be rude, Edward. But you should know by now. You're thirty-four, even if you do say you're thirty-one.

EDWARD: How do you know?

PAMELA: I always know these things. I will go to bed in a minute, so let yourself out when you've finished, will you?

EDWARD: Sure.

PAMELA: Why don't you go back to your famous bachelor pad. Sue'll be in a state if she doesn't know where you are.

EDWARD: I'll let myself out.

PAMELA: You ring her and say you're on your way if you like. Shall I?

EDWARD: You know, Pam, I've always thought you were a very sexy kid.

PAMELA: You told me the other week for about five hours. Well, I'm rather disappointing, I believe, and I'm twenty-six and I'm no kid.

EDWARD: You're not twenty-six but you've got a lot going. I never saw Orme in *Macbeth*. What was he like?

PAMELA: The best.

EDWARD: So they tell me. Bit before my time.

PAMELA: Too bored to bother, you mean.

[He picks up cutting book]

EDWARD: Here he is. Playing Arthur Bellenden. Of the Twenty-first London Regiment. Act One. Nutley Towers. A Friday evening. He looks quite something.

PAMELA: He was—he was ravishing.

EDWARD: Act II. The Conservatory, Nutley. Sunday evening. Act III. The Marskby Drawing Room. Fitzroy Square. Monday evening. What's it called?

PAMELA: *The Call of Duty.*

EDWARD: Good stuff. Orchestra under the direction of Mr. Reginald Garston. What's this entracte?

PAMELA: Quite ravishing.

EDWARD: Shaftesbury Theatre, May 7, 1922. Here's a good one. *The Undecided Adventuress.* Wonder what she couldn't decide.

PAMELA: Marry or a life of sin. Great long thighs.

EDWARD: "Master, you owe on the firm seven thousand pounds. If it's not deposited in the company's bank by midday on Monday, you shall have to face up to the dishonour. Your rank is nothing to me. I will brook no arguments, no entreaties. Not even for the sake of Effie." Effie! "You have brought disgrace enough on her already." I'm sorry. I didn't mean anything.

PAMELA: Why not try Abigail again?

EDWARD: She's tired.

PAMELA: Tired. I'm sure she'd accommodate *you* if you persist.

EDWARD: She's not all that great at it, anyway.

[Phone rings]

EDWARD: Don't worry. I'll go. Shall I take it?

[She nods. He takes phone]

EDWARD: Yeah . . . Hang on . . . Pauline.

[PAMELA goes]

PAMELA: What is it? I'm asleep. I'm asleep. I'm trying to stay asleep. . . . When? Why didn't you ring before . . . I could have come then. . . . No, I'll come down later . . . I've taken a pill. Oh, Mother can make all the arrangements. She'll enjoy all that. . . . No, don't put her on. . . . Hello. . . . No, well, I mistimed it, didn't I? . . . Please don't get hysterical *now*, it's bad timing. . . . No, I can't. . . . Get Andrew . . . get Andrew to come down. . . . Yes. . . . Later. *[She puts the phone down]*

EDWARD: Pamela. I'm so sorry. I suppose you're not surprised. Can I get you a drink?

PAMELA: There's one more bottle of champagne in the fridge. *[EDWARD goes to get it. She looks at the open cuttings book, while he opens the fresh bottle]* A Weekend Gentleman.

He was a vile seducer in that. "And your unborn child. You shall never see it, Gerald. I shall see to it that it grows up in sweetness and ignorance, far, far away from where your guilty hands can ever find her." Sounds like a paedophiliac or whatever.

EDWARD: What's that?

PAMELA: Someone who likes children. No, he wouldn't have played that. He would have thought it most improper. Besides, it would have made him giggle. He was a terrible giggler. He must have been the other man. They didn't like him to be a rotter. When he was, he was a frightful flop. And he giggled too much. *[She raises her freshly filled champagne glass]* Oh, Orme. . . . Orme . . . my darling. . . .

EDWARD: Shall I stay a little?

PAMELA: If you like. We can finish this together.

CURTAIN

ACT TWO

Same scene. Some weeks later. PAMELA *is in a nightdress and dressing gown. It is late afternoon. She is drinking a glass of champagne. In the room are* EDITH *and* PAULINE. EDITH *is rather formally dressed. Even* PAULINE *is slightly subdued.*

EDITH: I still think you should have come.

PAMELA: So you said.

EDITH: There were quite a lot of people there. After all, when you think he hadn't been on the stage for about ten years. And a whole generation have hardly even heard of him.

PAMELA: You sound as if you're surprised there was anyone there. After all, you're the one responsible for the thing happening. Orme would have hated the idea. I don't think he ever went to a memorial service in his life. He'd have laughed his head off at the idea, rows of his friends having to listen to Handel and Wesley and knighted actors reading the lesson. He'd have thought it very common.

EDITH: I don't think he'd have said that.

PAMELA: Well, it wasn't for me. It was for Orme.

EDITH: I saw Constance there.

PAMELA: Well, she likes a good blub. It's like singing the "Red Flag" to her.

EDITH: And that man in the opposition Front Bench. The one who's so hot on the arts. You always see him at Covent Garden.

PAMELA: Can't think. Tory poove I suppose.

EDITH: After all, he *was* knighted himself. He can't have been that aloof.

PAMELA: Mama: only because he knew you wanted it so much. Which is why he kept turning it down until after you'd broken up.

EDITH: I hope that's not true. It sounds very petty. And if it is true, it isn't kind to point it out.

PAMELA: Wit very often is petty, mama, and, knowing him, I can't honestly believe it hadn't occurred to him. I told him it was petty myself. And rather common. However, he didn't make too many mistakes. And today's circus he can't be held responsible for. That's your fault.

EDITH: In that case, there may be a certain ironic justice in it.

PAMELA: You really didn't like him, did you? How's the bookshop, Pauline?

PAULINE: Oh, I goofed over that. I went broke in two weeks. Don't know why. Business was fine. Management, I guess. That's what Dave thinks.

EDITH: Have you been out, Pamela?

PAMELA: Out?

EDITH: Since the funeral. You never seem to answer the telephone.

PAMELA: I take sleeping pills during the day and turn off the telephone. Constance doesn't like it. I think she's terrified the prime minister will ring up and there's no one to take the message. She's getting an answering service.

EDITH: Very wise. I should think you must be losing offers, don't you?

PAMELA: Work? I shouldn't think so.

EDITH: I mean people will probably think of you at the moment.

PAMELA: People never think of me as Orme's daughter. There's too much space between us. Besides, you don't get offered work like compassionate leave. They leave you alone. They'd rather. It only reminds them. So what are you doing, Pauline? Changing your scene then?

PAULINE: Yes. Dave and I thought we'd try the sun for a bit.

PAMELA: Oh, yes, I've had offers of going to the sun. It's a little like when your chap has left you. They suddenly remember you and see if you're on top again.

PAULINE: Oh, Spain. Somewhere. . . .

EDITH: But you'll need to work again soon, won't you? You haven't done anything for ages.

PAMELA: That's right.

EDITH: I mean you do know Gideon's left hardly anything except a few debts and mementoes, which he seems to have left mostly to you.

PAMELA: They're not worth much. He had a comfortable retirement.

EDITH: Don't you think you ought to be looking? Seriously?

PAMELA: Don't worry, mama. I shan't come to you for anything.

EDITH: Isn't your agent, Bernard what'saname, doing anything for you?

PAMELA: If there's anything, he'll come and knock the door down and wake me up. I think the time comes when you no longer follow the sun. Orme and I used to go to the west coast of Scotland—at least we did a couple of years running. I'm rather bored with my useless golden body. It's had thousands lavished on it in air fares and sun oil and hundreds of broiler bikinis. I think I shall use a sunshade. I'm tired of juggling face down with my bra straps and all that. I think a sun tan is definitely vulgar. It's like dieting. *That's* vulgar. It's just uncollected effort.

PAULINE: You're lucky.

PAMELA: No, I'm fastidious, fortunately I don't like rich food. And I don't like getting drunk in a certain way. That's vulgar. You and Dave both diet, don't you? I'm not surprised. He's far too fat for a man of his age. What is he—twelve? He eats too much and drinks too much. You can't eat *and* drink. One or the other. Orme drank. Better for you. If you drink the right thing.

PAULINE: Dave doesn't drink.

PAMELA: Well, sitting around smoking pot in groups is vulgar. So are nervous breakdowns. Meretricious. I've had at least three. I lay in them like I used to water ski and play tennis. Like I made love at your age. With those acrobatic, expert wogs in Milan and Paris. Mind you, I always *used* people like ski-instructors. I promised them nothing and gave them nothing. Instructors. Like theatre directors. Only faggots and middle-aged women in books written by faggots have affairs with ski-instructors.

EDITH: But what are you going to do, Pamela?

PAMELA: I told you. I shall probably take my sunshade to the South of France for a week or two. It's warm and I can drink champagne and swim. I like to swim still. And I can usually avoid anyone I know. I'll wear a black armband. I've got a couple of nice new frocks that will go very well with it.

EDITH: You don't have any work, any aim, hardly any friends now, except for a few——

PAMELA: Homosexuals? Well, they've mostly given me up. I'm ultimately unrewarding to them. Which is just as well. Except for Bernard, of course. If you're a woman or a moll, you do have to spend quite a lot of energy flattering them with your sympathy and admiration and performing like captured prize dogs for them. I think Bernard's different. But they do conform to their archetype. Like most sizeable pressure groups, I suppose, and not even poor liberal Constance can really escape the fact, beyond all her parliamentary recommendations, that as a group they *are* uniformly bitchy, envious, self-seeking, fickle, and usually without passion.

EDITH: You do generalize, Pamela.

PAMELA: Mama, if you've never had the discomfort of having what are commonly known as crabs—which I know you haven't—do listen to someone who has suffered from them constantly. Even Bernard agrees with me. In fact, I think he said it to me.

PAULINE: Is Constance going to marry that guy?

PAMELA: I expect so. Yes, I expect I shall have to change my scene. Constance is very accomplished. She can cook every sort of cooking, write books, give you an opinion on anything from Marxist criticism of the novel to Godard, she's even managed to get herself a child, an ex-husband, and now a well-thought-of lover.

EDITH: Perhaps you should try writing a book. You could do a biography of Gideon. Who could be better?

PAMELA: Not me. He wouldn't want it either.

EDITH: Or a novel. Look at the people you've met in the past ten years or so, not just in your own line.

PAMELA: You're like Constance.

EDITH: Well, she's right. You don't look at all well. Staying indoors, sleeping all day for weeks on end, living on champagne. Which you can't afford.

PAMELA: One of the several reasons I am getting out of here is that I fancy Constance is going to write a book with me in it. You should always beware of lady writers. They hover and dart about like preying fish in a tank. They've their eyes on you and little tape recorders whining away behind their ears by way of breathing apparatus. Then they swallow you up whole and spew you up later, dead and distorted. Nothing has happened to you in the meantime except that they turn you into waste material. Because the trouble with lady writers is they've usually no digestive juices. They're often even surprised you're not pleased. There, I gobbled you up whole. Aren't I swift, don't I move, don't I watch. Like hell you do. You just can't deal with it decently once you've got it. That friend of yours—oh, Mildred—that one did it to *me* once.

EDITH: I didn't think she meant it was you.

PAMELA: She wasn't sure whether to be pleased when people recognized me, or to just pass it off as her own inventive craft.

EDITH: I can't remember.

PAMELA: She even described me physically—she's a mess herself, of course. Then a quick rundown on my character and finished up patronizing me for being less intellectually perceptive, and so ending up as a puppet—and I mean puppet —in her clever dickdyke thirty bobs' worth, and not being similarly bright enough to write a book about her and the mess *she* is.

EDITH: You're not being fair to Mildred. She's got quite a reputation.

PAMELA: She has.

EDITH: You're unfair to everyone. Including yourself.

PAMELA: I hope so. Help. You've seen I'm still around, mama, why don't you get back. Your old man must be worried about you.

EDITH: I'm concerned about you, Pamela.

PAMELA: Well, don't be. We've managed quite well without each other for about twenty years.

EDITH: It's not been easy.

PAMELA: I couldn't have changed it.

EDITH: What's going to happen to you?

PAMELA: I shall go on as I have done for twenty-nine years.

EDITH: As you say, you've never married or had children. Well, that's all right, there's no reason why you should if you don't feel the need to. At least people are beginning to realize a woman isn't a freak if she wants other things out of life. But there *are* other things, like work, yes, and having affairs and even making love. You can't want to stop all that at your age. You're young and intelligent and healthy and attractive. And a lot of people like you. Constance adores you. She says lots of people do and you aren't always aware of it.

PAMELA: Constance somtimes has her ear to the ground of the wrong building.

EDITH: You seem to have no impulse about these things, or even ordinary things like whether to move or take a holiday, go out or sit in the sun. I know you're upset about Gideon but you'd been like this for a long time before.

PAMELA: I shall manage within my own, my own walls. I've no ambitions. I've told you: I love acting. I'm not so keen on rehearsals. I don't wish to be judged or categorized or watched. I don't want to be pronounced upon or do it for anyone.

EDITH: Will you go back to your house?

PAMELA: I suppose so. At least it's mine.

EDITH: Won't it seem strange without a man about the house.

PAMELA: Really! Edith. No, it won't seem strange at all. *[Phone rings]* Answer it, will you? I'm out.

PAULINE: Hello. . . . Just a minute, I'll see. . . . It's your agent, Bernard. I thought you'd want to. . . .

EDITH: We'd better go,

PAMELA: It's nothing you can't hear. *[On phone]* Darling! How nice . . . Oh, I'm all right . . . Yes, really . . . Well, I've not been answering the phone . . . Well, I'm glad you didn't . . . I couldn't afford to get the door fixed . . . Oh, you went? . . . No . . . I know Orme wouldn't have gone for it . . . What made you go? . . . Oh, well, I'm glad you enjoyed it . . . It seems to have been a success. I thought it was all frightfully respectable. Who let you in, you great Jewish queen? . . . Oh, don't you start "what's your scening" me, baby! Well, you're a very mutton old hippy dressed up as lamb! And how are things for you? What a love life you do have . . . How do you find the time? No, I'm twenty-nine this week. Period of mourning has aged me for a bit. Till next week . . . You must tell me all about it . . . Yes, all the details . . . you know I must have them . . . I'll tell you . . . what . . . nothing . . . only my stepmother . . . yes, and my little stepsister . . . oh, years younger . . . can't you hear her shaking her cannabis rattle? *[Enter MURRAY front door. She motions him in]* All right, listen, Bernie . . . you know that address book of yours. The one with names of the gentlemen in it. Yes, Ladies' Services. Can you give me a few numbers and which names to mention when I ring? . . . No, of course I'm not, darling. After all this time . . . Yes, for a little friend . . . All right, ring me back. But don't leave it . . . Yes, well it *is* urgent. It always is, isn't it . . . Oh, and I'm changing my address. No, not scene, I'm going back to my house . . . Yes, of course, I'm all right . . . Right . . . soon now, mind . . . Hello, Murray. You know my mother and stepsister, Pauline.

MURRAY: How do you do.

EDITH: We'd better go. Do try and answer the phone. And let me know when you go back to the house. And try to get something to eat.

MURRAY: I'll see she gets something.

EDITH: I wish you would. Thank you.

MURRAY: Good-bye, Mrs—— . . .

[*Nobody helps.* EDITH *goes to kiss* PAMELA]

PAMELA: I haven't cleaned my teeth, mama. [*She lights a cigarette*] I'll give you a ring. [*The other two* WOMEN *go out*] You needn't bother to follow up that offer,

MURRAY: Are you sure?

PAMELA: Quite.

MURRAY: Do you think you should be drinking that?

PAMELA: Certainly. It's very good. My agent sent it round as a present. I think he must spend all his commission on it for me. I pay him ten percent and I seem to get it back in crates.

MURRAY: Was that who you were talking to?

PAMELA: He'd been to Orme's Memorial. He can't resist that sort of thing.

MURRAY: Connie went. I couldn't manage it.

PAMELA: She couldn't resist it either. I saw her all dressed up for it this morning. I went back to sleep.

MURRAY: What was, was that about Ladies' Services?

PAMELA: None of your business. Have some of this.

MURRAY: It is.

PAMELA: It was a private telephone conversation.

MURRAY: I can't pretend I didn't hear it. Come on. What are Ladies' Services?

PAMELA: What do you suppose?

MURRAY: Pamela?

PAMELA: What are you doing here?

MURRAY: Don't be pompous suddenly. I came to see you.

PAMELA: Constance will be here soon. She's only gone to a meeting. It was after Orme's do. I wish you'd go away. This, of course is the, I mean, this is it, the disadvantage, this is why you shouldn't, this is sharing with, with, yes, look, Murray, don't stand there just arrived, I don't need anything, yes, I'm

in the club, everything's in control, I'm sitting here with a
drink, I've got the telephone, I've got friends, I like you
quite a lot, but I'd like some, oh, privacy, I guess. Anyway,
I'd like to be alone, and not stared at, please go away, ring
up Constance, no, waylay her outside and take her to a movie
in Westbourne Grove or something. Things . . . are very . . .
easy.

MURRAY: Oh, Pamela, what's happened to us?

PAMELA: Don't "oh, Pamela" like that. You're another Constance.
We *aren't* alike. Nothing much has happened. I'm getting
out this evening. My mama decided me.

MURRAY: You mustn't do that.

PAMELA: I'm not getting out of anything that's necessarily happened. I'm just getting back to where I used to live, such as
it was. Not very much. But I can warm it up after a day or
two.

MURRAY: I'm going to tell Connie, I don't care what you say.

PAMELA: Do what you like. If you do, you're more feeble than I
thought.

MURRAY: You think I'm feeble then?

PAMELA: Oh, yes. Don't you?

MURRAY: What do you mean?

PAMELA: You just want to be spoilt and cossetted because you've
convinced Constance and I suppose others I don't know about
that there's something special about you. What it is I don't
know.

MURRAY: And *you* don't want spoiling?

PAMELA: No. And you couldn't do it, anyway.

MURRAY: We could do all sorts of things.

PAMELA: Like?

MURRAY: Like, for instance . . .

PAMELA: Spare me a list . . .

MURRAY: What do you mean: feeble?

PAMELA: Immature, I suppose.

MURRAY: That's what women usually say about men when they
can't keep up with them.

PAMELA: I dare say. We don't match up, you see.

MURRAY: What are you going to do?

PAMELA: I wish everyone would just stop asking me: what am I going to do. I am going to get up and I am going to go to sleep, if I've got enough to knock me out. I'm going to speak to Bernard and get his list of Ladies' Services.

MURRAY: And then what?

PAMELA: I shall go back to my little house and one day I shall pick up the telephone when it rings. And if it doesn't ring, never mind. I may have to ring someone else instead. If they're in . . .

MURRAY: I shall come round to the house.

PAMELA: Oh, for God's sake.

MURRAY: I mean it.

PAMELA: Then I suppose I'll have to go and stay with Bernard. He'll look after me and he'll get the police on to you. He'll enjoy that.

MURRAY: I do love you.

PAMELA: Well, even if you do . . .

MURRAY: What is it?

PAMELA: What is what?

MURRAY: Haven't you got anything to say to me?

PAMELA: No, Murray. Not really. We've had a good time together, because we've hardly been together——

MURRAY: We could be . . .

PAMELA: Well, we won't be . . .

MURRAY: Why not?

PAMELA: My nose says so.

MURRAY: Mine says the opposite.

PAMELA: Well, I rely on mine. Not yours. But, anyway, it's had its pleasure. Don't renounce them. I've been looking at Abigail's notices. Before my mama and little sister arrived.

MURRAY: You want me to stay with Connie?

PAMELA: No.

MURRAY: Well?

PAMELA: You will find each other. Or not. I don't want to talk about it. I won't be involved in your life, or hers. I'm sorry for both of you. *Not* much. A bit. You'll manage, so shall we all. Just remember: what I should do now or at any time is nothing to do with either of you. I owe you no confidence.

MURRAY: Pamela, let's talk about it.

PAMELA: You always want to talk about it. I don't want to, I'm not going to. Now go or talk about something else. Anyway, I'm getting dressed. And I don't like being watched.

MURRAY: You'll change your mind. You will. There's always time for that. I know the handling of you. I really do.

PAMELA: Good. Like a horse. Did you go to Abigail's play? Oh, yes, you went with Constance. She didn't seem to like it much. Did you?

MURRAY: Quite. She seemed to enjoy it to me.

PAMELA: Ah! She said it was really about a sort of regional mysticism that didn't or couldn't, er, engage her, oh, attention, her full interest.

MURRAY: I don't think the play was really about regional mysticism. Whatever that . . .

PAMELA: Indeed?

MURRAY: No, it was surely about . . .

PAMELA: I can't wait. Tell me.

MURRAY: I don't understand you, Pamela. You seem to treat people as if they weren't there sometimes. As if they were just walk ons. What's happened?

PAMELA: Oh, Murray, do stop.

MURRAY: All these gibes, and immaturity—and your paternalist female ripeness.

PAMELA: Oh, very good, Murray. You sound like the character in your play.

MURRAY: You haven't even read it.

PAMELA: Yes, I have. I read very slowly. Like everything else.

MURRAY: You can't be serious about Ladies' Services?

PAMELA: My dear, it's like going to the crimpers. Only more expensive. I may have to borrow some money from you.

MURRAY: I'll give it to you, of course.

PAMELA: You'll lend it to me. No, you won't. I'll borrow it from Bernard. I owe him enough already, but never mind.

MURRAY: You must.

PAMELA: I mustn't anything. I'd go to Wee Willie Wonder—

MURRAY: Wee who?

PAMELA: Wee Willie Wonder. My gynaecologist. But he'd only give me a lecture. Oh, he'd do it.

MURRAY: Is he a moralist too?

PAMELA: Not he. He's not one of those bear down and be joyful queens. He'd just lecture me.

MURRAY: What about?

PAMELA: Like you, like mama and Constance. Except that he knows me better. Anyway, he's a nice sensitive man. He'll worry about me and reproach himself and I'll have him coming round to the house.

MURRAY: How did it happen?

PAMELA: What? Oh, guess.

MURRAY: Has it . . . ?

PAMELA: No, it's never happened before. At least I've not dried up like an old prune, after all. You've proved that. That should please you. Still, even Wee Willie nods sometimes. And it's a mysterious, capricious place in there. Especially mine. Not surprising. It feels like a Bosch triptych often enough. It's been better lately, I thought it was odd.

MURRAY: What do you mean: that should please you?

PAMELA: Oh, your eyes. Not just now. I used to see it in my previous gentleman's face sometimes—before he left me. When he was making love to me. He never said anything. He was too reticent. I suppose it's a question of if you become literally substantial they can luxuriate in their abstraction with a nice trailing guide line to mother earth. Trailing guide line, I've said that out of your play. There, you see, I read very carefully. Do go, Murray. I want to get undressed and I feel shy with you about the place and Constance will be back and it's quite clear you're longing to tell her. Well, I can't stop you. But I don't want her solicitude and being practical and sustaining all of us. I'm quite practical enough for myself. And I don't want to sustain all of us. Even if you two do, and I know you will. You're all bent on incest or some cosy hysteria. She's bound to blub. You're not above it, and we'll all end up on the floor embracing and comforting and rationalizing and rumpled and snorting and jammed together and performing autopsies and quite disgusting, all of it. You both are. Don't indulge her. Just because she demands it.

MURRAY: What?

PAMELA: She was brought up on the principle of fulfilment in as many spheres as possible. As a statutory obligation. I'm only saying don't always give in to her, and not now. There isn't any statutory level of fufilment we're entitled to. I've tried to explain it to Constance. I've told her it leads to excess and deception. It's difficult to talk to her about a lot of things. She either reduces them to worthy sounding principles or theorizes them so that they relate to any old thing. She's a very coarse woman, I'm afraid.

MURRAY: Have you ever told her?

PAMELA: No. It would hurt her. She'd mind. Besides, I'm fond of her. I used to think we were alike. I take so long to find things out. Dear God, I am always so far behind. She's also rather coarse when she talks about sex. Oh, I know what you think. Lust is o.k. by me. But not when it's ambitious and gluttonous and avaricious. Then it's vulgar. Very vulgar indeed. You shouldn't wear those shirts she gives you. If you want to look really sharp, and you obviously do, you need something a bit more expensive than that. Give me your measurements. I'll go to Jermyn Street in the morning. It'll give me something to do.

MURRAY: Pamela . . .

PAMELA: I haven't cleaned my teeth. Something in silk. A very pale brown I think. And a dark, velvety tie. It would look terribly good. You've not been around long enough. I usually refit most of my gentlemen completely. Pity. Your wardrobe needs a bit of a cast out. Don't let Constance buy too many things for you. And simply remember, you should know by now, you're twenty-nine, you're only a few years older than me: one and one don't make two or three. They sometimes don't even add up to one. [Phone rings] Answer that, there's a good boy. If it's my mother, I've had an enormous bowl of nourishing soup, a boiled egg, and gone to bed to sleep it off.

MURRAY: *[On phone]* Yes? Your agent . . .

PAMELA: Darling . . . That's good . . . Please . . . You're quite wrong . . . No, don't come round . . . Listen, could you hang on a minute . . . Murray, are you going?

MURRAY: I suppose I'd better.

PAMELA: You didn't mean that about coming round to my house?

MURRAY: I don't know. Perhaps not, after all.

PAMELA: I wouldn't put it past Constance. Oh, and there's Edith. Cheer up. We'll go out together sometimes. Not the three of us. My nice coloured gentleman will be back soon. You'll like him. He's frightfully New Statesman. Nice though. Fastidious.

MURRAY: 'Bye, Pamela.

PAMELA: 'Bye. *[On phone]* No, Bernard, it's someone here. Murray . . . Yes, that one. Some of my friends have got real brains, they're not all sex-happy queens like you. Though he's very sexy . . . No, nothing for you, darling. At least, I don't fancy so . . . Actually, I've just read the play he's written. I think you ought to look at it. I know you're not but you might have some ideas. You know everybody. And if you do do anything for him, I want a percentage . . . I'm very poor, Bernard . . . What do you mean, I always . . . He's just going . . . I'll give you his number . . . It'll be worth your while. He's going to be very big. I know it. You know what a success nose I have with people. Didn't I tell you Abigail was going to be the biggest star since Garbo . . . ? I know I told you not to take her on . . . I'd have left you if you had . . . You're not that tasteless. Or greedy. *[To* MURRAY*]* What's your number, darling? *[He looks at her and goes out. To* BERNARD *on phone]* Oh, I think he's gone. I'll give it to you, the play. Look, darling, could you really help me? . . . Could I come and stay with you for a few days? . . . I told you, I'm fine. I just don't want to stay here any longer and I can't face that little house for a bit. My mama'll only come round and she doesn't know you . . . Well, that's your fortune . . . are you sure, really? . . . I won't stay long and I'll not inter-

fere with your love life, well I know that's impossible . . .
Who is he? . . . He sounds divine . . . bless you . . . yes, I've
got a paper and pencil. Right, Ladies' Services . . . Dr.
Gradski . . .

[CONSTANCE *comes in carrying parcels*]

CONSTANCE: Just missed Murray getting into a taxi. [PAMELA
blows her a kiss] Oh, sorry. [*She goes into the kitchen, un-
wraps parcels of food, coming in and out*]

PAMELA: [*On phone*] Yes . . . who do I mention . . . how much
. . . Dr. who? . . . You're kidding . . . yes . . . Don't seem
many Smiths or Browns . . . Sure these aren't the names of
agents you're giving me? . . . Oh, I know him, I met him with
you, the one who procures for you . . . oh, come off it . . .
Yes . . . another . . . That'll do. I'll try these first . . . and
then I'll . . . might as well shop around. No . . . Darling,
don't, please. I'll make my own way. There's not much to
talk . . . Oh, all right . . . half an hour . . . [*To* CONSTANCE]
How are you?

CONSTANCE: I'm fine.

PAMELA: What's all that?

CONSTANCE: Goodies. I've just been to Fortnums. We're all going
to have a smashing meal. I bought some Dom Perignon. I've
just put it in the fridge. That isn't the one you don't like,
is it?

PAMELA: That's fine.

CONSTANCE: I'll ring Murray. I've been thinking about you all
day. I rushed away from my meeting. There's some scent
for you.

PAMELA: Darling——

CONSTANCE: I'm going to look after you. I've been talking to Murray. He's very worried about you. I've been too soft with you.
I wished you'd been there this morning. I think you'd have
changed your mind.

PAMELA: I don't need looking after, darling. Lovely scent. I'll put
some on.

CONSTANCE: We owe it to one another.

PAMELA: No, we don't. You and Murray should have this place to yourselves.

CONSTANCE: Nonsense. What could be nicer? Besides, Murray's not getting rid of his flat. We both agreed on that.

PAMELA: I must go.

CONSTANCE: He doesn't want it.

PAMELA: Maybe not. I've got a few things packed.

CONSTANCE: But you don't mean you're going tonight? What about dinner?

PAMELA: I'm sorry, but I've got to have dinner with Bernard. He wants me to meet some film producer. It's rather important. I'll have some of the Dom Perignon with a bit of ice in it though. That's sacrilege for you.

CONSTANCE: Pamela, what's wrong? My darling. Tell me. Why don't you talk to me?

PAMELA: I've stayed long enough.

CONSTANCE: What is it? I thought you were happy with me. We do get on, don't we?

PAMELA: Sure. But I need to get away for a bit.

CONSTANCE: You mean a holiday? We could all go together. Why don't we? What a super idea.

PAMELA: I'm going with Bernard to the South of France. One of his friends has got a villa. I don't think it's what Pauline calls your scene. It's not really mine.

CONSTANCE: Murray would be fascinated, I'm sure.

PAMELA: I think Murray might inhibit them a bit. No, I'll just sit by the pool and become a golden girl again. I've been looking at my body . . . look at it. A sort of dirty yellow cigarette-stain colour.

CONSTANCE: You look stunning.

PAMELA: Sorry about your dinner. You and Murray can have a nice candlelight session alone together. You don't mind Bernard coming round?

CONSTANCE: No. I'm a bit dazed. I don't know whether I want to cook now.

PAMELA: You must feed up Murray. Spoil him. He likes spoiling. And why not?

CONSTANCE: I'll pack for you, if you must . . .

PAMELA: Don't bother. I'll leave most of it . . . for now. Just talk to me while I undress.

[She moves between her bedroom and the drawing room, dressing and packing in a casual way, talking. At one point in the bedroom she is naked. CONSTANCE *wanders about following her, rather helplessly, smoking and watching her every movement]*

CONSTANCE: I brought you the evening papers.

PAMELA: More rave notices for Lady Tinker-Bell, I suppose?

CONSTANCE: Oh, yes, "all that's permanently in the air."

PAMELA: Did you and Murray enjoy it?

CONSTANCE: I think Murray quite liked it. He liked her, anyway, you'll be sorry to hear.

PAMELA: I'm not sorry.

CONSTANCE: I think he thought she'd be good in his play. I think I see what you mean. But she certainly gets the audience and the critics.

PAMELA: You bet. Went out of their frigid little minds. Still, I suppose there's always hope on Sunday.

CONSTANCE: I see you've got all the papers then.

PAMELA: Yes, mama brought them. She seemed to think I'd want to see them. She's also a great fan of Abigail's too. Natch. Bet she wishes she had a daughter like that.

CONSTANCE: This one says something good about the play too . . . "Finely wrought and blessedly well constructed."

PAMELA: That means it's like a travelling clock. You can see all the works. That way you know it must keep the right time.

[She goes into the bedroom. CONSTANCE *watches her from the doorway with the papers]*

CONSTANCE: . . . "What a relief to hear every syllable superbly and uniquely delivered."

PAMELA: Why doesn't he own up he's deaf? He was the only critic who couldn't hear Orme. And he had a voice like a

ton of Welsh nuts. I don't mind people being old as long
as they're not bullying with it.

CONSTANCE: I think there's actually one with "mystery behind the
eyes." Yes, here it is: "a fugitive, self-scrutinizing mystery."

PAMELA: Self-absorbed he means. He's hardly taken his eyes off
the leading man all evening. He's the one who made that
little play I was in sound so worthy and full of painful si-
lences and hauntingly expressed, delicate agonies or something. Kept them away in droves. Mind you, it *was* a bit
worthy, all greys and browns and sort of obsessed with being
rarefied and staring you out with austerity. I got good notices,
specially from him. I knew I would. It was a sympathetic,
bearing-down part. All I had to do was upstage myself and
keep a straight back. Sounds like cricket, doesn't it. I got stuff
about my repose and troubled enchantment and the impression of a powerful intelligence in perfect unison with heart-
aching turmoil. Something like that.

CONSTANCE: Well, you remembered it.

PAMELA: Even I remember some jokes. Actually, I wasn't really
thinking about anything. I just kept trying to think what
Orme would have done. He didn't think too much of it. He
said, you're giving your critics' performance. So, I said I
know, but I've got to get on sometimes. And he didn't say
anything. Except: that's all right. As long as you know it.
Try and give the audience the real thing sometimes. Would
you like me to do Abigail for you? [CONSTANCE *laughs*] You
can't miss if you do that. They go off their heads.

CONSTANCE: Gosh, you've got a beautiful body.

PAMELA: As I say, you have to be frigid to be one of them.

CONSTANCE: You really are permanently brown all over. You
haven't got those awful bra cup marks.

PAMELA: You need to be three things: timid, aggressive, and frigid.
T.A.F. Like Welsh.

CONSTANCE: This one seems to have lost the point completely.

PAMELA: Probably wasn't listening, poor darling. Who is it? Oh,
he's the one who sends me those dreadful telly plays he
writes. Takes the part for the whole—as the actress said to

the critic. Don't look so glum. I've just made a joke. I thought
you were mad about jokes?

CONSTANCE: I hate to see you go. Do these upset you?

PAMELA: It takes more than an Abigail to make me give up. It's
all like the weather. As for them, there's something funda-
mentally wrong with you if you want to do that. Something
missing. I've noticed it. When you meet them. Impotence.
That's why when they've been really nasty, they try to in-
gratiate if you're ever unlucky enough to meet one. "Oh, did
I say that? I'm sure I've said other things. I've always ad-
mired your work."

CONSTANCE: You're looking better.

PAMELA: I feel it. Thinking of Abigail and all those people being
hoaxed. Put some ice in that lovely Dom Perignon.

CONSTANCE: Good idea. You seem almost superstitious about her.

PAMELA: How?

CONSTANCE: Well, it's as if she didn't take everybody in, you'd be
disappointed.

PAMELA: I suppose I would; they might have taste.

CONSTANCE: Wouldn't it be better if they did?

PAMELA: It would. But they haven't.

CONSTANCE: It seems to give you back your energy. You're so
afraid of losing it.

PAMELA: So would you. It's a delicate plant. Not like your great
climbing tree.

CONSTANCE: No. I have to flog mine. You're right. But good fortune, if you like, seems to fill you with dread.

PAMELA: Dread never is very far away, is it? Here's to success!
Um. Delicious.

CONSTANCE: It'll seem strange not having you drink champagne
about the place. We usually drink whisky when we're together. Murray, I mean. It's only when we're with you. Perhaps you've converted us. He really loves you.

PAMELA: You can't afford it. Champagne I mean. Well, not Dom
Perignon.

CONSTANCE: Darling, please stay. You need love more than anyone I've ever known. And looking after. We'll both do it.

PAMELA: You look after Murray. He's the sort who needs it. Clever men need a lot of pampering. They have a hard time in some ways, I think.

CONSTANCE: Pamela, why don't you play the part in his play?

PAMELA: I thought he liked the idea of Abigail? If he can get her.

CONSTANCE: I think you'd be much better.

PAMELA: Tell a management that.

CONSTANCE: Gosh, actresses get ready quickly.

PAMELA: We have to.

CONSTANCE: You did like it, didn't you?

PAMELA: Yes. I'm giving it to Bernard. He might have some ideas.

CONSTANCE: What did you think of it?

PAMELA: Actually, he did ask me if I'd do it.

CONSTANCE: Well?

PAMELA: I don't really understand it, Constance. Perhaps I'm not clever enough.

CONSTANCE: You don't mean it. You don't like it. Did you tell him?

PAMELA: No. Why? What's my opinion! You like it. I'm sure a lot of people will.

CONSTANCE: But why? He respects your opinion.

PAMELA: Well, tell him not to.

CONSTANCE: What's wrong with it?

PAMELA: Oh, please. Don't hedge me in. Authors should never go peddling in the marketplace.

CONSTANCE: I know. It's vulgar.

PAMELA: Quite. Oh, all right, if you must. I think it's, yes, clever. It's full of erudite banalities. It's not a play, it's a posture by a clever annotator, a labeller. People sit around and make up Freudian epigrams about one another. It's written by someone thinking about writing it instead of thinking about whatever it's about. Do I make myself incomprehensible? I'm afraid it's catching from that script. I'm sorry, darling.

CONSTANCE: It seems as if just everything is over. You're going away. The recess'll be over soon.

PAMELA: It was never to be a permanent arrangement.

CONSTANCE: No. Perhaps I had deluded myself that it would be, somehow.

PAMELA: It's always tempting but one must guard against the more likely possibilities.

CONSTANCE: Pamela, why were you taking down those phone numbers?

PAMELA: Oh, my God. I must ring them before I go. Ladies' Services, darling. Somebody in need.

CONSTANCE: Who?

PAMELA: No one you know.

CONSTANCE: Who?

PAMELA: Audrey—the girl in the crimpers. Silly girl. I thought they all took the pill those girls now.

CONSTANCE: Aren't you taking a risk.

PAMELA: Darling, I'm just helping the poor girl out. Hope she can afford it. Oh, don't look like that. What does one do— wait for the third reading in the Lords?

CONSTANCE: Darling, you will keep in touch, won't you?

PAMELA: Of course. I always do. Don't blub, darling. Have a nice dinner and a cuddle with Murray.

CONSTANCE: Sorry. I blub too easily.

PAMELA: Yes. You do. You must learn to do it without letting your mascara run. It's quite an easy trick. I'll show you.

[Doorbell rings]

CONSTANCE: Damn! Don't go yet. Please. When's Bernard coming?

PAMELA: I said half an hour. He'll be late.

CONSTANCE: Might be Murray. Hope so. I'll make *him* talk you out of it.

[She goes to the door. EDWARD stands there, slightly drunk, with ABIGAIL beside him. She is dressed in Men's Carnaby Street clothes. She also wears a theatrical moustache. It is almost possible to mistake her for a man at first glance, but only just. It is just the starlit ABIGAIL]

EDWARD: Hi.

CONSTANCE: Edward. Come in. What——?

EDWARD: Is Pamela up?

CONSTANCE: She's just dressing. I don't know . . . Is it . . . Why, Abigail!

ABIGAIL: Constance, love!

CONSTANCE: Do you know, I really didn't recognize you. Good heavens. You look, you look marvellous. What, what happened?

EDWARD: She looks a gas doesn't she? Pamela! *[To* CONSTANCE*]* Don't say anything—— *[They come in]* How are you, darling? Better?

PAMELA: Hello, Eddie. I'm all right, darling. Just coming. Constance, give him some of your expensive champagne.

CONSTANCE: I'll get it.

*[*PAMELA *appears. She stares at* ABIGAIL, *who is seated in the centre of the room]*

PAMELA: Who's your friend? Good God! . . .

CONSTANCE: I was wondering if you'd be taken in. I was. Just for a moment. Doesn't she look marvellous.

EDWARD: We thought it was fun.

PAMELA: Hilarious. Where have you been like that?

ABIGAIL: Well, darling, how are you, you look really beautiful, honestly more than ever. I adore your hair.

PAMELA: I haven't been to the crimpers for two weeks.

ABIGAIL: Well, we had this night last night, you see, what with everything.

CONSTANCE: Oh, congratulations.

PAMELA: Yes.

ABIGAIL: Thank you, my darlings.

PAMELA: Did you get my telegram?

ABIGAIL: Yes, darling. Bless you. Isn't it marvellous? I can't believe it.

PAMELA: I don't know why. I find it only too believable. I thought I'd forgotten to send that telegram.

ABIGAIL: Eddie's been super. We had an absolute rave night. The management gave a party. That looked like being a bit draggy.

EDWARD: I'll say.

ABIGAIL: No, but darling, everyone was so sweet. And, you know, all the old excitement, and, oh well, you know what it's like, Pamela.

EDWARD: Hey, Connie, where's your record player. We just bought a fabulous record.

ABIGAIL: Oh, yes, Eddie. Do play it for them. Pamela will adore it. I'm mad about it.

PAMELA: So you did what?

ABIGAIL: Oh, yes, well there was the first night, and, well it was extraordinary. I don't remember much. I know I cried at the call.

EDWARD: They were hanging from the ceiling. It was a cert. You could tell.

ABIGAIL: You know that feeling?

PAMELA: Yes.

ABIGAIL: Well, I couldn't get out of my dressing room for hours. Then we finally got to this party. They were getting a bit narked, I think, but it was lovely when we got there. Oh, everyone was so happy. Somehow, good things, well they simply change everyone, don't they? I mean they do. Everyone was just pleased and happy and I didn't care what happened. Then we left finally. Eddie drove us down to get the papers. Though everyone said we needn't bother. And, of course, it was super. We all went back, well, some of us, to Eddie's and we just went dotty all night. Eddie and I didn't go to bed at all.

CONSTANCE: How do you feel?

ABIGAIL: Wonderful! Oh, I do think people are really *it*. Absolutely. I do! Oh, champagne, how delicious. So, yes, we had champagne and Eddie cooked bacon and eggs with it for breakfast. And he said let's go out and buy anything we want. We're loaded. We can have anything we want. And, oh, so we did. We bought pictures and rugs and I bought a lovely ring and Eddie bought a fabulous cigarette lighter. Oh, we went to galleries and I bought some clothes. Then Eddie said we must have lunch at the Caprice. We hadn't

booked a table and it was packed but we just walked in.
We saw loads of people, didn't we, Eddie?

EDWARD: Yeh.

ABIGAIL: Then we saw a bit of some Swedish movie. It had some
thrilling things with a girl having a baby.

PAMELA: Really?

ABIGAIL: I thought it was rather beautiful. But Eddie got bored
and fell asleep and I woke him up, and we bought these
super records. And, oh, yes this, well, we thought it would
be fun if I changed. You know, there's a picture of me in
every paper today. So we dropped in at Wig Creations for
the moustache, then got a taxi to Carnaby Street. Walked all
the way to Charing Cross Road. Not a head turned. Isn't it
marvellous?

PAMELA: Fantastic.

ABIGAIL: That's right, Eddie. Oh, it's marvellous. Listen to this,
Pamela. You'll go dotty. Constance . . . Eddie.

[EDDIE and ABIGAIL dance to the record. CONSTANCE and
PAMELA watch]

EDWARD: [Presently] How are you, Pamela?

ABIGAIL: Isn't it divine? Yes, are you all right, darling?

PAMELA: Sure.

ABIGAIL: Oh, my God!

EDWARD: What is it?

ABIGAIL: Oh, my God. Pamela! What have I done?

PAMELA: Tell me.

ABIGAIL: I should have gone to your father's Memorial!

PAMELA: I shouldn't worry. You had a better time.

ABIGAIL: But I should have gone.

PAMELA: Why? He didn't want anyone to go. I'm sure he would
have approved of your day, Abigail.

ABIGAIL: But don't you understand. I was supposed to read one
of the lessons.

CONSTANCE: Abigail——

PAMELA: I'm sure there were too many.

ABIGAIL: How awful. Pamela, what can I say?

PAMELA: Don't.

ABIGAIL: But I was asked.

PAMELA: They must have managed. No one mentioned it to me.

ABIGAIL: Darling. Eddie, turn that off. He really was the most marvellous actor. My father was mad about him. I scarcely saw him.

PAMELA: No.

ABIGAIL: And are you all right, darling?

PAMELA: Fine.

CONSTANCE: She's a bit done in.

ABIGAIL: Eddie. Darlings, I must go. Look at the time. I've got a performance. Can we get a taxi here?

CONSTANCE: You'll get one in the street.

PAMELA: I should take your moustache off.

ABIGAIL: Darling. Bless you. *[Embraces all round]* Sorry we barged in. Just wanted to see if you were all right.

EDWARD: My idea really.

PAMELA: I know. Thanks, Edward.

ABIGAIL: 'Bye, darling.

[She and EDWARD do a musical exit. Then he comes back for the record. Pause]

CONSTANCE: I think they've finished off the champagne.

PAMELA: I've got a last bottle. At the back at the bottom.

CONSTANCE: I'll get it. Can't you put Bernard off? I'll ring Murray.

PAMELA: I'm all ready.

CONSTANCE: Don't let Abigail break everything up.

PAMELA: I don't think she has.

CONSTANCE: Don't be hurt by it.

PAMELA: My dear girl, I promise you I'm not. Bernard's bound to be late.

CONSTANCE: There: here's to us.

PAMELA: To us all.

CONSTANCE: Are you taking the books with you? Orme's?

PAMELA: Oh, they'll go in Bernard's car. In the back somewhere.

CONSTANCE: Why do you suppose he goes around with Abigail?

PAMELA: Why do you think? Why does Murray want her for his

play? At least she's alive in her way. Even he gets bored with his dollies. The thing about them is they really are mostly wooden. Abigail isn't wooden.

CONSTANCE: Please ring him up. Stay tonight.

PAMELA: It's too late. He'll be on his way. Look at that: Portia's solicitude for Brutus.

CONSTANCE: It looks a bit more than solicitude.

PAMELA: Oh, Orme couldn't bear her. He said her underwear was never clean. I can quite believe it.

CONSTANCE: What does he say about Abigail.

PAMELA: We don't talk about it. We didn't talk about it. Kingsway Theatre. Founded on the French of Gabriel Vardie. Queens Theatre. Meggie Albenesi. He knew all all about her. Remembrance. That sounds good. Oh, he's playing a wog here. Count Stefano Ciffoni. He liked that. There he is on the west coast of Scotland. That's his place. His bleeding piece of earth, he called it. Well, *he* thought it was funny.

CONSTANCE: What were his big roles, really?

PAMELA: He was big in all of them. Even when he was bad. Oh, I suppose you mean, well, Shylock, Macbeth, of course, Brutus, oh, yes, Hotspur, and a very funny Malvolio.

CONSTANCE: What was *that* called?

PAMELA: *The Real Thing.* Aah, here we are. The countess lights upon—lights upon already—the count in a compromising situation. Oh, Orme. She looks het up all right. Drunk I expect. Yes, look, see, he's having to hold her up. He always did. Yes, it's the last act. What's new in the next session?

CONSTANCE: Oh, pretty heavy.

PAMELA: You won't have much time then?

CONSTANCE: No, what about your film?

PAMELA: Don't know yet. I expect I'll do a telly. Here we are: *The Real Thing.* "Think, Ella, there *is* no inheritance, nothing, only my debts and no career. Just the poor son of a parson, an ex-captain. Now that Jock Crawley has deprived me of my one chance, my one hope of happiness and redeeming myself, there is nothing left for me to do. Only go out of your life. No, I want you. I want you to be my wife. That is not possible. I *want* your life. Ella, oh, Ella, you are a magnificent woman. A gem." *She* had mystery behind the eyes even then. "And so are you, David. All that a woman could ever want. A real gem. Not paste. But the real thing, Davie. The real thing."

CONSTANCE: Perhaps it should have been called *A Real Gem*.

PAMELA: No. *The Real Thing* was better. Oh, here's one of his great flops. His own adaptation of *The Brothers Karamazov*. Lost all his savings in that. Here we are, here's the critics: "A gloomy piece, which will only, we confidently predict, achieve a limited hold on the public." It certainly did. Lost all his savings. His own management, you see. And his own wife dunning him for money all the time. He was always having affairs with actresses.

CONSTANCE: Oh, Pamela . . . what are we all going to do?

PAMELA: You'll go back after the recess. That's what you'll do. It's getting better all the time.

CONSTANCE: Is it? I don't know.

PAMELA: Anyway, someone said, I think: "The worst has already happened." Or something. He adored actresses. But he didn't like the idea of marrying them. At least, I think he did, but he didn't meet her. That was the trouble with mama. Just because she was always on about Kokoschka and Thomas Mann and the texture of life in a Socialist society, he was taken in by it. He thought she was not only cleverer than his other ladies, but cleverer than him.

CONSTANCE: What's she really like?

PAMELA: Daft as a brush. The old man had more in the way he held a tennis racket than every letter she ever wrote to the papers. From unemployment in the Highlands to bed wetting. Thank God for Orme, I was born before Dr. Spock. He was through that. Please don't cry, dear. Or I'll have to go before Bernard turns up.

CONSTANCE: It all seems so wrong.

[Bell rings]

PAMELA: I'll go. *[She goes.* CONSTANCE *can't move. The door reveals* BERNARD*]* Darling, you're on time.

BERNARD: Darling—for you, anything. What are you up to, you naughty girl? I'm going to give you a tough evening.

PAMELA: Oh, no, you're not. You can just tell me the news and then I'm going to bed early. You'll have things to do anyway. You know Constance.

BERNARD: Hello. Where do you want to eat? Is that all the stuff you've got?

PAMELA: I'm sending back for the rest. How about the Armpit Restaurant?

BERNARD: My dear, I've got so much to *tell* you. How about Abigail Ratatouilles?

PAMELA: Don't tell me.

BERNARD: Shall I take these?

PAMEL: Darling, would you? I'll get my fur coats. Always need *them*. It gets cold, even in the South of France.

CONSTANCE: Won't you have a drink before you go?

PAMELA: Bernard doesn't drink, isn't it dreary? He's so obsessed with his figure, which isn't so hot anyway. And also his performance. About which who knows.

BERNARD: You might find out one day, darling. Don't think I can't. You're looking fabulous. Doesn't she?

CONSTANCE: She does. Pamela?

PAMELA: Could you take these, Bernard? I'll just say good-bye to Constance.

BERNARD: Right, I'll be downstairs. 'Night, Constance.

CONSTANCE: Goodnight, Bernard. *[He goes]* Oh, my dear. It isn't right.

PAMELA: Sh. There. I'll teach you that trick the next time. Take care.

CONSTANCE: Take care.

[They embrace]

PAMELA: Oh, Bernard will look after me.

[She goes out. CONSTANCE *drinks the rest of her champagne. She goes to the telephone and dials]*

CONSTANCE: *[On phone]* Darling? You're there . . . No, I'm o.k. . . .
I arranged a dinner for Pamela and she's gone . . . Yes, left
. . . I don't know . . . How do I know . . . I don't know what
she's bent on or anything . . . come on over . . . yes, now,
please . . . I love you . . . I ache for you . . . Do you? Thank
heaven for that . . . Darling . . . oh, my darling . . . Pamela's
going to give me a lesson . . . yes, right . . . Don't be long . . .

CURTAIN.

THE HOTEL IN AMSTERDAM

CAST

HOTEL PORTER
LAURIE
MARGARET
ANNIE
GUS
AMY
DAN
GILLIAN
WAITER

ACT ONE

The drawing room of a suite in a large, first-class hotel in Amsterdam. It is a fairly cheerful room, as such hotel rooms go, with bright prints, plenty of low lamps, and furnished in a rather friendly combination of thirtyish and tactful Hotel Empire. Three separate bedrooms lead off. The door to the hotel corridor opens and a PORTER *enters with a trolley filled with luggage. He is followed rather tentatively by three couples,* LAURIE *and* MARGARET; GUS *and* ANNIE; *and* DAN *and* AMY. *They are all fairly attractively dressed and near or around forty but none middle-aged. In fact, they are pretty flash and vigorous looking. Perhaps* GUS *and* MARGARET *less so than the others. This is partly because he is dressed a bit more conservatively than the other two men and she is visibly pregnant, though not unattractive. The* PORTER *looks for instructions about the baggage. He looks for the leader and decides on* GUS.

PORTER: Sir?

GUS: I'm sorry?

LAURIE: I think it's the baggage, Gus.

GUS: Oh.

MARGARET: Well, tell him darling.

GUS: No, it's all right. Now, let's see.

ANNIE: Well, don't let's make an operation out of it. Those are ours. There, porter. Those two.

253

GUS: Yes, ah, but where are we all going to go? We don't, I mean we haven't had a look yet.

LAURIE: Why don't we sort them out and decide afterwards?

MARGARET: Brilliant.

ANNIE: Some men are brilliant, aren't they?

AMY: Can I help?

MARGARET: No. Gus can manage.

GUS: Yes. Well, it's just a question of sorting out the rooms, isn't it? They're all there.

ANNIE: I should hope so. We're paying enough for them.

MARGARET: Well, don't let him stand there, darling.

GUS: Well, we think we'll have a look at the rooms first and then decide where we're all going and——

ANNIE: That'll take hours with Gus.

MARGARET: No. It won't. Look, porter, just put them all down on the floor and we'll sort them out ourselves.

PORTER: Yes, madam.

GUS: Oh, do you think we should?

LAURIE: Yes, much quicker.

GUS: We'll have to carry it.

LAURIE: That's true. I want a drink really. Have you got any——

GUS: What—a drink? No, but we can order some now.

LAURIE: No. You know. Change. Tip.

GUS: Oh, no, no, I haven't. Let's see. No, I used it on the taxi.

LAURIE: Darling?

MARGARET: You know I haven't.

ANNIE: I might have. Did you forget, Laurie?

MARGARET: Of course he didn't. He just didn't like to ask.

ANNIE: Why on earth not?

MARGARET: He's terrified no one's going to speak English.

ANNIE: You don't think they're going to speak Dutch, do you?

LAURIE: I suppose not. She's quite right though. I just feel I ought to and then I dry up. France is worst because it really seems so thick not to.

DAN: Like Americans.

LAURIE: Exactly. And they're so foul, the French I mean. If you do have a bit of a go, they despise you and pretend they

don't know. A waiter in Paris actually corrected me saying
Vodka once. After all, that's a Russian word.

ANNIE: I shouldn't let it worry you.

LAURIE: Well, it does.

ANNIE: Gus is very good. Bit slow but you're full of initiative always, aren't you, darling?

GUS: Yes, I don't think I have that trouble so much. You can
usually get someone to understand—especially nowadays.

LAURIE: That's the trouble. Amy, what should we give?

GUS: I looked up the exchange.

AMY: Here.

[She tips the PORTER, *who looks neither pleased nor dis-
pleased]*

ANNIE: Thank heavens. Now Laurie can breathe and we can look
around.

LAURIE: Just a minute. Do we all want a drink?

MARGARET: You mean: you do.

GUS: I don't know. Do we, darling?

ANNIE: You bet. After that journey. Aeroplanes!

GUS: Margaret?

MARGARET: No. I'm not.

GUS: Of course. Would you like something else?

MARGARET: Just mineral water. Perrier. Something.

GUS: Amy?

LAURIE: I know Amy will and Dan's tongue's dropping out.

MARGARET: You hope.

LAURIE: I can see it from here. Why don't we——

MARGARET: No. It's too expensive.

LAURIE: But we ought to celebrate getting here. After all, we're
all in one piece, we're all together, we've escaped and——

ANNIE: Nobody knows we're here.

LAURIE: No one. Absolutely no one.

MARGARET: Well, that's not true.

LAURIE: *[To* PORTER*]* Don't go. Well, no one who matters or will
let on. Amy saw to that, didn't you?

ANNIE: Oh, come on, let's order. I'll have a whisky sour.

LAURIE: Oh, isn't that going to be difficult?

ANNIE: Difficult? A whisky sour?

LAURIE: If we all have something different——

GUS: I see what he means.

DAN: Yes. Reinforcements.

LAURIE: Perhaps we could vote on it. All the same thing.

ANNIE: I *have* voted. I'm not being democratic just for convenience.

LAURIE: What about the rest. Amy?

AMY: I really don't mind.

LAURIE: Good girl. And Dan, you'll drink anything. Right? Scotch?

DAN: O.K.

LAURIE: Right, then so will I. Gus?

GUS: All right. But don't forget Margaret's Perrier.

LAURIE: Shall I?

ANNIE: We would like one whisky sour, one Perrier water, a bottle of J. & B. or Cutty Sark. Some ice and some soda. *[To* LAURIE*]* Happy?

LAURIE: Make it two bottles, we'll need them.

ANNIE: Two bottles.

LAURIE: And quickly please, if you can.

PORTER: Yes, sir.

GUS: Well now.

ANNIE: Let's look at the room. All right, Margaret?

MARGARET: Fine. Right.

ANNIE: You have first pick.

GUS: Oh, yes.

ANNIE: I don't mind. As long as the bed's big and comfortable.

LAURIE: I do.

MARGARET: You would; spoiled.

LAURIE: Well, let's get it over.

MARGARET: Don't fret, darling. Your drink will be here soon.

LAURIE: God, I hate travelling.

MARGARET: Well, you've arrived. Relax.

LAURIE: Yes, that's true, isn't it? I suppose we really have. What a relief. All those passports and tickets and airport buses and being bossed about. Air hostesses—I'd love to rape an air hostess.

GUS: Really? I don't mean about air hostesses. I rather enjoy all that travel guff.

DAN: You would. Public school.

MARGARET: Now then, Dan, don't be chippy. You're very lucky to be with your betters.

DAN: I know it. I hate the working classes. That's why I got out.

AMY: You can never get out.

DAN: I did. They're an unlovable, whining, blackmailing shower.

ANNIE: What's he talking about?

MARGARET: Just being chippy.

LAURIE: Don't keep saying that. You should see *my* horrible family.

MARGARET: I have and now you're both being chippy.

LAURIE: We're both just saying we've got horrible families and that you're lucky to have nice, gentle, civilized, moderate parents like yours. Right, Dan?

DAN: Right.

MARGARET: Oh, my goodness, class solidarity. Anyway, my mother's not that hot.

LAURIE: She's divine.

MARGARET: Well, you think so. She's just dull and sporty.

LAURIE: She's not. She's extremely attractive and intelligent.

DAN: Not like my mum—scheming old turd.

LAURIE: And your mum's so ugly.

DAN: Telling me.

LAURIE: Funny really because you're not.

ANNIE: He's beautiful.

LAURIE: Mine's got a very mean little face. Celebrates every effect, plays up all the time, to the gallery, do anything for anything. Self-involved, bullying.

MARGARET: Oh, come off it.

LAURIE: I suppose you think her face is pitted by the cares of working-class life and bringing up her sons on National Assistance. Well, it isn't. She has that face there because there's a mean, grudging, grasping nature behind it.

MARGARET: I don't know why nice men don't like their mothers.

ANNIE: Gus likes his.

LAURIE: That's because she's probably nice.

ANNIE: She isn't bad.

GUS: No. I suppose she isn't really.

LAURIE: And he's a bit queer too, remember.

ANNIE: That's true.

MARGARET: But you always say you are a bit.

LAURIE: So I am. But not as much as Gus.

AMY: What about Dan?

LAURIE: Well—either less than Gus or me. Or much more. He's more elusive. I mean Gus is so obvious. Those clothes. That's real conservatism.

GUS: Are they awful?

MARGARET: You look dishy.

LAURIE: I think my mother *would* have put me off women for life. I mean just to think of swimming about inside that repulsive thing for nine months.

MARGARET: Please.

LAURIE: But I think when I was quite young I must have decided she was nothing to do with women at all. That's why the real thing was such an eternal surprise.

MARGARET: She'd love this. You usually butter her up.

LAURIE: She doesn't give a twopenny fart. Excuse me—I think I'm going to . . . It's the idea of my mother. Don't worry, I'll tell her before she dies. No. I die. She'll outlive me for years.

DAN: My mother would have made a good air hostess.

LAURIE: Your mother! Listen, my mother should have been Chief Stewardess on Monster's Airlines. She'd have kept you waiting in every bus, withheld information and liquor, snapped at you, and smirked at you meaninglessly or simply just ignored you.

DAN: Have you ever thought of airlines for homosexuals?

LAURIE: I say: what a splendid idea. You could call it El Fag Airlines.

ANNIE: Gus could be a stewardess.

LAURIE: We'd design him a divine outfit. I say, I feel better already.

MARGARET: Don't get carried away. The holiday's only just started.

LAURIE: The great escape you mean.

GUS: You mean all the aircrew would be chaps?

DAN: *And* the passengers.

LAURIE: Why don't we start it? Fly El Fag. The Airlines that floats just for HIM!

GUS: It's not bad, is it? I say, we're getting our wind back, aren't we? Just starting to feel safe, I suppose.

DAN: We're really here.

LAURIE: Really here.

ANNIE: I don't know who's more astonished that we've all scarpered. Us or whether *he* will be.

AMY: K. L. will be pretty astonished when he finds out.

MARGARET: Let's face it: so are we.

ANNIE: We do sound a bit amazed at our own naughtiness.

LAURIE: No, we're not.

MARGARET: Yes, we are. Come on. You are.

LAURIE: No, we are relieved, unburdened, we've managed to slough off that monster for a few days. We have escaped, we deserve it, after all this time. Just to be somewhere he doesn't know where any of us are. Can't get near us, call us, ring us, come round, write. Nothing. Nix. For a few blessed days. No K. L. in our lives.

MARGARET: You make it more cowardly than it is.

LAURIE: So what if it is?

ANNIE: No. It isn't. We all deserve to escape. After all, he *is* the biggest, most poisonous, voracious, Machiavellian dinosaur in movies. And we all know what that means.

LAURIE: Quite.

ANNIE: Sorry, Amy. I know he's your boss.

DAN: He seems to be everybody's boss.

AMY: Poor Dan.

ANNIE: Yes. Married to the boss's secretary. That's probably the worst position of all.

MARGARET: You and I are in the same position.

GUS: I suppose we all play different roles to the dinosaur. But they're still roles.

DAN: Amy adores him.

ANNIE: So does everybody. I do. And Margaret does. Gus can't live without him. And Laurie tries to pretend he can.

LAURIE: I can.

ANNIE: I wonder if you will.

LAURIE: I have before and it sure didn't kill me.

MARGARET: I don't think I could bear any more recriminations.

ANNIE: But the rest of us are still supposed to be friends.

GUS: It's difficult, isn't it? Perhaps Laurie can come to some understanding.

LAURIE: Not this time, buddy. He's had it.

GUS: I don't know how we'll cope when we get back.

ANNIE: Darling. We've only just arrived.

MARGARET: How amused he'd be. Here we are congratulating ourselves on escaping from him and we've hardly stopped talking about him since we left Liverpool Street.

LAURIE: I wouldn't feel flattered to hear *what* we've said.

ANNIE: He'd be amused certainly.

LAURIE: Amy, you are sure?

AMY: Absolutely sure.

LAURIE: It would be great if he suddenly walked through that door while we were laughing and joking all together.

AMY: He won't.

GUS: What a thought.

MARGARET: Poor Amy. She's the real Judas amongst us. After all, she *is* his secretary. *We're* conspirators.

LAURIE: I don't see that she's been disloyal. So what if she has! That cock's crowed a bit too often for every one of us. *And* everyone else. Those he's victimized at one time or another. Oh, he'll find another spare eunuch knocking around London. The world's full of hustlers and victims all beavering away to be pressed into K.L.'s service. Someone always wants to be useful or flattered or gulled or just plain whipped slowly to death or cast out into the knackers yard by King

Sham. Well, let him go ahead and get himself crucified this
time. I know him not.

ANNIE: What do you mean?

LAURIE: What I say.

MARGARET: He won't.

GUS: Won't what?

LAURIE: Get himself crucified.

GUS: No, I suppose not.

ANNIE: No.

DAN: Pity.

AMY: He'll be all right. He'll find someone.

GUS: I say, do you know we haven't looked at the view yet. It's
rather good.

MARGARET: So it is.

AMY: We're really here.

DAN: I wish you'd stop saying that. Of course we're here. You
made all the superb arrangements didn't you?

MARGARET: Yes, thanks, Amy.

LAURIE: Hear, hear. Thank you, Amy.

ANNIE: Well, screw the view, we haven't looked at the rooms yet.

MARGARET: Yes, we must do that now.

ANNIE: Won't K.L. be furious when he can't get hold of you over
the weekend? He knows you never go away.

AMY: I said I was staying with some relatives in Yorkshire.

ANNIE: But you're a hopeless liar. You're so transparent.

AMY: I hinted it was really a lover.

LAURIE: Oh, he'd like that. More demolition around the joint.

AMY: Yes, he was rather intrigued. So he didn't ask any questions.

MARGARET: Not even where to get hold of you?

AMY: I said there was no phone. But I'd ring him.

MARGARET: Then won't you have to?

AMY: Well, of course, he'll be furious when I don't. I'll have to
say I wasn't well.

LAURIE: That won't wash. He'll ring Dan to stir it up.

AMY: I don't think he'd do that. He wouldn't want to mess things
up if he really thinks I've got a lover and Dan doesn't know
about it.

ANNIE: Don't fancy your first morning back, with your shorthand
pad, when your boss has been deprived and rejected of men
all weekend and you not on the phone, having a bit on the
side and not even confiding in him. He'll be *very* hurt.

AMY: Oh, dear. Yes. He will.

LAURIE: So what. Say you had the curse and it ruined the entire
rendezvous. That would appeal to him.

AMY: Wouldn't wash. He knows my calendar better than I do.

DAN: Knows your miserable little face, you mean.

MARGARET: Aren't they charming?

ANNIE: Did you know that air hostesses have holy travail with the
curse?

LAURIE: Really? Good.

ANNIE: Seriously. To do with the air pressure or something.

LAURIE: Good. Jolly good!

ANNIE: Either don't get it for months on end and worry themselves to death in case they're up the spout . . .

LAURIE: Fancy a pregnant air hostess. Think how high and mighty
she'd be. Putting her feet up and pecking at all the cus-
tomers' canapés.

ANNIE: Or they get it twice a week.

DAN: Do you mind? I feel a pain coming on.

ANNIE: Wish you did. Then you wouldn't jeer at poor little Amy
when she's boo-hooing all over K.L.'s office.

DAN: Thank God they don't have women pilots.

GUS: The Russians do.

LAURIE: Remember: never travel on Rusky Airlines. Keep to El
Fag.

DAN: Or you might go up front and see a little bundle of Russian
misery crying its eyes out over the controls.

LAURIE: All misted up and locking herself in the loo. Worse than
seeing a little yellow face turn round and grin at you.

ANNIE: Like the *Lost Horizon.*

LAURIE: Our bloody drinks are lost. Where is that hopeless Hol-
lander? Do you suppose he understood us?

MARGARET: Of course he understood us. This isn't Bournemouth.

[Knock. WAITER *enters]*

GUS: Ah. There we are. Good evening.

WAITER: Good evening, sir.

MARGARET: Now you can relax.

GUS: I say, this is Haig. Didn't you order——

LAURIE: Doesn't matter. It'll take hours. You know what——

GUS: Sure?

LAURIE: Sure. Open it, please, would you?

WAITER: Yes, sir.

GUS: I'm sure he'd change it if we ask him.

MARGARET: Laurie would die. Of embarrassment apart from anything else.

LAURIE: It's all right, leave it. I'll do it.

WAITER: One whisky sour.

ANNIE: Thank God for that. Thank you.

GUS: That's all for the moment. Oh—Perrier? Yes. Here you are, Margaret.

WAITER: Thank you, sir. Good evening.

GUS: Good evening.

[WAITER *goes out*]

DAN: I don't think he approved of us much.

LAURIE: Did you think so? Yes. I had that feeling.

MARGARET: Thinks we're alcoholics.

LAURIE: I thought he thought the girls were probably O.K. But not us.

ANNIE: Perhaps he thinks we're none of us married.

GUS: Oh, yes—having a real mucky weekend, gang bang stuff.

LAURIE: He looked very suspiciously at you.

GUS: Did you think so?

LAURIE: I noticed it. Thought you were a bit effeminate, I expect.

GUS: Perhaps he did. I think it's these bloody trousers, darling. You said I should throw them away. They don't do much for me, do they?

LAURIE: Nothing desirable.

ANNIE: Darling, you always look rather effeminate. You and Laurie both do. In different ways.

GUS: Ah, but Laurie carries it off somehow. I don't.

MARGARET: Especially to foreigners.

ANNIE: It's part of your masculine charm.

GUS: What do you mean?

ANNIE: Oh, I don't know. A kind of mature softness.

MARGARET: And peacockery.

ANNIE: Yes, a bit uneasy sometimes but gallant and foursquare all the same.

LAURIE: Doesn't sound too bad.

ANNIE: It's lovely.

GUS: You're quite right. I know foreigners think like that. It's hell when I'm in America.

LAURIE: They think I'm Oscar Wilde. It's very flattering.

MARGARET: And don't you play up to it!

LAURIE: Well, I mean you just have to, don't you? It's like they expect to see the Changing of the Guard.

ANNIE: Thank heavens for the charm and femininity of the English male I say.

LAURIE: Well, American women certainly don't have it. Poor sods.

MARGARET: I'll drink to that.

LAURIE: Perrier. Ugh!

MARGARET: I like it.

LAURIE: Everyone's glass charged? Right . . . Well, here we all are.

ANNIE: Here we all are.

LAURIE: Here's to all of us. All friends and all together.

MARGARET: Well, naturally.

LAURIE: No, it's not natural. It's bloody unnatural. How often do you get six people as different as we all are still all together all friends and who all love each other. After all the things that have happened to us. Like success to some extent, making money—some of us. It's not bad.

GUS: Bloody good.

LAURIE: Everyone's married couples nowadays. Thank heaven we're not that.

MARGARET: You're drunk already.

LAURIE: You know what I mean.

MARGARET: Yes.

LAURIE: To us, and may the Good Lord bless and keep us.

ALL: To us.

LAURIE: And preserve us from that dinosaur film producer.

ANNIE: I don't think I can quite drink to that.

GUS: It's a problem.

LAURIE: Well, suit yourselves . . . Ah, that's better.

GUS: Isn't it good?

LAURIE: All right, Amy?

AMY: Fine.

ANNIE: Guilty?

AMY: No. I'm forgetting it until Monday.

ANNIE: I wonder if you will.

LAURIE: Well, give her a chance. Dan?

DAN: Smashing.

ANNIE: You know what: I think people who need people are the ghastliest people in the world.

LAURIE: Absolutely. We all just happened to find one another. At the right time.

ANNIE: It sounds a bit Jewish show biz.

LAURIE: I thought it was a rather tense Anglo-Saxon sentiment myself. I mean you couldn't sing it.

ANNIE: Well, you could. It would be rather mediocre.

LAURIE: I mean you couldn't belt out a rather halting little comment like that. It's not poetic. It's just a smallish statement. About six unusually pleasing people. Well, five. God, I'm getting fat.

MARGARET: You've always been fat.

LAURIE: Really? *Have* I? I've deceived myself.

MARGARET: You're very attractive. Pleasing.

LAURIE: More pleasing than K. L.?

MARGARET: Yes. Don't know about more attractive.

LAURIE: Hell!

AMY: We really *are* lucky. I mean it's a splendid hotel and a lovely suite.

DAN: Which *you* can't afford.

LAURIE: You don't have to. *I* can. So can Gus. You made all the arrangements. And Dan's going to do all the talking.

AMY: I think they all speak English.

LAURIE: You must admit it's better than that rotten Paris.

ANNIE: I suppose we're all what's called spoiled.

LAURIE: What do you mean: spoiled?

ANNIE: Well, first-class hotels, great suites, anything we want to drink.

LAURIE: What's spoiled about that? I'm certainly not spoiled. I work my drawers off and get written off twice a year as not fulfilling my early promise by some philistine squirt drumming up copy, someone who's got as much idea of the creative process as Dan's mother and mine rolled into one lazy minded lump of misery who ever battened off the honest efforts of others.

ANNIE: Writers are born to be reviled.

LAURIE: No they're not. They sit in judgement on themselves all the time without calling in outside help. They need to be loved and cared for and given money.

ANNIE: We all love you and you make lots of money.

LAURIE: Where would K.L. be without me—where *will* he be without me to write his lousy pictures? Pretty all right, I guess. And without Gus to edit them into making sense and cover up his howlers? Of course, I suppose you'll go on doing it.

[Pause]

LAURIE: Well, not this one. Besides, he hates it if I make money. I think he tips off the tax man. We don't live in Switzerland any of us, do we? More sense but still. . . . Loaded with distinction and not a C.B.E. to go round. When I think of the rotten dollars I've made——

MARGARET: Don't.

ANNIE: And K.L.

LAURIE: Well, lolly doesn't worry him. He spends it. You just round up a few people like Gus and me here, turn them up on the gas and if you suck around the blood counter at the supermarket long enough, you've produced another picture. And you go on doing. What I do, I get out of the air. Even if it's not so hot always, I put my little hand out there in that void, there, empty air. Look at it. It's like being a bleeding conjuror with no white tie and tails. Air . . .

MARGARET: Hot.

LAURIE: It never pays what it costs . . . No. I'm feeling quite relaxed now. Sure you won't drink?

MARGARET: I do keep telling you.

LAURIE: Sorry. Actually, I do speak Italian quite beautifully, don't I, darling?

MARGARET: The accent's good.

LAURIE: Poor vocabulary. But they don't mind if you make it up. They love it. *[All very fast but clear]* Prego, prego. Si, grazie. Signorina. E machina bella. Grande film con regissori K. L. con attirci Inglesi tutte bellisima. Attrici Inglesi molto ravissante crumpetto di monde. Per che. Me Lauri scritori Inglesi famioso connossori, grosso. Molto experementi, Senza pommodori, si. Oggi declarimento attrice Inglesi crumpetto elegante, insatiabile, splendido lasagne verde antifascisti pesce Anna Magnani Visconti arrividerci con rubato grazie mille, grazie. There, wasn't that good! Allemange basta! Pasta per tute populo. Kosygin pappa mio. Si grappa, per favore.

MARGARET: I think I'm going to sort the rooms out.

LAURIE: Oh, leave it.

MARGARET: I want to unpack.

LAURIE: Oh, all right.

MARGARET: And I expect the others do. Unless they want an Italian lesson.

LAURIE: Shall we go to an Italian restaurant tonight?

GUS: That sounds good. Darling?

ANNIE: Perhaps we should try the local hostelries.

LAURIE: Yes. I expect you're right. I'm too fat for wop food.

MARGARET: Dutch food's rather heavy.

GUS: Enormous portions. Good beer. I've got an information thing here.

ANNIE: Oh heavens—don't start on that already.

GUS: Well, we'll have to make a decision.

LAURIE: I don't see——

GUS: Might have to book a table or something. If we want to get somewhere good.

LAURIE: Yes, I see.

ANNIE: You both make it sound so difficult.

LAURIE: My dear Annie, it *is* difficult. I can't think of anything that comes easily. It's all difficult.

ANNIE: You need one of those things that fortifies the over forties.

LAURIE: I'm not over forty!

MARGARET: Well, you look it.

LAURIE: What are you trying to do to me?

MARGARET: No, you don't. You look like a teenager.

LAURIE: Yes, a plump, middle-aged, played-out grotesque.

ANNIE: Never believe in mirrors or newspapers.

LAURIE: I thought I'd got the mirror fixed . . . I need another one after that.

MARGARET: Come on, let's explore this place and see what we've got for our money. Annie?

[ANNIE *follows her. Also* GUS *who looks helpful*]

LAURIE: Over forties. I heard a disc jockey the other day introducing a pop version of "Roses of Picardy." "Picardy" he said. "Where's that?" Help . . .

DAN: Do you ever look to see if your birthday's listed in *The Times?*

LAURIE: Always.

DAN: And is it?

LAURIE: They missed me out the year before last. Seemed like an obituary only no notice. When you do something, try to do something, take a look at someone else's efforts, you ask yourself, *I* ask myself: is there something there that wasn't there before? Well . . . I picked this damned paper up and it seemed I hadn't even been born any more. . . . Do you ever have a little lace curtain in front of your eyes? Like little spermy tadpoles paddling across your eyeballs? No? Do you think it's drink or eyesight?

DAN: Drink.

AMY: You ought to watch that.

LAURIE: I've been watching it for years. Fascinating. And tell me, do you ever either of you, no, you wouldn't, Amy, but you Dan, do you ever wake up with your finger tips all tingly and aching?

DAN: No.

LAURIE: Well, do you ever wake up with an awful burn in the stomach?

AMY: Yes, he often does.

LAURIE: And then what do you do?

DAN: Get up. Work. Paint if it's light.

LAURIE: This is about five o'clock, is it?

DAN: Usually.

LAURIE: And you can actually work, can you?

DAN: Not always.

LAURIE: Do you wake up, Amy?

AMY: I usually wake up.

LAURIE: And then?

AMY: I make coffee or give him a glass of milk.

LAURIE: And have a bit of a chatter?

DAN: That's it. Until it's time for her to get off to K. L.

LAURIE: I'm afraid I usually need a drink. It's the only thing that burns it out. Need to weld my guts with a torch. Then about nine, it eases off. I read the post. Try to put off work. Have a so-called business lunch. That's good waste of time. Then I know I'll have to sleep in the afternoon.

AMY: Does Margaret get up when you're like that.

LAURIE: She can't—poor old thing. You see she can't get off to sleep. So by the time I'm about to totter about downstairs, reading last night's evening papers, she's only just managed to get off. Especially now.

AMY: When she's pregnant?

[LAURIE *motions her silent at the word*]

LAURIE: So, I'm afraid we're a bit out of step with sleep. When I was eighteen I used to sleep fourteen hours on Sundays. When my mother would let me.

DAN: My mother made too much noise.

LAURIE: If *only* you can find enough energy. Where do you find it? Where's the spring?

AMY: You're loaded with it. You've got far more than Dan.

LAURIE: No, I haven't. Dan doesn't need energy. He runs perfectly efficiently on paraffin oil. You fill him up once a year and he's alight for another twelve months. With me, I need the super quality high-thing stuff poured into my tank twice a day. Look at K. L. He's unstoppable, you never have to wind him up. He just goes. Like that.

AMY: He gets very worn out.

LAURIE: I should think he does. If I did what he does in a day, I'd be in bed for a month.

DAN: He delegates.

LAURIE: Ah, yes—the operator's alchemy. Where do you get it? He takes it from *us*. We could be giving it to one another. He's been draining our tanks, filling his own. Filling up on all of us, splitting us up.

[MARGARET, ANNE, *and* GUS *return*]

MARGARET: Give what to each other?

LAURIE: A little vitality.

ANNIE: We're all right. And we're on hols. So we can recharge.

LAURIE: Yes, we've got away.

ANNIE: The rooms are fine. You and Margaret are having that one. Gus and I this one and we decided Amy and Dan would like that one with the view. It's nice.

AMY: Are you sure?

ANNIE: They're all nice. Now we can get our stuff in.

MARGARET: Gus has done nearly all of it already. Gus, you are a darling. Honestly, you two! Letting Gus do all the carrying.

LAURIE: Good for his figure.

MARGARET: Typical.

LAURIE: And bad for my kidneys.

MARGARET: Are you going to help me unpack?

LAURIE: Do you want me to?

MARGARET: No, I don't think so.

LAURIE: I can.

MARGARET: I don't doubt it.

LAURIE: Shall I talk to you while you do it?

MARGARET: No. Talk to Dan and Gus. I might lie down for a bit.

LAURIE: Let me——

MARGARET: Please stay where you are.

ANNIE: Ours won't take a second.

LAURIE: You seem to have brought an awful lot of stuff. What are you going to do? Play golf? Hunt or something?

ANNIE: Mostly Gus's stuff. Medicines, all chemists counter.

DAN: Got my easel?

AMY: Yes.

DAN: Right. Just in case. [ANNIE *and* AMY *go to rooms*] I'll never use it.

LAURIE: Working on your own. I could never live on my own. Oh, I have done. It's been all right for a time. But what about now and then, the steep drop and no one there. And no one to phone or too far away.

DAN: Or too early in the morning.

LAURIE: That's one of the few good things about movies. You do work with others. Bit like the army.

GUS: I suppose we really have made the right selection? Over the rooms?

LAURIE: Who cares? They'll all be the same.

GUS: I just thought Margaret ought to have a nice one. If she's not sleeping.

LAURIE: Gus, I know you mean well but please forget about it. I say, old Amy won't get the sack when she gets back to K. L?

DAN: No. He relies on her too much.

LAURIE: Do you mind?

DAN: Mind?

LAURIE: I shouldn't think you see much of her. His nibs keeps her at it. Seven days a week.

DAN: He pays her well. More than I earn. It works out.

GUS: Don't think that would suit me.

DAN: Annie can't see all that much of you.

GUS: Oh, a fair bit. He tries to keep me away from her, mind you.

You know: don't bother to drive home. Stay here and we can make an early start at breakfast. But I hardly ever do. I need a bit of looking after, I'm afraid. I hate staying in other people's houses. Unprepared and all that. No shaving stuff. Or someone else's. And I don't like really sleeping on my own. Somehow, well the quality of sleep is different. Do you know what I mean?

DAN: I can sleep anywhere.

LAURIE: I think I know. More drink—before they come back?

GUS: Well. It does seem a bit unfair to drink so much in front of Margaret.

LAURIE: It isn't. But just don't say so.

GUS: Oh? All right. Well, here's to all of us. Amsterdam . . . What a brilliant idea of yours. He'd never think of here.

LAURIE: No?

GUS: Not exactly his sort of place, I'd have thought. Not much night life.

DAN: Few bank managers dancing with each other and that's it.

MARGARET: *[Off]* Laurie. Would you ring down for some more Perrier for me?

LAURIE: O.K. darling.

[He hesitates, looks hopefully at GUS, *who responds]*

GUS: I'll do it.

LAURIE: *[Grateful]* Oh, would you? Thanks.

[He pours out for DAN*]*

GUS: *[On phone]* This is room 320. Yes. Oh, yes—room service, please . . . Hullo, can I have two large bottles of Perrier water. And, oh, yes, some ice. And a bottle of Cutty Sark. You brought Haig last time. Yes. Thank you. All fixed.

LAURIE: Thanks. And no one's to buy an English newspaper. Right?

DAN: Right. It's not your birthday, is it?

LAURIE: I wonder why she didn't ring down herself.

GUS: Unpacking, I suppose . . .

DAN: I was thinking the other day: do you think they make bicycle clips any more?

LAURIE: Hadn't thought of that. No, of course. All those little bare black ankles.

GUS: Bicycle clips . . . I think I've still got mine.

LAURIE: Like Picardy, I should think. No one would know. Like those things you used to wear on your sleeves.

DAN: I should hope not.

LAURIE: Well, of course, I never did. I'll bet *you* did.

GUS: What?

LAURIE: Wear those things. Up here.

GUS: No——I don't think so.

LAURIE: Do you have one of those little pocket diaries? You know, for appointments and things.

GUS: Yes.

DAN: No.

LAURIE: Well then, Gus. I wonder if this happens to you. You know how just after Christmas and you've got nothing to do except feel ill and miserable and dread those last days of December? If you haven't got to hell out of it. Well, I always start my new diary off before the New Year. Put my license number in it because I can't remember it. Why *should* I remember it? Then you put in your telephone numbers—I even put my own in. Otherwise I might ring one I had years ago . . . Well, and then there are the names of all those people, not all those people but some people, because I don't keep many in there and then you know—every year I sit down and there's not just one I don't put in again, there's four, five, six. I think there are only about eleven in this year —and that includes people like you and Dan and K. L. *He'll* be out next year. And my agent. And that's about it. Oh, and my mother . . . Hey, what are you all doing in there?

ANNIE: [*Off*] Unpacking!

MARGARET: [*Off*] What do you think?

LAURIE: Well, come back in.

AMY: Coming!

LAURIE: Margaret! We're all missing you. We're on our own.

MARGARET: *[Off]* No, you're not. You're getting stewed.

LAURIE: We're six and there are only three in here.

ANNIE: Bad luck.

LAURIE: We love you. Why have you gone and left us? We came here to be together. And you all disappear off to the bedroom or the bathroom and dolly about with your rollies and skin tonic. Come back in here! You're needed!

GUS: Yes, come back. Annie!

ANNIE: *[Off]* I'm unpacking all your laxatives and poove juices.

AMY: *[Appearing]* All done! It's a lovely room, Dan. Go and look at the view.

DAN: I will.

LAURIE: You deserve a lovely room, my dear. Come here and give me a kiss. Just for arranging everything if for nothing else ever. Not a hitch.

AMY: It was easy. K. L.'s got a good travel agent.

LAURIE: You didn't use *him!*

AMY: He won't let on. I briefed him.

LAURIE: Good girl. Well, if you lose your job, you'll have to come and work for me. Have a drink. Won't be as exciting as K. L. But you'll get more time off. *[Knock on door]* That's him. He's found out where we are. You've bungled it and he got on a plane and did it the quick way.

AMY: Come in.

LAURIE: Scusi, scusi. Momento, momento, tutte in bagno. Basta, per favore.

[WAITER *enters*]

WAITER: Whisky sour?

LAURIE: No, Cutty Sark.

AMY: Annie, did you order a whisky sour?

ANNIE: *[Off]* Yes. I knew you'd all forget me.

GUS: Why didn't you tell me? I've ordered.

ANNIE: *[Entering from bedroom]* Easier. Thank you.

GUS: I ordered. Cutty Sark. And Perrier. And ice. You won't forget!

WAITER: Very well, sir. *[Goes]*

GUS: Crossed lines. All right, darling?

ANNIE: Everything's out. Anything from bowels to athlete's foot.

LAURIE: Do you know there really is such a thing as writer's cramp?

ANNIE: Sounds rather comic—like housemaid's knee.

LAURIE: Not funny if you're a housemaid or a writer.

DAN: Have you had it?

LAURIE: Naturally. What's more I get psychosomatic writer's cramp.

AMY: You can type. I've seen you.

LAURIE: The commitment's too immediate. Horrifying. Like kissing someone for the first time and then bingo you're having to slap the breath of life into some rotten little fig of a human being that heaved its way between you five seconds afterwards. Do painters get anything like housemaids?

ANNIE: Aching backs I suppose on murals and things. Do you?

DAN: Not much.

LAURIE: That's because you work at a controlled pace, you see. Everything you do has rhythm, you see. Systematic. Consistent. *That's* the thing. Mine's all over the place.

ANNIE: You produce the goods.

LAURIE: Are—but do I then?

ANNIE: Don't fish. You know you do.

LAURIE: But what goods? I ask myself: can anything manufactured out of this chaos and rapacious timidity and scolding carry on really *be* the goods. Should it not be, I ask myself. What do I ask myself, perhaps I shouldn't be rhetorical and clutter conversations with what-do-I-ask-myselfs? Won't the goods be shown up by the way of the manner of their manufacture? How can they become aloof, materials shaped with precision, design, logical detail, cunning, formality. And so on and so on.

ANNIE: And so on. You're not such a bad tailor.

LAURIE: No, I'm not.

ANNIE: There, you *were* fishing.

LAURIE: *And* I provide my own cloth. Any clunkhead can cut. I don't mean in your sense, Gus.

GUS: What? Oh, no—you're right.

ANNIE: I've a feeling we're getting back to K. L. *You* said let's leave him behind. But you won't.

AMY: He will.

GUS: Well, it is difficult, you must admit. He rather makes one talk about him.

ANNIE: Perhaps we should go straight back to London and be with him after all.

GUS: Don't suppose he'd have us altogether.

ANNIE: Why were you doing your parliamo Italiano bit?

AMY: He thought it was K. L.

ANNIE: *That* would have fooled him!

GUS: You didn't really, did you?

LAURIE: No. Except with him nothing is so awful he couldn't visit it on you.

ANNIE: No one would think you'd been loving friends for ten years.

LAURIE: You can't be loving friends with a dinosaur.

ANNIE: What are you then?

LAURIE: A mouse—what else?

ANNIE: Some mouse. With the soul of a tiger.

LAURIE: A mouse. With the soul of a toothless bear.

ANNIE: What's Gus?

LAURIE: Gus? He's, he's a walking, talking, living dolphin.

ANNIE: Amy?

LAURIE: An unneurotic fallow deer.

ANNIE: And Dan?

LAURIE: Dan, he's a bit difficult. Rather cool, absentminded but observant. Orangutan.

ANNIE: You're a rather sophisticated mole who keeps pushing up the earth to contract all her chums in the right place at the right time.

AMY: And Margaret—what's she?

LAURIE: Don't know. That's a difficult one.

GUS: Something frightfully attractive but efficient.

LAURIE: A rather earnest chimpanzee. Practical, full of initiative.

ANNIE: Inquisitive?

GUS: I don't think chimpanzees are very attractive.

ANNIE: Neither are moles.

LAURIE: Oh, yes they are. I'd love a mole for Christmas. Perhaps you can buy rubber ones in Amsterdam.

DAN: I don't think Orangutans and what was it, fallow deer, are very well matched myself. It's the sort of thing a marriage bureau computer would come up with.

ANNIE: I don't think he was very good at all.

LAURIE: Dinosaur was good.

GUS: That was easy.

ANNIE: And you didn't characterize your dinosaur.

LAURIE: I will.

ANNIE: Don't. We know.

LAURIE: Perhaps he's not the same dinosaur to all of us. It's obvious but it may be his little tiny dinosaur's trade trick.

[MARGARET *enters*]

MARGARET: Was that the waiter?

GUS: Wrong order. Your Perrier's coming.

MARGARET: You rang down?

LAURIE: Yes. We did.

MARGARET: We?

LAURIE: Gus did. It's the waiter—he likes rough trade, don't you, Gus? [GUS *grins*] It's the beating at that prep school and scrumming down in the mud and being genuinely liked by the men, no?

GUS: I don't think the waiter's exactly my dish. But I quite like the Dutch, I think. Seem rather nice up to now.

ANNIE: We've not taken much of a sample. Taxi drivers, receptionists . . .

LAURIE: Air hostesses. International. But I think we're going to like the Dutch. I think we're going to have a lot of time for the Dutch, as my horrrible mother says.

ANNIE: Only means nasty contraceptives to me. And chocolate.

LAURIE: What, you mean chocolate coated ones? Oh, I see. Talking about that arse aching subject, somebody told me only very bovine girls can munch away at 'em. Air hostesses are made for the pill, for instance. Will you have a pill with your coffee, madam, with the airline's compliments. *They* take them. If you've any temperament at all, you just kick around in your stall like a racehorse. I mean you couldn't *give* the pill to racehorses.

DAN: Well, it would be doping them, wouldn't it?

GUS: I say, this is *good,* isn't it.

ANNIE: Don't say it—we're really here.

LAURIE: Well, we are.

[Knock at door]

ANNIE: Come in. *[*WAITER *comes in. To* LAURIE*]* Sorry. I thought we'd had enough of your Italiansprache.

GUS: Ah! Good evening. *[As if he hadn't seen the* WAITER *before]*

WAITER: Sir. *[He puts things down. Pause]*

GUS: Where would you recommend us all to eat on our first night in Amsterdam?

WAITER: It depends on what you have in mind.

GUS: Well, what we have in mind is absolutely the best, not necessarily the most expensive or the most famous. I mean: what would you suggest?

WAITER: It's difficult, sir. There are many excellent places to dine.

AMY: I've got a typed list here, Gus. More or less in order.

GUS: I just thought he might——

LAURIE: I should forget it.

GUS: What?

LAURIE: Amy's well trained. She always gets out a list of the six-supposed best restaurants for K. L. I've often wondered what he'd have done if his surname had been Young or Yeo or Yarrow.

GUS: Why?

LAURIE: We'd have called him K. Y.

ANNIE: *You* would.

GUS: What's K. Y.?

LAURIE: Gosh, these prep schools were tough, weren't they? Or did you use Matron's vaseline? You *do* like it rough.

GUS: Oh!

*[*WAITER *goes out]*

LAURIE: Oh. You know what its legitimate, well intended use is? Cleaning surgical instruments. Well, you remember that as-asistant K. L. had a couple of years ago . . .

ANNIE: What happened to him?

LAURIE: Stepped on the trap door in front of the desk one day, I suppose. Anyway . . .

MARGARET: I don't remember him.

LAURIE: Yes, you do. English faggot he picked up in Hollywood. About thirty-five, all tight pants and white socks and greying hair.

MARGARET: Oh, and that expression . . .

LAURIE: Yes, I think you called him the frozen Madonna. I called him Sibyl. He had a crown of sibilants over his head. He sounded like a walking snake pit. I mean, you could even hear him from one end of the Crush Bar at Covent Garden to the other—*packed*. So, Sibyl told me he went into this chemist and there was this other faggot behind the counter. He says: very dignified: can I have a tube of K. Y., please? The assistant doesn't say a word, wraps up package, gives it to him. Then as he drops his change into his palm, he says. . . . "Have fun." And Sibyl said "I looked and said 'What? Cleaning my surgical instrument?' "

MARGARET: Now, listen, I think Gus is quite right, we should have a talk about what we're going to do and then make a decision.

ANNIE: That could take hours.

MARGARET: Well, it mustn't. This is our first evening. We've made all this effort to get here and go through all these elaborate conspiracies not to let K. L. know where we are. Amy may have lost her job. *And* we haven't got all that much time.

LAURIE: I wonder where we'll all sit down and do this again.

ANNIE: If you'd said "when" I'd have belted you.

GUS: Tomorrow. Tomorrow.

MARGARET: Oh, come on. Amy, let's look at your list. I don't think we want to go anywhere too ambitious tonight.

GUS: All right, Margaret?

MARGARET: I just think we've been travelling and getting out of

London and we should go somewhere fairly quiet but very nice and—oh, I don't know. What have we got here . . .

GUS: We must go to the Rijksmuseum.

MARGARET: Yes, Gus, but not tonight. Rembrandts are for the morning.

ANNE: And there's the Stedelijk.

DAN: And those Indonesian places where you get thirty great dishes.

AMY: You're greedy.

MARGARET: This sounds the sort of thing: fairly conservative but attractive seventeenth-century surroundings, beautiful tables and candles. That sounds like us. Tonight anyway. Laurie, choose.

LAURIE: They all sound good. Like the waiter said. That one you said looks pretty good.

MARGARET: Annie?

ANNIE: Yes. That sounds what we'd like. Gus doesn't like too much noise. He can't talk *and* eat.

DAN: Anything will do us.

MARGARET: Right. Then let's get the concierge to book a table. As there's six of us. And it may be busy.

LAURIE: I'm on holiday. Amy will do it.

MARGARET: We're all on holiday. Why should she do it?

AMY: I'll go and ring down. Give me the list. *[Goes off to bedroom]*

GUS: Then we'd better talk about tomorrow. What people want to do. I mean some may just want to sleep or do nothing.

MARGARET: No. I don't think that's right. We should try and all do the same thing. Unless . . . Well, we'll see what everyone says.

ANNIE: I can tell you what everyone will do—just talk. About what to do, where to go, what we should wear to do it. And we'll end up getting drunk at lunchtime in the American Bar and eating in the Hotel Dining Room.

LAURIE: Sounds delightful.

GUS: I suppose it isn't very adventurous.

MARGARET: Annie, you'll have to help me.

LAURIE: We're here—that's adventurous.

ANNIE: We'll talk about tomorrow over dinner.

GUS: I'll bring my guide.

MARGARET: Amy!

AMY: Yes?

MARGARET: I know nobody knows we're here but we might get one call for this room. If we do it'll be for me. Perhaps you should tell them. Save confusion.

LAURIE: For you! But we agreed not to tell *anyone* we were here. Except the blooming nanny and she wouldn't get through. Who did you tell, for God's sake?

MARGARET: Gillian.

LAURIE: What did you go and tell your bloody sister we were here for?

MARGARET: Oh, don't be silly. I told her not to tell anyone we're here.

LAURIE: But what did you tell her *for?* She's not one of us.

MARGARET: Isn't she?

LAURIE: Well, she's not really anything to do with K. L. And, besides, she wouldn't like it. She thinks we're all a bit flippant and middle-aged. Not half as middle-aged as her.

MARGARET: Come on. You like her. It's just that she's been having a bad time lately.

LAURIE: What bad time?

MARGARET: I'm not sure. But this affair she's having——

LAURIE: Oh, fleecing another rich duke of five hundred pounds and clenching her fists because she didn't lose her cherry until she was twenty-eight and she doesn't think she gives satisfaction and she plays Bach fugues all night and doesn't wash her hair because it's all so difficult. Blimey! I think *I* complain. She needs a public recognition for the suffering she undergoes, that's all. Then she'll feel better. She should get the Golden Sanitary Towel Award. K. L. can give it to her at the Dorchester with all the past winners present.

MARGARET: Well, I told her if things got too bad to ring me.

LAURIE: You didn't say she could come here?

MARGARET: I said if things got too much for her, I'd get her a room.

LAURIE: Oh, lovely for your friends.

MARGARET: I don't think anyone will mind.

LAURIE: Did you ask them?

MARGARET: You don't have to ask friends everything.

LAURIE: Perhaps you do. If she comes out, we can all go home. Why don't she and K. L. get together?

MARGARET: She's my sister, Laurie. I'm not having anything happen to her. Just for want of a phone call.

LAURIE: She won't do anything to herself. Not till it's too late. Like getting laid.

MARGARET: I love her.

LAURIE: You can. Don't expect your friends to.

GUS: Poor girl. What is it?

LAURIE: She's just a star wrecker of other people's coveted, innocent little weekends, that's all.

GUS: Oh, if she turns up, we'll look after her. She can't spoil anything. It's all right.

ANNIE: Of course it is. I know how to deal with Gillian. Put her to bed, that's the best thing.

LAURIE: It's a long way to come to go to bed. I mean, I know people go to New York for haircuts——

MARGARET: Let's not argue, darling. I'm sure it won't happen. She doesn't want to worry me.

LAURIE: She wants to worry everybody.

ANNIE: Listen, Laurie, darling. We're together. We've got days ahead. No one knows where we are. Except your daft nanny. Now——

GUS: She's right. Oh, I'm sure that restaurant's first class and tomorrow we'll do just as we like and go round the Leidseplein and Rembrandtsplein and the discotheques and clubs. . . .

ANNIE: Drink up, Laurie. You'll feel better.

LAURIE: I shall, I shall. I feel better already.

GUS: Old K. L. wouldn't like this at all. He'd have wanted to be out on the streets by now. Not just sitting around talking. What *would* he do?

ANNIE: Oh, exhaust a list three times as long as Amy's in half the time. Play games into the night. Games with victims.

GUS: I mean he'd hate this. Just us: talking among ourselves.

LAURIE: Well, as we're all here because of him, because of him, let's drink to him. Don't go yet, Amy. Ladies and gentlemen, to our absent friend.

MARGARET: What's the time?

AMY: Six o'clock.

GUS: He must have rung somebody by now.

MARGARET: Perhaps we should have a little zizz before we go out to dinner.

ANNIE: Good idea.

GUS: He may not know we're *all* gone yet.

LAURIE: Not together, anyway.

ANNIE: I should think he'll go off to Paris or something. Anything. And when we get back just manage to make us feel foolish. We'll just say we went away for the weekend. Do we have to tell him everything? What am I saying?

MARGARET: What about Amy?

ANNIE: That's up to her.

LAURIE: Oh, he'll be adroit. But he'll also be maladroit. He won't be able to resist trying to discover where we've been and who with.

ANNIE: Perhaps he just won't care. As you said, it's not exactly his idea of fun. God, he'd be pleased and amused.

LAURIE: Oh, he'll appear to be innocent, rational, ill-used. Slightly impatient.

GUS: The trouble is he creates excitement.

LAURIE: Not half enough.

GUS: Perhaps we're all second rate and need second-rate excitement, sort of heats one's inadequacies.

LAURIE: He takes nothing out of the air round *his* head. Only us. Insinuates his grit into all the available oysters. And if ever any tiny pearls should appear from these tight, invaded creatures, he whips off with them, appropriates them, and strings them together for his own necklace. And the pearls have to be switched or changed about. Otherwise the trick, the oyster rustling would be transparent and the last thing he wants made known is his own function or how he goes about it. Where does he get the damned energy and duplicity?

Where? He's tried to split us up but here we are in Amsterdam. He has made himself the endless object of speculation. Useful to him but humiliating for us. Well, no more, my friend. We will no longer be useful to you and be put up and put down. We deserve a little better, not much but better. We have been your friends. Your stock in trade is marked down *and* your blackmailing sneering, your callousness, your malingering, your emotional gun-slinging, your shooting in the dark places of affection. You trade on the forbearance, kindliness, and talent of your friends. Go on, go on playing the big market of all those meretricious ambition hankers, plodding hirelings, grafters and intriguers. I simply hope tonight that you are alone—I know you won't be. But I hope, at least, you will feel alone, alone as I feel it, as we all in our time feel it, without burdening our friends. I hope the G.P.O. telephone system is collapsed, that your chauffeur is dead and the housekeeper drunk and that there isn't one con-man, camp follower, eunuch, pimp, mercenary, or procurer of all things possible or one globe-trotting bum boy at your side to pour you a drink on this dark January evening . . .

ANNIE: Well—Amen.

GUS: Gosh—it's started to snow.

LAURIE: I think I'm the only one who believed all that. Good, all the better. We can get snowed up.

MARGARET: Well, I'm going to have a zizz.

GUS: Yes. I should. And we can discuss the alts later.

LAURIE: Oh, yes, we'll discuss them.

MARGARET: Laurie?

LAURIE: Just finish this.

MARGARET: We don't want to go out too late.

AMY: I'll book the table.

[They go to their rooms]

ANNIE: Think I'll have one too.

LAURIE: Finish your drink first. I am glad it's snowing. How I hate holidays. Those endless, clouded days by the pool even when it's blazing sun. Do you remember doing it? All together—at K. L.'s villa? We drank everything you could think of from breakfast onwards after that vile French coffee. The deadly chink of ice in steaming glasses all day. Luxury, spoiled people. Lounging together, basting themselves with comfort, staring into pools. A swimming pool is a terrible thing to look into on a holiday. It's no past and no future. You can stare into a stream or a river or a ditch. Who wouldn't rather die in a ditch than in a pool? I'm too fat for pools and the pretty girls with their straps down and their long legs just make me long for something quite different. I always want someone to write me long, exhilarating love-letters when I lie there with the others . . . A handwritten envelope by your towel, curling up.

GUS: We didn't get on too well that time, did we? I'm sure it wasn't our fault.

ANNIE: We played too many games—too many bloody games, expected too much of the sun and each other and disappointed K. L. . . .

GUS: He asked us all again.

LAURIE: Yes. I read somewhere that one of those communications people, the men who tell you what it is we're all feeling now because of *the* media, said that marriage and romanticism was out. At least with the young people.

ANNIE: I suppose it was on the way out when we came in.

LAURIE: I wonder where we ought to go to live. All those sleepy-eyed young mice squeaking love, love. Scudding into one another, crawling over each other, eyes too weak for bright light, tongues lapping softly . . . all for love, a boy's tail here, a girl's tail there, litters of them.

DAN: Think I'll take a look at my things.

[He goes out]

GUS: Is he all right?

ANNIE: Yes. You know Dan.

LAURIE: I think he may be a very violent man.

GUS: Dan?

LAURIE: Fools make him suffer. So he paints or reads a book.

ANNIE: Or goes into his fallow deer.

LAURIE: Don't blame him.

GUS: Well, perhaps you'd better come with your whatever-I-was.

ANNIE: Yes.

GUS: So, shall we say seventeen-forty-five? First drink. Well, not first drink, really.

LAURIE: Nineteen-forty-five hours. First drink.

GUS: Good. Where's my street guide? *[He goes]*

LAURIE: Ought to have a bath, I suppose.

ANNIE: Not sleepy?

LAURIE: Yes. I wish I could live alone. Do you?

ANNIE: No. I never have.

LAURIE: I have sometimes. It can be all right for weeks on end even. But then. You have to crawl out of the well. Just a circle of light and your own voice and your own effort . . . People underestimate Gus, I think.

ANNIE: So do I.

LAURIE: Do you think *you* do?

ANNIE: I don't think so.

LAURIE: He doesn't exhilarate you like K. L.?

ANNIE: No.

LAURIE: No. Gus has created himself. Thinks he's nobody, thinks he behaves like it. Result: himself.

ANNIE: Do you think Margaret's all right?

LAURIE: No.

ANNIE: Can I do anything?

LAURIE: She doesn't like being pregnant.

ANNIE: Who does? A few mooish ladies.

LAURIE: She feels invaded, distorted. About to be destroyed.

ANNIE: Why do you both do it then? Was it the same with the others?

LAURIE: I thought we might get pleasure from it. She thought I would get pleasure.

ANNIE: And you haven't?

LAURIE: Perhaps they're like holidays or hotels.

ANNIE: No. Not hotels. You couldn't live without them.

LAURIE: I love Gus very much. I think he really believes most people are better than him . . . I only suspect it.

ANNIE: He loves you.

LAURIE: Good. Try not to be too restless. Don't do that. What were we all doing this time last year? I mean were we all together or separate?

ANNIE: Separate.

LAURIE: I wonder *what* we were doing. We'll have a good evening. I feel better already. The snow's stopped.

ANNIE: Good. Seventeen-forty-five then. Try and kip. *[She kisses him lightly]*

LAURIE: I will. And you, Annie. And you.

[She goes to her room, taking her handbag. The three doors are closed. LAURIE *looks out the window]*

CURTAIN.

ACT TWO

*The same. Two evenings later. They are all in the sitting
room, looking much more relaxed, enjoying the First Drink
of the Evening.*

GUS: Well, what's the schedule for this evening?

MARGARET: I don't care.

AMY: Neither do I. Everywhere's been good.

LAURIE: I know. Isn't it weird?

ANNIE: Why shouldn't they be?

GUS: Yes, well if we came up with an absolute dud at this stage
we could hardly complain.

MARGARET: I must say that list of yours has been infallible.

LAURIE: Brilliant.

DAN: All smashing.

GUS: Not a dud. I say, we really have had quite a time, haven't
we? Friday evening seems weeks away. So does K. L. Right
after the first evening. Not a foot wrong. We're jolly lucky.

LAURIE: I mean even that Indonesian place was quite funny.

DAN: Actually, it was a "lovely feast of colour."

MARGARET: All those dishes. How many do you think we actually
got through?

AMY: I think Dan had a bit of the whole thirty or whatever it
was.

LAURIE: Still looks as lean and clean as a brass rail.

MARGARET: And we got Laurie round to the Rikjsmuseum, without too much bitterness.

LAURIE: I felt at home in all that nonconformist gothic.

ANNIE: And there *were* the Rembrandts.

LAURIE: Yes. We needed a drink after that. I keep thinking of him watching his house being sold up. All those objects, all those pieces and possessions got with sweat, all going. K. L. would have enjoyed that.

ANNIE: Don't be unfair.

LAURIE: And his child dead. What was his name? Titus?

ANNIE: I liked the place with the bank managers dancing together.

LAURIE: That's because you danced with that chambermaid from Hanover.

ANNIE: It seemed only fair. It's a bit churlish to just go and gawp like a tourist. I think you were very mean not to dance.

LAURIE: No one I fancied.

MARGARET: Annie's right. You got frightfully stuffy and absent-minded all of a sudden.

LAURIE: I was worried about you and that lady in the black dinner jacket.

MARGARET: You didn't show it. I don't know what I'd have done if Gus hadn't protected me.

ANNIE: She really fancied you, didn't she?

AMY: I'll say. I've never seen anything like it.

DAN: She was just queer for pregnant girls.

MARGARET: I'd have thought that would have put her off.

GUS: Not at all.

ANNIE: What about tonight?

GUS: Yes. We must make a decision.

ANNIE: Where's the list, Amy?

DAN: Let's have a look. What are the alts?

GUS: We've still got lunch tomorrow.

LAURIE: Why don't we stay the extra day?

ANNIE: We've done all that.

MARGARET: Yes. Amy must get back.

LAURIE: But why? I don't see it.

MARGARET: Because she doesn't want to lose her well-paid job, which she also likes.

ANNIE: And she has obligations.

LAURIE: What obligations? You don't have obligations to monsters.

DAN: What about this? I don't know . . .

AMY: Why don't we go to the place we went to on the first evening?

LAURIE: That was wonderful.

DAN: At least we know it's first rate.

GUS: You don't think that being a bit unadventurous, do you?

ANNIE: Yes. Let's chance our arm.

LAURIE: Why should we?

MARGARET: I agree. We should try something different.

DAN: What for? Not that I mind.

LAURIE: You girls are so ambitious. Even if it's for others.

GUS: Really escaped, didn't we? I haven't laughed so much for months. Have you, darling? You said last night.

LAURIE: I still think we should go back a day later.

MARGARET: No.

LAURIE: Amy could fix it.

AMY: Of course. Why don't you? I could go. It seems silly when you're having such fun. Dan, you could stay with them.

ANNIE: I think we've voted on that one.

LAURIE: Oh, no, we haven't. I wonder when we'll all sit down like this again.

MARGARET: Damn it, we've done it enough times before.

ANNIE: Sure, we'll do it again.

LAURIE: Yes. But when? How? Where? How do we arrange it? I don't want to go back to London.

ANNIE: Who does.

LAURIE: No. I mean it. What is there there for any of us? We should all go and live together somewhere.

MARGARET: Where, for instance? Somewhere you didn't have to pick up the phone for room service.

LAURIE: We need a broken-down Victorian castle or something, oh, with all the plumbing and jazz we wanted. But lots of space around us. Acres of land around us, empty, chipped and scarred still by Roman legions.

ANNIE: Sounds freezing.

LAURIE: What would you prefer, a sonic bang up your lush, southern parkland? We could do what we liked, have lots of children.

GUS: There aren't many of us.

LAURIE: We'll think of some others.

ANNIE: But who?

GUS: K. L. would find out about it.

LAURIE: Let him. You'd all come, wouldn't you?

ANNIE: What about staff?

MARGARET: Good question.

DAN: You'd need lots of nannies.

LAURIE: Yes. Well . . . we'd get ex-stewardesses from El Fag Airlines. They're absolutely wonderful nannies. Poor old things will work for absolutely nothing if you get a really rejected one.

AMY: And the rest of the staff?

LAURIE: They must be people we know. People who'd fit in with everyone. I would learn carpentry. I've always wanted to do that. And brick laying. I could work on the house. Gus knows all about electricity. Margaret could drive. Except we wouldn't use the car much. Annie's the great horse expert. We could use them and maybe hunt if we got over our green belt liberal principles. And Dan could, well, he could just paint.

GUS: Who do we know?

LAURIE: Well, we ought to make a list. That's one thing, do you realize, we've escaped from? Margaret? My relatives and all those layabout people I pay to look after us. So that, the theory being, we are able to do other things, not bother with inessentials because we've *made* it.

ANNIE: I thought your Nannie was good?

MARGARET: She's very good.

LAURIE: Only she doesn't look after *me*. She looks after two creatures who don't even know yet they're being waited on.

ANNIE: I thought you didn't like being waited on.

LAURIE: I don't. But if I pay for it at home I expect it.

AMY: They're only tiny babies.

LAURIE: Darling, don't say "tiny babies." All babies are tiny compared to people. Even if they had to be landed like killer sharks, they're still tiny. What I hate about them, it's like my relations and K. L., you always, you're expected to adjust to *their* mood, their convenience, their bad back, or I-don't-know-I'm-just-depressed. What are they going to be like when I ring the bell, when I open their letters. They never anticipate *you*.

ANNIE: Gus never anticipates for himself.

MARGARET: How?

ANNIE: He's always taken by surprise by situations and people's reactions.

MARGARET: Laurie rehearses them all.

GUS: Am I?

ANNIE: He was cutting some trees down just by the pond one day. And he'd keep stepping back. Just about a foot away from the pond. "You will mind the pond" I'd say to him. "What? Oh. Yes." Then he'd do it again. "Don't forget the pond." "No . . . all right" . . . Always a bit surprised. I watched him for two days and then I thought, I can't go on. I'll leave him to it. He missed it by inches for a whole morning. And then fell in.

GUS: Yes. That's quite right. I did feel surprised when it happened.

LAURIE: The mistake is to feel guilty. That's always been my mistake. He's driving you about because you're cleverer than he is. And though I say it, he can't even drive as well as I can. That's why he's a servant, she says. Well, why can't he be a good one, I say. I wouldn't want him to wait on me. I don't know though. Why do it at all? There are third-rate servants. Perhaps I've got the ones I deserve, like the relatives I deserve.

DAN: As the old saying goes, we're all bloody servants.

LAURIE: You're right. Deliver the goods or the chopper. I suppose that's right. Do we deliver the goods?

ANNIE: If someone's cooked you a meal decently and woken you and been able to smile as well, that would be delivering the goods.

MARGARET: It would.

LAURIE: *Are* we spoiled?

ANNIE: Staying in a luxury hotel on the Continent because you're afraid of your servants?

LAURIE: That does make it sound stupid. Very.

GUS: But that wasn't the main reason.

LAURIE: Yes. I just send my nasty relations a cheque. I never see them. They certainly don't want to see me.

DAN: What are they?

LAURIE: Retired rotten, grafting publicans, shop assistants, ex-waitresses. They live on and on. Having hernias and arthritic hips and strokes. But they go on: writing poisonous letters to one another. Complaining and wheedling and paying off the same old scores with the same illiterate signs. "Dear Laurie, thank you very kindly for the cheque. It was most welcome and I was able to get us one or two things we'd had to go without for quite some time, what with me having been off work all this time and the doctor sends me to the hospital twice a week. They tell me it's improving but I can't say I feel much improvement. How are you, old son? Old son? We saw your name in the paper about something you were doing the other day and the people next door said they thought you were on the telly one night but we didn't see it, and Rose won't buy the television papers so we always switch on to the same programme. Rose doesn't get any better, I'm afraid. I brought her a quarter bottle the other day with your kind remittance which served to buck her up a bit. Your Auntie Grace wrote and said she'd heard Margaret was having another baby. That must be very nice for you both. We send our best wishes to you both and the other little ones. Hope you're all well. Must close now as I have to take down the front room curtains and wash them as Rose can't do it any longer, but you know what she is. Bung ho and all the very best. Excuse writing but my hand is still bad. Ever. Your Uncle Ted. P.S. Rose says Auntie Grace said something about a letter from your mother which she sent on but I'm afraid she sent it back unopened. She just refuses to pass any comment. She told me not to say anything about it to you but I thought I'd just—*PASS IT ON TO YOU!*" [*He gestures towards them*] Pass *that* on!

MARGARET: Oh, don't talk about them. They're so depressing.

ANNIE: They sound quite funny.

LAURIE: They're not quite funny, Annie. They're greedy, calculating, stupid, and totally without questions.

MARGARET: They're just boring.

LAURIE: They're not that even. They're not even boring. Now *I* am boring. I am quite certainly the most boring man you have ever met in your lives. I see you're not going to contradict me so I won't let you.

GUS: As a matter of fact, I was going to contradict you because I am infinitely more boring than you could ever be even on a bad day. Not that I think you could be even then.

MARGARET: You're both drunk.

LAURIE: No, we're not. At least Gus may be a bit. I am just straightforwardly boring. Look, some people when they're drunk are dreadfully boring, especially when they're supposed to be freewheeling and amusing. Now, drink doesn't do that to me. Drink doesn't change one, does it?

ANNIE: Not much.

LAURIE: There you are. I am just as boring drunk as I am sober. There is no appreciable difference. If I could tell you, if I could, how much I bore myself. I am really fed up with the whole subject . . . I am a meagre, pilfering bore.

DAN: Well, don't be a bore and enlarge on it any more.

LAURIE: You're drunk! [*Laughs*] I say Dan's drunk. We really are having a time. . . .

MARGARET: Did you see Terry had married that girl friend of K. L.'s?

ANNIE: Yes.

DAN: Not that horrible Tina What'saname?

AMY: The same.

LAURIE: That's the movie business. Where the producer persuades the director to marry *his* crumpet.

MARGARET: He hasn't got a very strong character.

LAURIE: What does that mean?

ANNIE: I think he'll survive her.

LAURIE: I mean K. L.'s got a *strong* character. Hasn't he? Does it mean simply someone who can impose their will on others? Can be politic and full of strategy!

MARGARET: You know what I mean about Terry.

LAURIE: I saw something very interesting the other day. No, somebody told me.

AMY: About air hostesses?

LAURIE: No, about nurses. Is this boring? That's the window sign of a bore. He always says to you at some point, is this boring?

ANNIE: Fascinating.

LAURIE: Yes, well I think it probably is. Because it may affect us all in some way. Well, apparently if you've got the real incurables, the carcinoma or some dance like that going on inside you, the doctors very sensibly start pumping things into you at the right time and make you as thumpingly stupid as possible. Unfortunately, the nursing profession, being imperfect, like El Fag Airlines or any other concern, contains a considerable and dangerous fifth column of popish ladies in starched collars and cuffs who'll fail to give you your shot of blissful dope come six o'clock. Nothing to call on in the small house but a couple of codeine and an Irish lilt. So, do you know what they do, the clever ones, the doctors? Well, if they should decide they'd rather a patient didn't lie in agony, they insist on a roster of Australian nurses. They're the best. The Aussies. They'll give you enough for you and your horse if you tell 'em. So, if you ever wake up after you've been in hospital for a little while and one day a little cobber voice says to you "And how are we today, Mr. so-and-so?" you know you've scored.

ANNIE: Yes. That's better than the lady pilot.

LAURIE: Annie?

ANNIE: What?

LAURIE: You're called Annie, and I'm called Laurie.

ANNIE: What are we supposed to do?

MARGARET: Hadn't you thought of it before?

LAURIE: No. Isn't that odd? Had you?

GUS: Not me. I don't think. Annie mentioned it to me one day.

LAURIE: Dan?

DAN: I've got used to it. The trouble with being spontaneous, or even trying to be, and I think one can, the trouble is it does put you at the mercy of others. That's not the same thing as being a bore.

LAURIE: What do we ever go back to England for? What do we do it for?

ANNIE: I thought you never wanted to come away.

LAURIE: It's the bitchiest place on earth.

MARGARET: That's the name of the place you come from. Now, what have we decided?

GUS: About what?

LAURIE: We haven't decided anything. Um? *[Holds her hand]*

MARGARET: I mean where are we going for our last night?

[Knock on door]

LAURIE: You didn't order anything, did you?

GUS: No.

AMY: Probably the maid with all those clean sheets for when we go.

ANNIE: Come in.

[The door handle rattles]

GUS: No key. Well, if it's K. L., he's too late. We've done it.

[He goes to the door, opens it. A girl of about thirty, GILLIAN]

LAURIE: Gillian.

MARGARET: Darling.

GILLIAN: I'm sorry. I should have warned you.

MARGARET: *[To her]* My darling, what's the matter? You look ill.

GILLIAN: I didn't have a chance. I'm all right. I couldn't remember how long you were staying.

MARGARET: Why didn't you ring me? Come in and sit down. Take your coat off.

GILLIAN: No. I think I'll keep it on.

LAURIE: Oh, sit down and take the bloody thing off. It's hot in
here.

GILLIAN: I'm sorry. I should have rung first. I couldn't find the
number.

LAURIE: Just the name of the hotel?

MARGARET: Laurie, give her a drink.

GILLIAN: No, I'll have a Perrier.

LAURIE: Don't tell me *you're* pregnant.

MARGARET: Give her one.

GILLIAN: Just a small one, very small.

LAURIE: Did you bring your own nose dropper?

GILLIAN: Well, how are you? Have you had a good time?

LAURIE: Fanfuckingtastick! Never stopped laughing, have we?

AMY: We've had a marvellous time. Why didn't you come?

GUS: I think you'd have enjoyed it. We've done quite a lot in an
easy sort of way, done what we wanted——

LAURIE: After discussion.

GUS: After discussion. And all the places we've been to have been
tremendous fun—thanks to Amy's list.

DAN: I liked that place like the Brasserie at Joe Lyons where
everyone sang Tipperary—in English.

GUS: Yes, I think you'd have liked it—don't you, darling?

ANNIE: I don't think she'd have liked that place much, Margaret
didn't.

GUS: Oh, well, Margaret didn't feel so hot for a while.

MARGARET: I just can't stand the smell of beer and all those awful
swilling, ugly-looking people.

ANNIE: I think the men enjoyed it rather more.

AMY: I loved it.

DAN: You even sang—as usual.

LAURIE: What do you mean—the men liked it?

ANNIE: I mean you sometimes try and fumble your way back to
childhood while we watch and get impatient and wait for
you to stop.

LAURIE: Perhaps you should try coming along.

ANNIE: Yes. We found two really remarkable restaurants, we discovered a new game, or rather Laurie invented one, and Gus

had us in stitches telling us stories about his regiment in the
war, with two versions to every story, one tragic and one
comic, the tragic one always being comic and the comic one
always tragic. Laurie's starting a new airline and Dan's putting out a new scent. They'll tell you.

GILLIAN: I'd like to go to the Rijksmuseum.

LAURIE: There are other things here besides Rembrandt. We
needed a drink after him. Drink?

GILLIAN: Thanks.

LAURIE: Too much?

GILLLIAN: No, fine.

LAURIE: Only I don't want you leaving any because I'm an im-
poverished writer with a wife, children, useless servants, a
family of ageless begging letter writers, a trencherman nanny,
and three dogs as big as you. I haven't yet found my voice,
I write too much not enough, I have no real popular appeal,
I take an easy route to solutions——

ANNIE: Stop being paranoid.

LAURIE: Why? If a man is ill he isn't a hypochondriac. And if he's
attacked he's——

MARGARET: Oh, shut up, Laurie. Can't you see there's something
the matter?

LAURIE: Who with? Annie?

GILLIAN: I told you—honestly—everything's fine. I just thought I'd
come suddenly.

MARGARET: Darling, I've known you all my life. Something's very
wrong. Do you want to tell me?

LAURIE: Oh, leave her be.

MARGARET: I know her. You don't.

GILLIAN: I wish I *had* come. You all look as if you've had a super
time.

LAURIE: I'll bet we do—now. [*To* MARGARET] You're right—it's
not a very convincing performance.

GILLIAN: Tell me what else you've been doing. It does sound good.
I've always wanted to come to Amsterdam. [*She leans forward avidly. The others decline visibly. She has broken the
fragile spell*] Did you go on the canal?

DAN: Yes.

GILLIAN: And that modern art gallery, whatever it's called. Can't
pronounce Dutch. And the harbor, or where is it, where all
the tarts sit in the windows looking like dolls. This hotel looks
splendid. They were terribly nice downstairs. They seemed
to know all about you lot up here. They smiled the moment
I said who I wanted. Do you think I can get a room? Perhaps
I could get one down the hall. All I need is a little room. I
suppose I could come in here with you most of the time.
Don't let me interrupt what you're doing. I'll just finish this
and change, I think. Perhaps I could have a bath in your
room, Margaret, if Laurie doesn't mind. What time are you
going out? I don't want to hold you up. I needn't unpack.
Unless you're dressing up. I could change in your room
though and see about the room later. Do you know where
you're going tonight? . . .

GUS: We were—just discussing the alts. Perhaps we should go
somewhere you'd like.

GILLIAN: Don't change anything because of me. It's my fault for
turning up like this. Just do what you would have done by
yourselves. Please don't let me change anything . . .

LAURIE: Gillian, for Christ's sake burst into tears . . .

[Slowly she crumples and they watch her]

GILLIAN: Please . . . take no notice. I'll get a room down the hall.

*[*MARGARET *puts her arm around her and leads her into her
bedroom and closes the door]*

LAURIE: Drink, anyone?

ANNIE: Yes, please.

GUS: Poor girl.

DAN: Just as well we're going tomorrow.

AMY: I wonder what it is.

LAURIE: Oh, either her lover's married and can't or won't get a
divorce or he *isn't* married and she can't bring herself to
offer herself up to something total. Variations on some crap
like that. But I tell you, she's not going to blight our week-

end. We've had ourselves something we want to have and we made it work and she's not going to walk in here on the last night and turn it all into a Golden Sanitary Towel Award Presentation.

ANNIE: I'm afraid she's done it.

LAURIE: Well, we mustn't let her. Look, Gus, flip through that list and we'll decide where to go and either she can come with us and put on a happy face or——

ANNIE: Oh, not that.

LAURIE: No, I agree—the miserable one's better. You and Dan can talk to her a bit about the Rembrandts and painting and Dutch domestic architecture and what Marshal McLuhan said to Lévi-Strauss while they were on the job. Otherwise, she can just shut up and leave us to it. Or Margaret can stay with her arms around her in the bedroom all evening.

GUS: That's not very fair on poor old Margaret.

LAURIE: Her sister's not being very fair to us.

ANNIE: That's not her fault.

AMY: No. Dan will talk to her and cheer her up. He's good at that.

LAURIE: Why should he?

DAN: Sure. I don't mind.

ANNIE: Why should we? We do. Listen, Margaret will listen to her and calm her down. Then we'll take her out with us. She'll be all right.

LAURIE: But will we be? If I didn't know I'd think it was a last-minute joke of K. L.'s on us. Blimey, she's turned it into Agony Junction all right. Look at Gus. Dan, have some more in there.

GUS: Oh, she's not such a bad girl.

DAN: She's brought London with her . . .

GUS: Perhaps we should go to the place we went on the first night, anyway.

LAURIE: I suppose so.

GUS: I think she'd like it. It's quiet and the food—did you have those herrings?

AMY: My chicken in that pastry thing was wild.

LAURIE: Oh, she'll be sick or pushing her food away or leaving it and pretending she's enjoying it and filling us up with guilt and damned responsibility. Damn her, we've just got together again, she's an odd man out, we haven't got time to take off for her coltish, barren, stiff-upper quivering lips and, and klart-on. Am I unsympathetic?

ANNIE: Yes.

LAURIE: I'm sorry . . . all of you . . .

DAN: Not your fault.

GUS: Not anybody's fault.

LAURIE: Beaudelaire said: can't remember now.

GUS: Someone said the other day: "What do you do if you live in San Francisco, you're twenty-one, and you go bald . . ."

LAURIE: He said, I know, "beauty was something he only wanted to see once."

ANNIE: She's quite attractive.

LAURIE: Gillian?

ANNIE: Um.

GUS: Very.

AMY: Not as much as Margaret.

ANNIE: She's prettier than she thinks, that's the trouble.

LAURIE: She should take some pretty pills. So should I. I'm all water. Heavy. Bit of underwater fire like North Sea gas. Not much earth or air either . . . What a *precious* remark—that's her fault. Did I tell you about the boy with the crocodile shoes?

ANNIE: No, but it's too long. I've heard it.

DAN: Tell them the one about the nun in the enclosed order.

GUS: Wish I could remember jokes.

LAURIE: Young nun enters an enclosed order with a strict vow of silence. The silence can only be broken once every three years with two words. So: after three years the girl goes to the Mother Superior, who says: "Now, my child, three years have passed since you entered the order. You have kept your vow of silence. It is now your privilege to say any two words you wish to me." So the young nun pauses painfully, opens her mouth and says: "Uncomfortable beds." So the Mother

Superior says: "Right, my child, and now you may go back to your work." Three more years pass and she comes before the Mother Superior again. "You have observed the rule of this order for three more years. It is your privilege to say two words to me—if you wish." So the nun hesitates and then says: "Bad food." "Very well, go back to your work, my child." Another three years pass and the nun is brought in front of the Mother Superior again. "Well, my child, three more years have passed. Is there anything you wish to say to me?" The nun raises her eyes and, after an effort, she whispers: "I want to go home." "Well," says the Mother Superior, "I'm *glad* to hear it. You've done nothing but bitch ever since you got here . . ."

ANNIE: Why don't you go in and see how Margaret's managing?

LAURIE: I don't think I'm what's wanted in there. Margaret will call if she wants me.

ANNIE: Are you sure?

GUS: Shall I knock?

LAURIE: No, leave them. Did you like her, Amy?

AMY: Gillian? I don't really know her. I felt sorry for her . . . when she was sitting there trying not to spoil everything.

LAURIE: But doing it pretty well all the same.

DAN: Why did you ask Amy?

LAURIE: Because Amy likes nearly everyone.

ANNIE: You make her sound imperceptive, which she's not.

LAURIE: No. I think she is blessed with loving kindness . . .

DAN: So—we've decided on the first night place? . . . Laurie?

LAURIE: What?

ANNIE: Yes.

GUS: Well, we thought so, Dan. Unless you'd like to suggest something else. We thought . . .

ANNIE: Discussion.

DAN: Perhaps we'd better start getting ready slowly. Amy?

AMY: Yes. Right. Now.

LAURIE: You two really are a lecherous couple.

AMY: Me?

LAURIE: Me? Yes, you two. You toddle off to the bedroom every evening twenty minutes before the rest of us.

ANNIE: Good for them.

LAURIE: Perhaps you simply organize these things better. Is that it, Dan? I'd never thought of it before. Perhaps, working efficient secretaries make the ideal wives. I mean it does need fitting in with everything else. How long have you been married?

AMY: Nine years.

GUS: Marvellous. Is it really?

ANNIE: Nine isn't so long. Some people have golden weddings.

LAURIE: Golden Sanitary Towel Weddings. I think Dan's pretty formidable. I bet if you looked at his sexual graph of desire his would be steady, unchanging up there like Nelson on his column and there'd be mine bumping about among the lions.

DAN: Wish it were true.

LAURIE: Well, get along then.

AMY: Actually, I wanted to write a couple of postcards.

GUS: *Are* you? I don't think you should write postcards from here somehow. I haven't. Deliberately. It seemed like giving evidence that we'd ever been here, all of us.

LAURIE: Yes. Well, go and do it, whatever it is. Only don't keep us waiting.

ANNIE: Oh, who kept who waiting last night?

LAURIE: I did.

AMY: See you then.

GUS: Seventeen-forty-five. *[They go, closing the door behind them. Pause]* What'll you do when you get back?

LAURIE: Don't know.

GUS: No, *we* weren't sure. Were we, darling?

LAURIE: I've tried not to think about it.

GUS: Perhaps we should all have dinner the first night back. Where could we go?

LAURIE: I'll ask Margaret.

GUS: That new place you took us to the other week was nice. I wonder if K. L.'s discovered it.

LAURIE: Hope not.

ANNIE: I expect he has.

GUS: I wonder if he'll ring when we get in.

LAURIE: Sure to.

GUS: Perhaps he'll wait for one of us to ring him.

LAURIE: He can.

GUS: Well, it worked . . . Are you going to work as soon as you
get back?

LAURIE: If I can. You?

GUS: I've got to. I should be there tomorrow really. Do you know
what you're doing next weekend?

LAURIE: Margaret would know.

GUS: Perhaps we could do something.

LAURIE: Maybe. We'll talk about it on the train . . .

GUS: I think I'll go and have a bath. A *real* bath, I mean. What's
the time? Yes, seventeen-forty-five. I'd better book the table,
hadn't I? Best not disturb Dan.

ANNIE: I'll have one after you.

GUS: What?

ANNIE: A bath, my darling.

GUS: O.K. Well, I'll have one first, then I'll run one for you and
I can shave while you're in it.

ANNIE: Right.

GUS: You might as well stay and have another drink with old
Laurie.

LAURIE: I'm all right. Perhaps she'd like a kip.

ANNIE: Bit late now.

GUS: Do you know what you're going to be wearing this evening?

LAURIE: No. Oh, the same as the first night I expect.

GUS: Yes. I see. I remember. Only it helps me when I make up my
mind what to put on. It's that chocolaty mohair kind of
thing?

LAURIE: That's the one.

GUS: That's good. Well, fine. See you then.

ANNIE: And, darling—wear your purple tie.

GUS: Are you sure?

ANNIE: It suits you.

GUS: Not too——?

LAURIE: Yes. Divine.

GUS: Oh, all right. Annie gave me that. It's awfully pretty. She's
got the most amazing flair and taste in things like men's
clothes. In everything, come to that.

LAURIE: Except men.

GUS: Yes. Well, blind spot in us all. I'll call you when I've run the bath, darling. And I'll put some of that oil in, shall I? If there's anything—with Gillian—you know, I can do, give a knock.

LAURIE: Go and have your bath. I want to see you properly turned out for our last night.

GUS: Right.

[He goes into his room and closes the door. Pause]

ANNIE: Are you sure I shouldn't go into Margaret? Girl stuff.

LAURIE: If you want to. *[She doesn't move]* You haven't been married before, have you?

ANNIE: No.

LAURIE: I have.

ANNIE: It's quite a well-known fact.

LAURIE: Yes. It's like having had a previous conviction . . .

ANNIE: Of course, I lived with people before Gus.

LAURIE: Many?

ANNIE: I don't think so; some would. But I don't think it was inordinate—no. I lived with each one an inordinate time.

LAURIE: I wonder what my other wife thinks of me.

ANNIE: Has she married again?

LAURIE: Twice. I wonder what my name even means to her.

ANNIE: Ever see her?

LAURIE: No. I dread bumping into her somewhere. Even here the other night, I thought I saw her in that smart place.

ANNIE: Why do you dread it?

LAURIE: I don't think she likes me.

ANNIE: Why not?

LAURIE: I imagine I wasn't very kind to her.

ANNIE: Weren't you?

LAURIE: I don't know. I wish I could really remember. I try to. I hope not. But I'm sure I was.

ANNIE: It doesn't mean that *you're* unkind.

LAURIE: Doesn't it?

ANNIE: Oh, come. Just capable of it. Like everyone.

LAURIE: Amy is never unkind.

ANNIE: You don't want to be like Amy.

LAURIE: Don't I?

ANNIE: No . . . It will be all right . . . when we get back.

LAURIE: Yes.

ANNIE: Don't grieve.

LAURIE: Annie. Laurie. I do.

ANNIE: I know.

LAURIE: You live with someone for five, six years. And you begin
to feel you don't know them. Perhaps you didn't make the
right kind of effort. You have to make choices, adjustments,
you have requirements to answer. Then you see someone you
love through other eyes. First, one pair of eyes. Then another and more. I was afraid to marry but afraid not to. You
see, I'm not really promiscuous. I'm a moulting old bourgeois. I'm not very good at legerdemain affairs. . . . Do you
like Margaret?

ANNIE: Yes . . . Have you been unfaithful to her?

LAURIE: Yes.

ANNIE: Enjoyable?

LAURIE: Not very.

ANNIE: Often?

LAURIE: No. Not inordinately.

ANNIE: When was the last time?

LAURIE: Six months. Just a few times.

ANNIE: Before that?

LAURIE: Not for ages.

ANNIE: What's ages?

LAURIE: When she was in the nursing home . . .

ANNIE: In the nursing home? You mean, not——

LAURIE: Yes.

ANNIE: I see.

LAURIE: Are you shocked?

ANNIE: No. Surprised . . . Not really.

LAURIE: I thought you might say: men!

ANNIE: You're not men! I'd better go and change.

LAURIE: Gus'll call you. Have some more . . . I've wanted to tell
you.

ANNIE: Have you?

LAURIE: No one knows. You won't tell Gus, will you?

ANNIE: I won't tell anyone. . . . Why did you want to tell me?

LAURIE: Why? Because . . . to me . . . you have always been the most dashing . . . romantic . . . friendly . . . playful . . . loving . . . impetuous . . . larky . . . fearful . . . detached . . . constant . . . woman I have ever met . . . and I love you . . . I don't know how else one says it . . . one shouldn't . . . and I've always thought you felt . . . perhaps . . . the same about me.

ANNIE: I do.

LAURIE: When we are all away—you are never out of my heart.

ANNIE: Nor you out of mine.

LAURIE: So there it is. It's snowing again . . . I wonder what it'll be like in London.

ANNIE: God knows.

LAURIE: If we were going by plane, I'd say perhaps it'll crash. Or we won't be able to take off.

ANNIE: We'll have longer on the train together.

LAURIE: Together? Yes, and we can all get drunk on the boat.

ANNIE: Perhaps we should change and go on the plane after all. I don't know that I can face the journey with you there . . . sorry. A touch of the Gillians.

LAURIE: A touch of the Annies.

ANNIE: I love you . . . I can never tell you . . .

LAURIE: Thank you for saying it . . . Bless you, Amsterdam. Wouldn't K.L. be furious?

ANNIE: Because it's happened or because he doesn't know?

LAURIE: Both.

ANNIE: I think he'd be envious because it's happened. I fancy he's suspected for a long time.

LAURIE: Do you? [She nods] Yes. He doesn't miss much. Do you think Margaret knows?

ANNIE: I think she might. I would.

LAURIE: And Gus?

ANNIE: No.

LAURIE: Good . . . I think we need another . . .

[He pours for them both. Looks down at her]

ANNIE: Don't look at me.

LAURIE: I'm sorry. I shall never be able to come back to this place again.

ANNIE: Which?

LAURIE: Both. The hotel. Amsterdam.

[MARGARET *comes in*]

ANNIE: How is she?

MARGARET: Oh, she's a little better. Some of it came out and, oh, dear, I don't know why some people's lives have to be difficult. I'll tell you about it later. Anyway, she's resting on our bed. I thought she might be able to have a little zizz and then, if she's all right, she can come out with us. If not, I'll stay in with her.

ANNIE: But you can't do that. We must all go out, together, on our last night. You've got to.

MARGARET: Oh, we'll see. We'd better get her a room. Laurie, can you ring down and ask reception if there's a single room down the hall near us she can have?

LAURIE: O.K. Like some Perrier?

MARGARET: No, thank you, Laurie, are you all right?

LAURIE: Fine.

MARGARET: No, you're not, I can see. He doesn't look well. Does he, Annie?

ANNIE: I think he's just getting a bit seasick already.

MARGARET: It's not that. Even Laurie waits till the same day.

LAURIE: Who is it this time?

MARGARET: What? Oh, Gillian. It's too complicated, now.

LAURIE: Nothing's too complicated now.

MARGARET: Darling, I think you started drinking too early. You started right after breakfast. . . . Oh, yes, she saw K. L.

LAURIE: Saw him. How?

MARGARET: He asked her round for a drink.

LAURIE: When was this?

MARGARET: Friday.

LAURIE: I never thought he'd ring *her*. She didn't tell him where we'd gone?

MARGARET: Yes, Laurie, I'm afraid she did.

LAURIE: She did! The stupid, dopey mare!

MARGARET: Oh, stop it, Laurie. It doesn't really matter as it's turned out. He didn't ring or *anything* did he?

LAURIE: You mean she told him the hotel, the lot?

MARGARET: You know how clever he is at winkling these things out of people. She said he seemed so concerned about us all, and she was, oh, distraught about her own weekend. He managed to convince her that we'd really want him to know.

LAURIE: Don't tell me she's having an affair with him. They deserve each other. Except he'd spit her out in one bite.

MARGARET: Listen, Laurie, I'm worried about that girl. She's my sister and I love her, and I think she came very close to doing something to herself this weekend.

LAURIE: Don't you believe it. She just models for it. People like her don't go home and do it. They choose a weekend when there's someone likely to come in the flat or they don't take quite enough.

MARGARET: Don't be such a bitch.

LAURIE: Well, I am.

MARGARET: You certainly make the same noises sometimes.

LAURIE: You're sure she didn't spend the weekend with our friend K. L.?

MARGARET: She was all on her own. I should have found out she was feeling like this. I'd have made her come with us.

LAURIE: Nice for us.

MARGARET: Leave her alone. There are some problems you've never had to face.

LAURIE: I should hope so. [*The telephone in the sitting room rings. They stare at it*] Who the devil's that?

MARGARET: Well, you'd better answer it.

LAURIE: She hasn't told anyone else where we are?

MARGARET: No. No one. She hasn't spoken to anyone. Well, pick it up.

[ANNIE *does so*]

ANNIE: Room number . . . what's this one? Three two O. Yes . . . No . . . Just a moment. It's for Amy.

LAURIE: Amy!

ANNIE: Amy! Phone! It's for you.

[They wait. AMY *appears putting on her dressing gown]*

AMY: For me? How do they know?

LAURIE: I'll tell you.

*[*AMY *picks up the phone.* GILLIAN appears *in the doorway of*
MARGARET's *bedroom]*

AMY: *[On phone]* Hullo . . . Yes . . . Speaking . . . Oh, hullo, Paul.
Yes . . . I see . . . no, wait a moment . . . let me think . . .
their number's in a bright green leather book on his desk . . .
yes, in the study . . . no, I'll try and get a plane earlier . . .
no, don't do that. . . . Stay there and I'll call you back. *[She
puts the phone down]* That was Paul. K. L.'s chauffeur . . .
He's killed himself. He found him half an hour ago.

[Pause. DAN *comes in, in dressing gown]*

LAURIE: How did he find the number?

AMY: It was written on a pad by his desk. By his body. *[*LAURIE
starts to pour drinks for them all] I suppose I'd better make
some ticket arrangements.

LAURIE: Have a drink first. Here, sit down. Margaret.

*[*GUS *appears at his door]*

GUS: Annie? Hullo. I didn't hear someone on the phone, did I?

ANNIE: K. L. has killed himself.

GUS: But how?

AMY: Sleeping pills. Sleeping pills and aspirin.

LAURIE: Come in. Have a drink. You too, Gillian. Dan . . . Sleeping pills, aspirin, bottle of whisky, half a loaf of bread to
keep it all down . . . give the housekeeper the weekend off,
turn the extension off in your study and lock the front door
. . . Well, cheers . . .

[Silence]

AMY: I think I'll talk to them downstairs from my room. Save
you having to listen. I expect you'd all like to go back together if I can fix it?

MARGARET: Of course.

DAN: I'll come with you. *[He follows her to their bedroom door. He says, a little drily]* I wonder: if we'll ever come here again?

MARGARET: What—to this hotel?

DAN: To Amsterdam . . .

LAURIE: I shouldn't think so. But I expect we might go somewhere else. . . .

[DAN closes his bedroom door]

CURTAIN.